The English

God bless 'em!

To my family

By the same author:

Italians First! (From A to Z), Renaissance Books, Hardback, 1989 and Paperback, 1994
The Italian Achievement, Renaissance Books, Hardback, 2007
Italy's World of Wines, Renaissance Books, Hardback, 2008
Quanto Siamo Str…. – in Italian – Amazon, Paperback and Kindle, 2014

Writing as Richard Goodall:

The Comfort of Sin: Prostitutes and Prostitution in the 1990s, Renaissance Books, Hardback, 1994 and Paperback, 1995
The Divorce Dilemma, Renaissance Books, Hardback, 2000
The English and Sex, Amazon, Paperback and Kindle, 2013
The Virgin Phoenix, Amazon, Paperback and Kindle, 2013

NB. For the sake of simplicity (and not to be politically correct), I have used the masculine personal pronoun even where – context permitting – the sentence can include also one or more persons of the female sex.

Cover by Fiona Lonsdale

Acknowledgements

My thanks are due to Gerald Rothman, who has been good enough to read the text and correct some of its more glaring omissions, excesses or inaccuracies despite not agreeing with many of its conclusions. But then, what are friends for…?

I am grateful to my elder son, Franco, for reminding me that a few of my long-standing beliefs about the English might not correspond to present-day reality; I have duly taken his thoughts into account (where I could…).

My son Paolo has shown himself, as usual, to be an outstanding proofreader.

Finally, I thank my assistant Stephanie Farrer for her continued patience and accuracy.

Contents

Introduction

I do not dislike Jeremy Paxman. I know that there are some who consider him a little supercilious, perhaps; but if that feature is true, it has never bothered me and it is probably in keeping with the remainder of his personality.

I read with great interest his book 'The English – A Portrait of a People'[1]. I am duty bound, however, to point out immediately that he repeated (perhaps a Freudian slip...?!) a very common English mistake when he quotes (page 27) Dr Johnson as saying that 'a man who had not visited the Continent was always conscious of an inferiority from his not having seen what is expected that a man should see'. Incorrect, I observe, since what Dr Johnson said[2] was that 'a man who has not been <u>in Italy</u> is always conscious of an inferiority from his not having seen what it is expected a man should see..... All our religion, almost all our law, almost all our arts, almost all that sets us above savages, has come to us from the shores of the Mediterranean.'

That is by the by. I learnt a great deal from his book. But when I came to the end of it, I felt that the elements and features of this 'portrait of a people' were incomplete and, despite a criticism here and there, his overall tone was too eulogistic, faults were glossed over and problems, some

---

[1] *Michael Joseph 1998, Penguin 1999*
[2] *Boswell's Life of Johnson, Thursday 11th April 1776*

even major, were not discussed, but rather set aside as though they did not exist. Put differently, the portrait was too perfect: no wrinkles, no moles, no inevitable traits of age; or even no cruelty, dishonesty or sexual impropriety.

The English people I know, or the English as a people, are not quite like that. It should not be thought for a moment that, having put him right on what Dr Johnson said, I am setting out to criticise the English or his view of them.

That is not my intention. The reader should know that I have been living in England long enough to consider myself British, though I could never be English. I was born in London of Neapolitan parents (both born in Italy). My wife was also born in Italy, is Italian, but my three children and six grandchildren were born in England.

I see myself as partaking of both the English and the Italian culture, nor do I find anything odd about that. Most of us, in any case, have, or ought to have, two parents. I completed all my education in Italy where I obtained my first law degree; continued in England where I was a barrister (Lincoln's Inn) for five years and a solicitor for 45 years.

I am now retired, which has given me a lot of time to crystallize my thoughts about the English, developed over a very long stay in this country.

I have worked in London. I love England.

True, I get annoyed by the present mood of materialism, self-aggrandisement, aggression and enslavement to the USA. I regret the loss of that greatest British asset: not the Empire, but solid, reliable common sense. Nevertheless, I love England despite the break-up of the middle class centre ground and the erosion, and, regrettably, the disappearance of those traditional values that made the country great.

I love too the English countryside, despite the way successive Governments have been causing it to change beyond recognition. To the ravages of the Dutch elm disease we are now adding the destruction caused by reliance upon misguided policies (I can only hope that Philip Larkin's pessimistic views about our beautiful countryside prove misguided).

I must make it perfectly clear that I consider myself to be Italian by tradition and English (British) by custom. I see no contradiction whatsoever in this, any more than the Welsh or Scots do when feeling that they might partake of two cultures. Despite the fact that at the moment there are at least 2.7 million children in England having a single parent[3], I still subscribe to the view that the majority of people have, or ought to have, two parents, anyhow: accordingly, I see nothing unusual about my cultural ambivalence.

---

[3] *Haskin, John- 'Population Trends' Vol.91 Spring 1998 ISBN 11-6209690*

Both on a personal and on a professional level, I have met many English people, male, female and of different varieties either as clients, opponents, employees, or in other relationships; I also have, I am pleased to say, a number of English friends and I hope they will continue to remain such hereafter...

So much for the record and by way of introduction. If and insofar as any comments I make could be interpreted as too critical, then I beg forgiveness of those readers who might resent them. But I urge them to consider whether I might perhaps be right in what I say. If I reach any conclusion about the English, it is not a hurried one and I certainly would not wish to fall into the same category as a foreign journalist I know who, having spent a mere two and a half years in England, decided that he was qualified to express views on this and that aspect of English culture, even in fields where I myself would prefer to abstain from rushing to judgment.

It is, of course, almost an impossible task to project the portrait of a people. Despite the fact that we all have formed a mental picture of various countries and that we associate different nationals with certain patterns of behaviour and outlook, and despite the inevitability of such a process of generalisation, the task of characterising a whole people is an exceptionally difficult one. I come to it, let me say immediately, with great humility, conscious of the fact that Dr Johnson is on the record as saying 'there is no permanent national character; it varies according to circumstances'[4].

As I recall writing elsewhere, generalisations are normally just as useful as they are dangerous. For example, the average Italian associates the English with reserve, democracy and an Empire and, until recently, believed that London was perpetually shrouded in fog, as in Sir Arthur Conan Doyle's books. It is my experience that the English reserve evaporates under the influence of alcohol, our British democracy is under considerable pressure at the moment and, as everyone knows, we no longer have an Empire. Of course, the 1956 Clean Air Act has seen to it that the 'pea-souper' fog periods have disappeared...

Until recently, most people tended to associate the French with high fashion and first class cuisine. It seems to me that few people nowadays can afford the former and indeed, when it comes to it, Italian fashions at the moment, at least for the average man or woman, are a great deal more popular than French; and when we consider the latter, I would bet that the man in the street, if he had to choose between going to an Italian or a French restaurant (or indeed, any other...!), would prefer the former. In any event, the French were taught the art of cooking by the Italians.

---

[4] *Boswell's Life of Johnson, Saturday May 9th 1772*

In case the reader is doubtful about the validity of the statement just made, he should know that it was an Italian gentlewoman, Catherine de Medici, who brought refined cooking to France when she married (on October 28th 1533) Henry II of Navarre taking with her, maybe as part of her dowry, her retinue of Italian cooks who introduced to France even new vegetables such as artichokes, garden peas and truffles and specialities like 'zabaione'. The Encyclopaedia Britannica, under the heading 'gastronomy', will no doubt confirm... (By the way, I should mention that her chefs also introduced to the French what has become one of their most popular dishes, namely onion soup...)

Especially in England, we associate our German cousins with militarism and efficiency. As a cynic, I allow myself the remark that despite those alleged strengths, they managed to lose two great wars; and so it goes on.

I don't believe that I shall fall into the generalisations trap and if I do, I seek pardon of the reader as from now.

The difficulty I have encountered is the same to which Jeremy Paxman himself adverts, namely to try to identify who the English really are. I believe there is no answer to such a question. The mixture of races that has, over the centuries, made up what we call the English is such that it is impossible to relate back to a particular blood line. Or, as Daniel Defoe[5] put it in his 'A True-Born Englishman', there

---

5 *Daniel Defoe, 'A True-Born Englishman: A Satyr', 1701*

is no doubt that the mixture of races that went into making 'that vain ill-natured thing, an Englishman' was exceptionally great, from the Romans to the Normans and taking into account Saxon, Dane, Scot, Pict and Irish blood.

Certainly, we may distinguish between the English in one part of Britain, and the Welsh, the Scots and Northern Irish in the others. That is comparatively easy. Equally, we can distinguish between the English and the British generally (excluding the Welsh, the Scots and Northern Irish), i.e. between the true natives and those who have acquired British nationality in one form or the other. That is also easy. But there simplicity ends. Even the way this island is described does not help: England, Britain, Great Britain, the British Isles, the United Kingdom; let alone Albion, perfidious or otherwise (a point already made by George Orwell in 'The Lion and the Unicorn'[6]).

In his book[7] Norman Davies dedicates twenty-two pages of the Introduction to his bibliographical and library researches into how the history of the British Isles is catalogued. He highlights the complications starting with the American Library of Congress, continuing with the Oxford Library recording system, and ending with his identification of at least sixteen states that have existed in the British Isles from 1169 to 1922. Equally difficult, it seems to me, is a classification of who the English are.

---

[6] George Orwell, 'The Lion and the Unicorn', Secker & Warburg, 1941
[7] Norman Davies, 'The Isles - a History', Oxford University Press, 1999

The Romans were here between 43 and 410AD, as most English schoolboys know, but it is impossible to assess the extent of the intermingling of local with Roman blood. All one can say is that as they had done to other provinces the Romans, especially after the arrival of Julius Caesar in 55AD, brought civilisation to the British Isles; they brought their system of government, of law, of building, their roads, their art, their technology, as well as Greek medicine.

I should not omit to mention what is probably one of the Romans' more important contributions to the well-being of England, namely their introduction of new crops: from cabbages, cauliflower, cucumbers, lettuce, onions, parsnips, turnips and swedes to cherries, figs and plums. The Roman introductions have stayed with us and have become 'anglicised'.

They built posts, forts, roads, camps, towns, baths, villas and palaces; they established agriculture, medicine, architecture and discipline.

They endeavoured to create that 'pax romana' which, centuries later, the British Empire was to convert for all its possessions into 'pax britannica'. They extended to Britain their maxim 'civis Romanus sum', namely they granted their citizenship in the same way as British nationality was later to be extended to all races in the Queen's dominions.

Overall, the historical consensus is that the English adapted quite well to Roman dominance. There is evidence of this in the numerous excavations of Roman villas and mosaics which were clearly owned by the English as well as by Roman generals. The city of Bath is the best possible example of how the English related to Roman civilisation, let alone the fact that Edgar I (or Edgar the Peaceful, as he was otherwise known) was crowned with Roman solemnity in Bath itself.

I suppose that this was the first instance of an approach to political and social life which was later encapsulated in the well-known expression 'if you can't beat them, join them'.

Above all, they came with a firm belief in their own ability to mould history, in their nobility of spirit and of caste and in their outstanding military techniques and discipline.

It is interesting to note that when Britain found itself in a position to establish an empire of its own, it claimed, and indeed displayed, all the virtues which the Romans had brought with them many centuries before. One could say that, in the political sense, there is no doubt whatsoever that Britain at that stage of its history became the successor of Rome.

After the Romans left, the island was prey to the well-known invasions. The Angles and the Danes came over from Frisia or Friesland, and they mingled with the Germanic settlers, attacking and settling in southern England.

The most famous of the Danes was King Canute who, I suppose, could be termed the first 'Englishman' to endeavour to establish some kind of empire. Apart from becoming the overlord of Scotland, he was King of England, Denmark and Norway which, for those times, was a fairly extensive territory.

The Norse people attacked and settled in the whole of eastern England, as well as in western England, the Norwegians settled in other parts, including western Scotland and eastern Ireland, the Irish Picts and other Saxon people kept raiding the country, and they all took advantage of the fact that the Romans no longer protected Britain in the way they had done for just under four centuries.

Incidentally, it is interesting to note that the expression 'the English' is derived from the word 'Angle' which, in turn, comes from the Latin 'anglus', namely an inhabitant of 'Angul' – Angul being a district of Schleswig-Holstein that is now in northern Germany which, in turn, derived its name from the fact that it was like an angle in shape. It was easy to add to it the ending '-ish' and get Anglish that later converted to English.

Having said all that, it seems to me that essentially the English are a Germanic race, similar in many respects to the Germans of whom they could be termed if not brothers, then certainly cousins (a 'relationship' confirmed by the coronation of George I, the son of Sophia, Electress of

Hanover, in 1714 who inaugurated the Hanoverian phase of the British monarchy. The reader will recall the Act of Settlement of 1701 whose purpose was to overcome the absence of heirs and to allow the importation of a foreign royal family, as well as of Protestantism. Thus was inaugurated what was to prove a fairly successful period in British history, namely that of the Georgians. At the same time, however, it might be worth mentioning that perhaps on that coronation there occurred the first 'official' example of English xenophobia... because there were many people who clamoured against it...).

This is not meant to be a historical overview, because this writer is no historian. Its sole purpose is to make two fairly essential points. The first is that the island races, as they are called, which developed generally in the British Isles, were founded on settlements, or invasions if you prefer, by continental people. The second point is that the intermingling of blood that went into making what one may term loosely the English race was very great indeed.

Nothing unusual in that. Racial purity could only be dreamt up by mad men, of which Hitler was a prime example.

I am ignoring any reference to the Vikings, popular though they may be, for the simple reason that the Norsemen and the Danes were, in fact, Vikings. They were Scandinavians, and that's it. One terms them Norwegians or Danes, but Norway and Denmark at the time did not exist, any more than Sweden did and, in any event, they were ultimately defeated by one of the greatest 'Englishmen', King Alfred, who did much for English unity and for the language. One wonders how influenced he was by what he saw in Rome on the occasion of his second visit.

The monk Bede, writing in the 8th Century, identifies the Germanic origin of the English people by explaining that they were a mixture of Angles, a German tribe, Saxons, who came from Lower Saxony also in Germany and Jutes, who are believed to have originated in the Jutland Peninsula of Denmark, also a people of Germanic origin. The love/hatred relationship which has always existed between the English and Germany, and the so-called mutual respect that persists between the two countries, apart from their sporting antipathy, that is said to have prevailed even during the Second World War, lends support to the concept.

Furthermore, this common origin also explains in part the disdain that the English have always felt for the enemies of the Germans, the French, and by extension, for Latin people generally. Before the reader rushes to deny that any such antipathy exists, he should pause and consider, if he would, how much closer any individual Englishman feels to a German or a Swede than he does to an Italian or a Greek; but let's leave that aspect aside, at least for the time being.

It is conceivable that the intermingling of races in the British Isles may have gone some way towards creating a people who, having learnt to repel invaders and, where that was not possible, to join forces with them, has established a kind of almost conceited belief in its own ability. Coupled with the fact that the Roman influence remained prevalent for centuries even after the Romans had left, thus creating a common feeling for Roman military efficiency, organisation and laws, this may have contributed to the idea that just as the Romans had done, the English could develop an empire which covered substantial tracts of the known world, which has prompted the historian Norman Davies to remark[8] that *'the British in general and the English in particular, saw themselves as an imperial race'*. This may well be true, but no one can say for certain (and in any event, I would turn his past tense into a present indicative. As I shall endeavour to show, most unfortunately the English <u>still</u> see themselves as an imperial race).

On such basis, I shall take it as my starting point that the English are, in fact, an amalgam of Germanic and northern races, which became established some fifteen hundred years ago. That is their origin. One cannot obviously discount the impact of other influences, whether they be Mediterranean or not: and I do not for one moment ignore the effect on national characteristics of the numerous immigrants, whether Jews (Ashkenazim and Sephardim), Italians, etc. Many of them, in any event, have changed their names, so it is somewhat difficult to be too specific.

---

[8] *op.cit. p149*

However, one must draw the line somewhere. Therefore, I stand by the conclusion which I have reached for the purpose of trying to identify certain common traits. How far the English differ racially from the Welsh, the Scots and the Irish is a point that I would find much more difficult, if not impossible, to determine but which for present purposes is almost irrelevant.

According to another definition, less popular, the English are in great part the successors of those Roman soldiers who stayed on after the official withdrawal of Rome from Britain in 410 A.D., as well as of the Vikings, the Saxons, the Normans, the Dutch and any other citizens of any other country who were born here and through, say, five generations were almost completely anglicised. I believe it would take about a hundred years for the national characteristics of one particular type of immigrant, leaving aside the matter of colour, to be blended in with the locals and disappear or at least to mellow with the passage of time. After all, in his 'The true-born Englishman' Daniel Defoe described his compatriots as 'your Roman – Saxon – Danish – Norman – English'!

I believe too that it is almost impossible to define the character of a people. The only way one can do so is negatively, by referring to their history, thus adopting a canon of construction of the people as a whole which however is no guide whatsoever to the temperament or character of the individual.

Take, for example, the fact that Britain created a great Empire. Is it to be believed that it succeeded in doing so because of its innate ethnic or racial superiority? Or is it more likely to be the reverse, namely that because it managed to establish an empire, the country was able to develop a sort of ethnic and racial superiority mentality which perhaps was latent and might not have come to the fore but for the historical accident of the Empire?

I suppose one way of looking at the problem would be a negative one, namely to define the English as all those people who live in the British Isles, who are not Welshmen, Scotsmen or Northern Irishmen, nor of different ethnic origin, nor immigrants who, for one reason or the other, have become British subjects. This is not a terribly satisfactory way of doing it, but it is workable and it is the definition I shall adopt. A fellow like me with an Italian name and ancestry, although he may speak English well, is not English. Would I have become English if, way back in 1961 as Leonard Caplan, a leading member of the Bar, had suggested to me, I had anglicised my name into Arthur Baron? Yes, as far as the rest of the world was concerned, no as to temperament, character, etc.: I could change my name, not my blood and my psychological heritage.

Would the suggested change have had a significant impact on my acceptability as a person and as a lawyer by the English people? Somehow, I don't think so...

It is quite clear therefore that the description 'The English' in the title is an elliptical and, indeed, inaccurate formulation but for present purposes I shall also ignore that recent scientific studies have shown that the 'northern' if not Germanic and Scandinavian influence on the English race is possibly less significant than believed, more particularly since at least two chromosomes found in the English blood are said to originate from north-west Spain... (from the Basque region, in fact): in my view, it remains a fact that the Anglo-Saxon influence on the English is fairly substantial. Even if it is not truly genetic, it is definitely cultural and social in origin.

A true Englishman, of course, does not exist, in the sense that there is no purity for any race; the fact remains that the identification in the English of a Germanic influence, despite the blending of cultures generally in the country, is not too difficult to make. Apart from the invaders already mentioned (essentially starting in the 9th Century with the arrival of the Vikings and in the 11th with the Normans) we must not ignore the numerous religious sects of the 16th and 17th Centuries nor the influx of the Huguenots. It was inevitable that, after the Reformation, there would develop in England a kind of Englishness and Anglicanism which were quite distinctive so that an English culture followed naturally.

The Jutes and the Anglo-Saxons mixed over the centuries with the new influxes and, if not absorbed, were certainly affected by new blood as well as, over the centuries, by the plurality of religions.

Hence, although the expression 'the English' is quite imprecise, it is all-embracing at least negatively – that is to say, by excluding from the present analysis first or second generations of black, Asian, Arab or Mediterranean origin and concentrating solely on the English who are the successors of the northern invaders.

To the English as so defined I dedicate the following observations, also because I firmly believe that they have always been the object of some fascination, both to their compatriots and to foreigners, given the varied nature of their characters and temperament.

This fascination has often manifested itself in the numerous books and magazine articles that appear from time to time to try to explain what are the essential features of so-called Englishness. In addition to those writers mentioned in this text, there have been very many others who have tried to identify and explain away some of the essential features of the English people.

From Nancy Mitford to George Mikes, from Kate Fox to Jilly Cooper, from Bill Bryson to Alan Bennett, much has been said and written to explain why the English are stated to be gregarious or to have a sense of humour or to be fond of their privacy, to be handicapped by their reserve, to manifest hypocritical attitudes, to have a practical and common sense view of life, to be ridden by class problems, to be fair-minded and courteous; the list could be added to. In fact, it is not too difficult to agree with many of the descriptions that are given of the English for, in most situations, they are self-evident.

The problem however arises when these writers try to analyse the reason why English people behave in a particular fashion. What are in fact the original causes, say, of the Englishman's alleged hypocrisy?

When one gets to the stage of causation, the unanimity which exists amongst analysts of the English temperament and character begins to show signs of cracking, because every single writer whom I know has tried to identify what he thought was a principal but different cause of a particular type of behaviour. For some, it is the latitude of the British Isles and their totally unpredictable weather patterns; for others, it is some kind of psychological imbalance that causes the English reserve suddenly to be transformed into a violent, hooligan-type behaviour that is clearly antisocial.

The schizophrenic nature of the Englishman doesn't really help in this context. One can pray in aid the history of the country and claim that it is an essential part of the English background. But other countries have a history as well. Other countries are placed at different latitudes on the world map. What has geography got to do with football hooliganism or with what clearly is the Englishman's fear of his emotions? So it goes on.

I myself shall not indulge in any such exercise, firstly because I do not consider myself competent enough to do so and, secondly, because I don't think it would add much. I suppose that if the truth be told, and if pressed, I might be tempted to say that all the alleged causes of the English people's nature are true though a predominant one may well be the weather. But there can be a major argument on that as well...

What I shall try to do, however, is to highlight rather more than the obvious merits of the English people – discipline, courtesy, patriotism, positivity, practicality, individualism, tolerance, a keen sense of humour, the often inexplicable love of the underdog, the almost absurd fondness for the understatement (which causes many problems of comprehension especially to foreigners), friendliness and, at times, also kindness – some of their negative features, not because I am over-critical but simply to remind the reader that there are two sides to every coin. This is often forgotten, because the English people have a tendency to concentrate solely on their virtues and not on their vices. Nowadays, however, for a number of reasons, some of which I shall be considering, their 'vices' are becoming much more evident and more significant in the history of England. I can only hope that in my enthusiasm for truth – as I see it... – I shall not go over the top...

I will not be swayed by easy language and, where appropriate, I shall call a spade a spade.

Food

Salads, and eggs, and lighter fare, tune the Italian sparks'
guitar.
And, if I take Dan Congreve right, pudding and beef make
Britons fight.
Matthew Prior (1664-1721), Alma (1718)

This is a very interesting topic, at least for a Mediterranean who has seen how, since the end of the Second World War, English tastes in matters of gastronomy have changed.

I am old enough to remember the days of food rationing and the early beginnings of what was to prove a very slow revival of appreciation for good things as soon as that came to an end.

When I recall that certainly until the middle 1950s there were just about one or two Italian food shops in Soho, garlic, though not unknown, was nowhere to be found as a prescription in English cooking or recipes, parmesan was believed to be a citizen of Parma and not a cheese, and the average English housewife was extremely puzzled, if not shocked, when she saw anyone buying an aubergine at the greengrocers, I look back in wonder and observe that perhaps some of us are allowed to smile, condescendingly, at all the present-day 'English' recipes calling for basil, extra virgin olive oil and garlic.

With the advent of mass tourism, starting in the early 1970s, the English began to appreciate that there was, after all, something to be said for variety and that, good though they may be in their own way, roast beef, Yorkshire pudding and two veg, liver and bacon, toad in the hole, apple tart, spotted dick, bangers and mash and fish and chips are, to say the least, a trifle boring.

(Although one could observe, in passing, that like all other traditions, even the gastronomic ones, in England, die hard. I have an English friend who has travelled the world extensively, but still maintains that his most enjoyable food consists of a chip sandwich...)

The success of supermarkets with year-round availability of foods, initially exotic but now accepted elements in patterns of eating that are becoming fairly well generalised in the British Isles, has been a major contribution to a complete overhaul of English eating habits. And why not, since there is no doubt that the English love food. Don't be misled by the fact that most of them content themselves at lunchtime with a pre-packed salad or a sandwich. That is because either they have no time for something more substantial, or can't afford it because they're spending their excess money on other things. Give them a chance and the English will eat as much as anybody else, if not more.

But they do so not as a matter of routine, as might happen with the French or the Italians: rather, they look upon food as an event. Going out to dinner is becoming nowadays as eventful for the average Englishman/woman as an evening out drinking in the pub.

This is good. As the French gastronome Brillat-Savarin put it, who in fact was a lawyer before becoming an epicure, 'tell me what you eat and I'll tell you what you are' (I am ignoring the variant on that theme, namely 'tell me how you eat and I'll tell you who you are'). The English are becoming more and more international in matters of food: but are they becoming more discerning?

The answer must be in the affirmative. The English are learning fast. Suffice it to look at the shelves of most supermarkets to see the variety of foreign food products on display. I read recently that the most popular foreign 'take-away' in England is Indian. I don't know whether that is true; personally, I should have thought that it would be Chinese; but tastes are becoming more cosmopolitan and, in particular, the impact of the Continent is quite astonishing. It is apparent both from the continuing stream of foreign food recipes available in newspapers and magazines and, above all, on television, and by incidental portrayals in soap operas and similar programmes. Nothing is more common these days, whether it be in Eastenders or Coronation Street, for one of the characters to put a 'lasagne' (sic) or a pizza in the microwave and uncork a bottle of wine.

I often ask myself, inwardly smiling, how the English managed before the continuous availability of extra virgin olive oil, garlic, basil, ciabatta bread and cappuccino. What did they eat? Whilst it is true to say that perhaps the older generation are more reluctant to abandon established eating habits, there is no question that, over the past forty years – that is to say, from the early seventies – the English culinary scene has undergone a metamorphosis which is explicable only on the grounds that what was being fed before to the residents of the British Isles was fairly limited in scope. This is not to be taken as a criticism of good, solid, healthy English food, but simply as an observation of how tastes have changed. We now have the Mediterranean diet[9] and even (anathema to an Italian!) Mediterrasian cuisine.

(If I wished to be a chauvinist, I should observe that to refer to a Mediterranean diet is inaccurate (maybe another Freudian slip): the proper expression ought to be 'an Italian diet'…! But I may be going somewhat over the top…!)

With such change there has arrived in England a different perception of food, almost an acknowledgment that amongst the many traditions for which the English are famed, good cooking was lacking.

Such different perception, if not appreciation, is reflected in the increasingly popular success of television programmes of one kind or the other, and on all networks.

---

[9] *First scientifically observed – and so termed – in the region of Calabria, in Southern Italy, by the American nutritionist Ancel Keys, though of long-standing in many other regions of the Mediterranean*

Ordinary cooks, top-class cooks, famous actors, simple housewives, youngsters, students, lawyers and other professional people, old-age pensioners, food writers, 'gourmets', in fact anybody with the kind of face and tone of voice which is considered popular or is known to the general public, must take part in cooking performances.

The general public watches such programmes with an interest and an intensity which are truly extraordinary. The amount of time spent watching television cooks bears no relationship whatsoever to the consequent effort dedicated to real cooking in front of a stove; the viewer is under the illusion that what is shown on television can be replicated at home.

It is, in fact, more than an illusion: it is folly to suggest that the ordinary housewife or single mother has the time or the inclination to repeat the success of Raymond Blanc and his pineapple parfait. The public is effectively being brainwashed into believing that it can achieve the same results as seen on television. It is a fascinating experience for those who understand what cooking is all about and, in a strange sense, a sad commentary on the state of 'family' cuisine in the British Isles. But we mustn't be too hard on the poor viewers, especially female, since the programmes transport them into dreamland, a land of magicians and of fables which, if they knew anything at all about cuisine in the first place, they wouldn't really waste time on watching. But perhaps I am being unkind.

The spread of foreign restaurants in this country has obviously contributed to a greater appreciation of the finer things in life by the English, even though very often the foreign cuisine has been bastardised to suit local tastes. What, however, the English cannot perceive is that, leaving aside the absurdly expensive restaurants that qualify for this or that accolade in food guides or magazines (a true rip-off, believe me), the run-of-the-mill foreign restaurant in the British Isles (whether it be French, Italian, Spanish, or whatever, it does not matter) reflects a fall in original standards.

This is a concomitant of the fact that the English man or woman, who orders, say 'spaghetti al pesto', has probably only tasted the kind of pesto that has been made in England by a restaurateur who knew in advance that he was dealing with a very generous and tolerant public, a forbearing customer unlikely to complain if the quality was not up to standard; alternatively, pesto sold in a jar in the supermarket. The kind of customer I am describing would not complain essentially for two reasons: the first is that when it comes to food the English are undoubtedly amongst the most tolerant people in the world and will put up with quite a lot in circumstances where a continental would react perhaps with vigour; the second reason is that the standard by which the performance falls to be measured is not known to the English man or woman, simply because of the lack of a strong gastronomic tradition, or of knowledge of the particular dish.

The English cannot solely be blamed for this kind of situation, save in the sense that with more women going out to work and the family unit being gradually destroyed, it is much more difficult to maintain standards. I have always believed that good food is the result of good cooking which, in turn, is a cultural and emotive fact, as well as a physical one. It is born, and it dies, within the family, and, whatever television cooks may say or do, is a labour of love. It is taught by mothers to daughters and it represents the distillation of all the teachings and remarks by whosoever spends most of 'her' life in front of a stove. It is not learned from a book or a newspaper article or from television programmes any more than it is learned by part-time mothers/wives.

Cooking, like looking after a family, is a full-time occupation which cannot be left in the hands of anyone, male or female, who has already spent some eight or ten hours in an office or has been busy at some other job. People who get home in the evening after a full day at work are tired; they do not want to cook, though they might just about want to eat. If they have to prepare a meal, theirs is not a labour of love, but of hasty necessity. Thanks to the microwave, they cut corners, they lose their critical sense, their touch and, above all, their own appreciation for what they are doing.

Where the housekeeper is at work there can be no real cuisine. Hence the ready-made, pre-packed, pre-cooked, pre-frozen, so-called food which has no taste, no style and no freshness. It suits those who buy it, who end up getting exactly what they deserve.

Inasmuch as the family (and extended family) has ceased in England to have any real significance for the most part, there cannot possibly be any appreciation of good food where such circumstance prevails.

It is against the background of such a view that I maintain unhesitatingly that, as far as the UK is concerned, if blame is to be determined for inferior foreign food, it must be pinned firstly on those foreign restaurateurs who, regardless of their nationality, are much more interested in making a profit than in educating the public; secondly, on the supermarkets which are 'appropriating' foods that should be lovingly prepared with those that can be sold pre-packed to a lazy public (I shall revert to this matter of appropriating...); and finally, and most importantly, on the changed social structures. I suppose that cannot be helped. Still, there is hope. The fact that there are so many English people nowadays who also take a marked interest in food and wines generally, and especially other than French, is indicative of the development of a sensitivity to food and drink that was certainly lacking, say at the end of the Second World War, or perhaps when rationing ceased.
To that extent, as they have done throughout their history, the English (and the Americans in like manner) are profiting considerably from what is offered by other nationalities, and are almost making their own what they are finding, or at least, do not know where what they now have originated.

For example, I heard it said recently that pizza originated here. Admittedly, it was a young lady speaking who displayed the kind of 'culture' which, I am sure, would have allowed her to say, had she been asked, that jeans were invented by the Americans (they were not – we owe them to the Italians; the name originates in Genes, the city of Genova where the blue cotton cloth was first produced[10]). But she was symptomatic of the phenomenon I have been describing, namely of the manner in which the English throughout their history have been successful, indeed, brilliant, in making their own what initially was someone else's.

As I have already observed above, I shall revert to this acquisitiveness in a later chapter.

It is a trait, as far as food is concerned, which results in a much better standard of living and of health for the British people as a whole. By eulogising the Mediterranean diet and making it part of a suggested form of healthy living, the British are undoubtedly reaping the benefit of a tradition going back thousands of years. One could say that the olive and the grape are taking over from the barley and the lard or margarine. This is undoubtedly true. I remember the days when people shopped for lard, suet, dripping, bacon fat, goose fat (not always available to the average housewife), butter and margarine. A good percentage of

---

[10] *So much so that when, in 1860, Garibaldi left that city with his 'thousands' to go and conquer the Kingdom of the Two Sicilies, his soldiers already wore 'jeans', adopting the usage of a particular type of corduroy trouser worn by local sailors.*

them now buy olive oil (always extra virgin, of course…) or vegetable oils (some of them not so healthy) of various kinds.

This is all to the good and full marks should be awarded to the English (or the British) for the admittedly belated realisation that their gastronomic knowledge requires improvement.

Such improvement is often to be credited to foreign cuisines, not only the Mediterranean ones. But oddities occur…

The Thai restaurant that forms an annex to the charming small pub in our country village, provides inexpensive, good food six days a week. On Mondays, however, it advertises its 'English menu'. Customers will undoubtedly be surprised to learn that the first item of its English menu is… 'lasagne'.

I trust I may be forgiven a small 'plug' for Italy, whose contribution to better and healthier eating habits is very substantial, if not unique.

It is not merely a matter of parmesan cheese, known in England since the 14th Century, or Parma ham, also known in England since the 17th, or Bologna sausages, known here since the 18[th][11]. One need only take a stroll through the aisles of any British supermarket to find out how and what present-day English families are eating. It is no longer toad-in-the-hole, acceptable though that may be. It is not even, really, fish and chips or rhubarb and custard, enjoyable though such dishes can be. Just consider some of today's Italian additions to the English language: aceto balsamico, borlotti, bresaola, bruschetta, cannellini, cappelletti, carciofini, cassata, cavolo nero, ciabatta, gnocchi, gnocchetti, gorgonzola, grissini, lardo, lasagne, latte, macchiato, mascarpone, mortadella, mozzarella, pancetta, pandoro, panettone, panforte, panna cotta (not one of the most exciting Italian sweets but oh, how suitable to the English palate), panini, parmigiano (and grana padano), passata, pasta (in all its multifarious shapes), pecorino (romano, sardo, toscano; you name it, is now available...), pesto, polenta (unknown in England until not too long ago and now an essential adjunct for bulk and colour to many main courses otherwise lacking in character), prosciutto, ravioli, ricotta, risotto, rucola, salami, taleggio, tiramisu, torrone, tortellini, tortelloni. (I am, of course, ignoring the cappuccino and the espresso...)

(It is interesting to observe that some of the Italian words that I have just mentioned have become such an intimate part of the English language as to cause amusing situations. As an example, may I record a rather odd occurrence on the

---

[11] *For this last statement, v. Boswell's Life of Johnson, Saturday May 9th 1772, where, referring to Bologna, the learned doctor says in terms 'the sausages there are the best in the world'.*

occasion of a Celebrity University Challenge Programme on BBC2 on Monday April 7th, 2003 at 20:00hrs. Both the TUC team and Jeremy Paxman himself identified the pseudonym of a well-known Italian painter coming from Parma as 'Parmigiano' instead of 'Parmigianino'. Parmigianino is the artist's name of Girolamo Francesco Maria Mazzola (more commonly also known as Francesco Mazzola). A forgivable slip; one must nevertheless admire their gastronomic taste in being aware of one of the finer ingredients of Italian cuisine...)

The connection between England and Italian food is, in fact, of longer standing than might appear. It is well known that when the Great Fire of London occurred on September 2nd 1666 Samuel Pepys borrowed a cart to 'carry away all my money, and plate, and best things'. The following day he got hold of a barge to remove his wine and his 'parmazan' cheese and other items of value. The fact is that the wheels or rounds or parmesan cheese were exceptionally valuable items, so much so that they were also used as gifts in diplomacy. In 1511 the Pope made a gift to Henry VIII of one hundred parmesan cheeses and in 1556 the Pope made gifts of eight great parmesan cheeses to Queen Mary of England. The strength of Italian gastronomy lies in its variety and simplicity. Hence the enormous success of our pizza: so quick to prepare, so enjoyable, so filling, so ideal for children. Such a boon for busy housewives with a young family...

Buon Appetito!

The Pub – English Drinking Culture

It is most absurdly said, in popular language, of any man, that he is disguised in liquor; for, on the contrary, most men are disguised by sobriety – Thomas de Quincey, 'Confessions of an English Opium Eater', 1822.

I hope I am right in suggesting that the English owe their traditional pub to Cromwell's beliefs. Let me explain.

Until, say, the 16th Century the traditional forms of large-scale recreation for the English masses, and probably also for the nobility, were associated broadly speaking with the church. There were celebrations on the feast days of saints, for the blessing of harvests, at burials, at weddings. This is not to say that there were no forms of private amusements or theatres, music and dancing; but open public entertainment was very often sparked off by some religious occurrence.

The church had been, for centuries, the centre of village life in England, as in many other countries. But in England the impact of Puritanism and the severity of thought, behaviour and attire that followed from it, coupled with the dissolution of the monasteries in Elizabethan times, resulted in the decreasing importance of any activity connected with churches and churchyards. At the same time, local squires and magistrates were concerned about any kind of behaviour that could be termed either riotous or disorderly and, whilst they appreciated that one of the causes of such types of behaviour was, in fact, the consumption of alcohol, they found it increasingly difficult to place restrictions upon a simple and universally acceptable meeting place like the local inn or public house. In particular, the inn that provided services, such as stabling for horses and accommodation, food, drink and, at times, even sexual facilities, became increasingly popular since it offered benefits that could be utilised by rich and poor alike, by peasant and nobleman. Indeed, where the local squire was powerful and the village not too big, it was probably in his interest that people should congregate in the pub rather than elsewhere, that he could frequent himself, where he was more likely to exercise control and, above all, to learn about what was happening in the village.

The pub was the meeting place for the locality at large, where business could be discussed, farmers could congregate to compare notes, and the inn itself could serve as a focus for other activities, such as markets and fairs. The examples in English literature are legion. What grew with the spread and the significance of the local public house was a gregarious kind of mentality, encouraged, of course, by alcohol, but initially almost independent of the provision of drink, at least in the sense that people did not necessarily go to an inn in order to get drunk. They might go to play cards, dominoes, darts, skittles and later pool; alcohol was the catalyst of social intercourse, as it has continued to be throughout British history. Not for nothing, Samuel Pepys described the pub as 'the heart of England'.

In fact, a major merit is claimed for the English pub generally, especially its more modern versions. It is said almost repeatedly that congregating in pubs contributes to a reduction in class barriers. Whilst there is an element of truth in this, I find it difficult to accept it as a valid generalisation. It is not the pub as such which is a leveller of humanity: it is the intake of alcohol. In any event, pubs themselves have different types of bars and purchasing a drink at the counter of one bar, rather than the other, is of itself almost a mark of 'class' distinction; or at least, so it was until more recent times.

What cannot be denied, however, is the fact that the pub, as an institution, is a major element in the creation of certain features of Englishness which are undoubtedly unique. All foreigners remark on the beauty of our villages. That goes back a long time, typically to the coexistence of the church and the pub. Later, the cricket green was added but there is no doubt that these three elements – the church, the pub and the cricket green – are as representative of Englishness as fish and chips.

The licensing laws endeavoured (in my view, unsuccessfully) to reduce the damaging impact of alcohol and the consequent drunkenness; but they could never eliminate it until very recently. It is only over the past ten years or so that the licensing laws have become almost a dead letter. But until even as late as the sixties pubs did not open until 11 o'clock in the morning, 12 noon in Scotland, then closed at either two thirty or three in the afternoon, opening again at either five or six o'clock and closing at some time between 10 o'clock (Scotland) and 11 o'clock in the evening in London, whilst a few areas exercised the 'local option' to remain alcohol-free.

Only the most expensive restaurants had special licences that permitted them to serve alcohol with food, otherwise you had to turn up with your own bottle (and pay a corkage charge), since the overwhelming majority of cafés and eating places were prohibited from serving alcohol.

It was as late as 1964 that the ten-minute drinking time after three pm or ten pm, or whatever the applicable closing time, was added during which drinks could still, and indeed had, to be consumed and there were more limited opening hours on Sundays.

In Scotland and Wales, pubs closed on Sunday but bars attached to hotels were permitted to serve bona fide travellers who, in theory, were supposed to sign a register to indicate that they had travelled more than three miles. By the latter part of the sixties this rule was followed by nobody and it became known that there were certain bars where one could freely drink on Sunday, whether one had travelled or not. At the same time, there were established, in the principal cities, various types of drinking clubs with more or less lax membership rules, where one retreated when the pubs closed, if one wanted a drink. There was yet another 'fiddle', namely, that it was possible for certain premises offering snacks to serve alcohol for one hour beyond whatever the legal limit was in the locality.

England may have been swinging in the sixties (more about this later), but limited drinking hours certainly contradicted the free and easy atmosphere.

The practice prevailing as regards the sale of alcohol in other countries did have overall a good effect on England, but could not prevent the British getting drunk. Male or female, this was and has remained a national trait if not a major problem, as witness the behaviour of the free-thinking and -behaving young and not-so-young girls on Saturday nights.

For that, it has always proved difficult to find a cure. The problem affects both men and women; indeed, not too long ago, the Cambridge College of St Catherine's carried out a survey which showed that its students (women) were exceeding any reasonable limit in their consumption of alcohol. It is, of course, well known that alcoholic drinks are the best possible social lubricants; nor is there anything either wrong or exceptional about that. But it does seem that in the British Isles this kind of lubrication lends itself to more problems than elsewhere, whether it be in the behaviour of football hooligans, rapists, rioters, violent husbands, or motorists 'over the limit'.
There are at least another two reasons why the English pub became such a prominent feature of the country. Alcohol was needed, it was safer to drink than water and cheaper

than tea or coffee. Real men, strong men, working class men drank beer, which was believed to add to strength; and if people got drunk, it did not matter much since the occurrence was frequent and almost universal. Wealthier people, and the nobility, had a tendency to prefer port, sherry and Madeira wines.

The second reason is that pubs became sports centres, in the sense that, where they could, they provided the traditional blood sports and when those became illegal, concentrated on traditional pastimes such as skittles or darts. Amongst the pastimes, football and cricket clubs became centred on the pub because, at least initially, the pub was the only establishment in the village that provided toilets and possibly changing facilities, into which one could retreat after the game for a drinking session.

Not all pubs organised sporting events, but some did, once they could convince the magistrates to grant suitable licences. Even when licensing laws were tightened, special licences were usually granted without too much difficulty for particular events. The licensing laws were tightened towards the end of the 19th Century because the country fell into a temperance mood. Quakers and Methodists, as well as Anglicans, felt that drunkenness should be avoided at all costs, a sort of moral backlash aimed at demon alcohol.

However, a principal drawback of the reforming temperance mood was that pubs ceased to become family centres because the age at which children could be admitted was gradually increased. There was thus established that particular feature of England, namely the severance of parents from children when it came to wining and dining, which can be said to date from 1882 when pubs were forbidden to sell beer to those under the age of 13; the situation lasted essentially until the late 1990s. To a Latin, that is one of the principal causes which has encouraged the Englishman to get drunk so easily. Mothers and fathers did not wish to be seen getting drunk by their children: the children stayed at home or outside, often locked in the car.

This in turn created a situation which persists to this day, when the children of British parents are more likely to misunderstand the significance, the nature and the effect of alcohol, simply because they haven't been used either to drinking it or to seeing it drunk within the bosom of the family (a situation which is typical of northern countries in any event, and not exclusive to England).

Digressing, I observe that another custom that Latins find almost incomprehensible, which is almost related to the desire of English parents, (to some extent, of course – it was not common to all English parents, and pertained mainly to those coming from wealthier families), is the sending of their children to educational establishments away from home, very often some distance away, where bed and board are provided. This custom was fairly well established by the time of Elizabeth I. We know about it because some of the most interesting observations on what was occurring in England during the 16th Century come from the 'relations' of the Venetian ambassadors. These 'Relations of England' are all important because they provide an insight into what the English at the time were like.

Obviously, some descriptions are totally out of character in present times, but some still fit to this day. Allowing myself a further small digression I should note that in one of these reports, that unfortunately is unsigned, we are told that the English were 'extravagantly foolish and superfluous in apparel'; furthermore, they were exceedingly 'fantastic and absurd in the way they were dressed'.

Some two centuries earlier, an Italian envoy had recorded:
> *'There is no country in the world where there are so many*
> *thieves and robbers as in England; insomuch that few*
> *venture to go alone into the country excepting in the middle of the day, and fewer still in the towns at night,*
> *and least of all in London'.* [12]

(The reader should not however think that these 'ambassadors' were prejudiced against the locals. A Venetian ambassador to England, Andrea Trevisano, wrote

---

[12] *Henry Stanley Bennett, Life on the English Manor (A Study of Peasant Conditions 1150-1400), OUP, 1937*

in 1498 'whenever they see a handsome foreigner they say that he looks like an Englishman'.)

The same author (in his 'Relation…' to his government) reports that the English were intemperate in their eating and drinking habits, but more particularly, in the present context, he records a tendency of the English to send their children away from home when they reach the ages of seven or nine, in order that they might improve themselves. This separation on a regular basis for long periods of time, of parents from children, in English society, has had a number of extremely important social and psychological consequences which, regrettably, it would be outside of the scope of this work to analyse but which, for a Latin at least, make more easily understandable a number of common English traits.

By the way, I read somewhere that the National Society for the Prevention of Cruelty to Animals was founded in 1824; the National Society for the Prevention of Cruelty to Children was established in 1884, 60 years later. Perhaps jocularly, the writer who provided this information hinted that there was the proof that the English loved their animals more than their children!

I do not share his belief. I think the English love their children in the way most parents do; whether they manifest the same feelings of love and affection in visible form is a totally different issue.

My view is that whilst the English love their children, their treatment of them follows on from the general tendency of the English people not to make a fuss. The English don't make a fuss of their children in the same way as a number of other nationalities do. Not for the English the constant outward manifestations of affection that are more common in Latin countries. But then, it is a national trait that the English avoid making a fuss in all sorts of situations. This is a fundamental reason why they are unlikely to complain, especially in restaurants when the standard of food or of service is not adequate. It is not that they don't realise what's going on, it is simply that they do not wish to attract attention to themselves and to the situation that has arisen. In a strange sense, it could be said that this attitude is the behavioural equivalent of their fondness for the understatement. It is quite often the case that an Englishman may be tempted to comment on a performance of any kind (artistic, sporting, political and so on) by saying 'not bad' whereas deep down he feels that he ought to say 'bloody good'.

Anyone who has observed English parents with their children would agree with the statements I have just made. There is, however, a drawback to this attitude; not so much in the sense that it can create difficulties in the overall parental attitude to children, but, more particularly, as far as third party observers are concerned. It may be the result of a misunderstanding of this attitude, rather than the conclusion to be drawn from a number of cases of maltreatment of young children by their parents, that has resulted in the proposal made in March 2014 for what has become known as the Cinderella Law.

It is now suggested that, well apart from physical ill-treatment of children – which is, in any event, well covered by existing legislation – a new law should be passed to deal with *'emotional abuse and cruelty'* by parents towards their children, which could land husband or wife or even both in prison for up to ten years! The difficulty is that it will, in most cases, be almost impossible to prove lack of love or care as distinct from physical abuse or neglect of children; there are so many variables in parental manifestations of either discipline or concern, ranking from the irritation caused by a youngster running through the supermarket aisles to the weepy, if not capricious, behaviour of young children.

It seems to me that this proposed law is further evidence of two factors that have recently become quite prominent in British society, namely the desire of the nanny state to interfere in every aspect of our lives on the one hand, and – this is much more serious – the breakdown of the family throughout the UK, which results from the 1969 divorce legislation and has become more and more marked since the 1970s. It would probably be somewhat trite of me to observe that a single mother caring for two or three toddlers with little support from their father, and possibly in receipt of a pittance in benefits from the State, would have to be a saint if she did not allow, occasionally, her anger at the children's behaviour to boil over from time to time. I don't think that any social worker or similar 'authority' will ever be in a position to determine whether her reactions amount to emotional cruelty for which she could be sent to prison (and, if so, what's going to happen to the children? The State will take over, of course...).

On the cynical side, however, it may well be that my assessment of the English attitude towards children is mistaken, hence the need for the State to intervene... I sincerely hope that that is not the case...; otherwise, it will be another opportunity for our too numerous busybodies.

But these attitudes cannot be helped. In a strange sense they are genetic; aggravated perhaps in a society where examples of sexual excesses abound whilst manifestations of nobler feelings are ignored.

Going back to the pub (as I must: my apologies for the rather lengthy digressions), such separation was, until recently, strictly enforced where children had to remain outside whilst their parents partook of alcoholic drinks. It was only recently, say over the past 15 years or so, that pubs began catering for families, clearly reaping the benefit of their Continental experiences.

The impression remains, however, that English parents would prefer not to have their children around when they go drinking at the pub, a sort of haven for the tormented soul, perhaps.

The pub is obviously keeping up with the times. Particularly by way of catering to the restrictions on smoking in public places, we now find establishments which are still called pubs but are in reality eating places (one cannot always describe them as restaurants) which have retained the main counters, providing drinking facilities, where beer is still drawn off the keg. Children are no longer discouraged although some pubs actually display notices barring the access of children under a certain age; but that is not related to the drinking laws, simply to the fact that perhaps the establishment has no desire to cater for children for whom their parents expect smaller portions at a cheaper price, or wishes to avoid the noise inevitably made by babies and young children.

Having said that for completeness, one concludes by observing that there is no doubt that the English pub is an extraordinary and unique institution which finds no equivalent in any other country in the world. I know that in some foreign places (holiday resorts, capital cities, etc.) there are attempts to replicate the 'English pub' but they are, in the main, both fraudulent and unsuccessful. They are fraudulent because the atmosphere of the English pub, especially the village pub, can never be replicated on Corfu or in Barcelona, or even Valbonne; they are unsuccessful because they do not provide the unique environment which embraces people, of all classes, all races, and of both sexes.

There can be no argument that the pub is a typically English institution, a classic manifestation of the Englishness that it is true to say foreigners, as a rule, cannot really understand and some of whom might also be envious of our communities that congregate in pubs. It is sometimes said that given the individuality of the English people, especially of the males, the existence of the pub is almost a contradiction since it is there, in a strange sense, almost akin to what happens with clubs, that the English person can find the environment where he feels both at ease with fellow drinkers and protected almost by their proximity.

The long-standing tradition of 'buying rounds' is proof of the need to strengthen the relations and the friendships that pub drinking endorses. True, it facilitates alcohol abuse and often drunkenness, but it is almost like a glue that binds those who regularly frequent such establishments.

What can be readily identified in English pubs are the distinctions, both of class and of wealth that divide the nation. To that extent, the English pub is a microcosm of British society and the best way to end this chapter is to remind the reader that in the early 17th Century the Duc de Sully wrote that 'the English enjoy themselves sadly, according to the custom of their country'...

We must, of course, take with a very big pinch of salt the vision that he projects of the way the English enjoy themselves; I would suggest that it is not that accurate and it might reflect the prejudice that the French have always manifested vis-à-vis their neighbours across the Channel.

Nevertheless, – and clearly out of context – I observe that there is an element of sadness about the current British social situation. For example, statistics published in April 2011 show that no less than 31% of habitable units in England are in the occupation of one person only.

Later statistics published in November 2012 indicated that nearly 2.5million adults between the ages of 45 and 64 live alone, such figure representing an increase of over 50% since 1996. There are, no doubt, strong social reasons (the destruction of the family unit by divorce, economic circumstances and so on) why this situation pertains; but we should not rule out the possibility that there is a genetic sadness factor about certain aspects of English life.

It may well be that this is one of the principal reasons why English pubs, despite the losses that have occurred in their numbers over the past 20 years, continue to be an essential feature of England. May they carry on being so...

On 'Arriving' Back in England

'Home, sweet home.'

One always knows when one is back in England. There are so many indicators, apart from the signs at the airport or elsewhere being written in the English language! But one would realise it even without the writing...

In theory, one should be pleased to be back home, although present-day queues at passport control, lasting occasionally well over one hour, are quite disheartening and, I would suggest, unnecessary. Once upon a time – before there was a distinction between EEC citizens and others – I had developed a technique to avoid even the smallest delay when getting back in the country, namely, to try and choose a queue where there were no children and no persons who, because of their attire, demeanour or colour, were less likely to have a British passport. Nowadays this gimmick no longer applies: there are usually delays.

Before the advent of common and comparatively inexpensive air fares, say in the 1950s, one crossed the Channel from France. Getting off the train at the French ports (Calais, Boulogne, Dunkerque) one always found the typical French confusion with porters rushing up and down in what appeared to be almost a chaotic fashion, much to the discomfort of the old or the inexperienced people from... more primitive countries who merely went along with the masses and followed, so to say, the tide.
At long last, one managed to board the old British Railways ferry where, especially in the early '50s, the prevailing smell was of diesel, tobacco and tea made with Carnation condensed milk.

There were women dressed as nurses, probably nurses, walking around the boat to help those who might get or be seasick. In the '50s the ponderous British Railways ferries did not have the kind of stabilisers that are more common in the 21st Century, so some of the crossings could be particularly difficult, especially in winter time.

When fog or mist permitted, one caught sight of the white cliffs of Dover, an imposing romantic view and one realised that home was close.

The tidier system of porterage (half a crown or five 'bob' were sufficient to cover most luggage) prevailing at Dover or Folkestone was again a reminder that we entered a different world and the typical, acrid smell of the coal engines and the steam vapour from the boilers of the trains were still fairly noticeable, if not almost romantic, after the electrified railways of the Continent. One might approach London again in fog and get out at Victoria, but from the moment one boarded the ferry everything seemed to slow down somewhat, to be calmer, more relaxed.

And then, as George Orwell puts it[13], one knew one was at home anyhow because 'the beer is bitterer, the coins are heavier, the grass is greener'. How things have changed! The coins are much lighter nowadays and about to disappear and lager and wine are almost replacing bitter and stout, and tastes are getting softer in the same way as the country is.

---

13 *The Lion and The Unicorn, p10*

But one knew instantly that this was a civilised country, where policemen patrolled the streets unarmed, they were all at least five foot ten inches tall (1.78cms), many 'Dixon of Dock Green' types, still used bikes, there were few policewomen, there were not many cars and they seldom got stolen save by criminals who needed to rob a bank, doorways to offices and homes were normally left open or unlocked, as were cars; entry phones to office buildings didn't exist; condoms were purchased at the barber's; the national anthem was played at the end of all cinema performances.

The policemen were polite; they were not armed. The arming of policemen came about, as had been correctly anticipated by those who objected to it, as a direct consequence of the abolition of the death penalty in 1965. Until then, criminals knew only too well that the rope was waiting for them if in the course of the commission of a crime they or their associates were found to have had a weapon, whether it was used or not. The case of Bentley became quite famous, for he was hanged despite maintaining that he did not have a weapon and that his crying out to his mate 'let him have it' did not mean that he should use his gun but that he should drop it. The presiding judge at Bentley's trial was Lord Goddard, known for his strictness in treating criminals.

We had no identification documents, were not obliged to carry our driving licence and did not even feel we had to provide evidence of identification or our name if stopped.

People were extremely friendly, tolerant, well-behaved, quiet. Television viewing was not yet either available or widespread and the public relied for much of its information on daily newspapers. In fact, newspapers were so common a source of information that London in those days had three evening newspapers (and they were not free). They were the Evening Standard, the Evening News and The Star and had come into being way back in the 1880s. Apart from the first one, they no longer exist, The Star ceasing publication in 1960 and the Evening News merging with the Standard in 1980.

I wonder how many youngsters nowadays can possibly be aware of how different life was in those days. The post was delivered in the morning, soon after the early morning delivery of milk, and for a second time in the afternoon.

The arrow-type indicators on cars were considered so unreliable that one was not allowed to pass a driving test without knowing how to use one's right arm...: straight out to turn right, moving about in circular anti-clockwise fashion to turn left and up and down to slow down...

Wing mirrors were not fixed to cars as standard equipment: they were an optional extra. Practically never would it cross a motorist's mind to park, even partly, on a pavement...

The first section of the M1 London-Leeds motorway was opened in 1959 and was rather slowly extended northwards, road humps were unknown as were fixed speed cameras. The breathalyser had not yet become available and anyone suspected of being so to say over the limit was often taken to the nearest police station and asked to walk straight on a line painted on the floor of the station... Of course, a blood test was also administered if thought appropriate. A more 'romantic' approach?

Cities and villages had not yet been invaded by motor cars, so parking was not a problem. There were, of course, no parking meters and one almost never saw motor vehicles double-banked or positioned either halfway or fully on pavements.

Trams were still in use in most major cities and even in London, especially in its southern section, and when a bus conductor issued a ticket a gentle bell was rung by him when punching the ticket, the sound of which seemed to interest children.
People very seldom kissed each other when they met, contrary to what is so customary (and sometimes so annoying) nowadays when one has to decide on which cheek to start and whether to kiss on one or both or occasionally three, if not four times. In fact, even a handshake was not that normal when meeting a stranger and especially not for a man when meeting a woman.

The entertainments available to youngsters on Saturday nights were much more sedate than todays. Drugs were not common, the use of knives only occasional and violence occurred mainly outside pubs at or after closing time.

The more enterprising young boys and girls would usually go dancing on a Saturday night. In London, at the Hammersmith Palais and other venues; in the suburbs, perhaps at Richmond.

Most of us were really quite naïve...!

Visiting any NHS dentist was free and the relative treatment was a mere one pound (raised to one pound and ten shillings in 1961...); no dentures could cost more than five pounds.

London telephone exchanges, in particular, had numbers preceded by 263 quaint names (shortened to the three initial letters) like Abbey, Arnold, Belgravia, Colindale, Covent Garden, Gulliver, Grosvenor, Juniper, Museum, Shepherd's Bush, Victoria, Viking, Western and so on.

The road layout at Marble Arch, London, was the same as had stood for years and Speakers' Corner was as busy as ever. All kinds of view were voiced there and protests were usually verbal – no fisticuffs.

Nowadays, it looks almost deserted by comparison, its most visible elements being not the number of speakers on stands but the occasional, almost lonely ice-cream or hot-dog van.

One final, striking thought. Football was played for the sake of the game and of sport, and certainly not to make money. I was reminded of this quite recently (February 27th 2014) at the funeral of one of our greatest and probably most-loved footballers, Tom Finney, when the broadcaster remarked that in his day Finney was paid £14 per week…

It struck me as absurd that, a few days before, another footballer of today was said to have negotiated a new contract at a fee of £300,000 per week.

Finney was often chosen as a left-winger for the national team. I remember with nostalgia the front set-up of our very successful national football team: Matthews, Mortensen, Lawton, Mannion and Finney. What a difference from today…

This is probably a nostalgic view of a country which has changed dramatically over the past 50 years. The advent of the aeroplane and the speed of progress have contributed to the modernisation of England, but at what cost? I am not saying that the English have completely lost their national characteristics but the Englishness of the country is reducing all the time.

I have often thought that such trait began diminishing as the English countryside seemed to be denuded after the practical disappearance of the Elm. I have always considered the Elm one of the most beautiful of our trees.

Every time I saw one stirring in a gale, I was reminded of the beautiful statue of the Nike of Samothrace, now dominating proudly the staircase of the Louvre in Paris.

How apt is its description given by the Italian writer Gabriele D'Annunzio as 'clothed in wind' ('Vestita di Vento'). Nothing but a memory left...

The English Weather

Is there in the world a climate more uncertain than our own? And, which as a natural consequence, is there anywhere a people more unsteady, more apt to discontent, more saturnine, dark and melancholic than ourselves...?
William Congreve, 1698

I have always considered that it is most important not to discount the effect of the weather on the temperament and the character of the English people. With warm fronts, cold fronts, occluded fronts, alternating at great speed over the whole country, frequent and sudden variations in temperature (especially downwards...), it is not surprising that writers have found it difficult to determine whether the British Isles had a climate or a weather system or merely a history of warm fronts. Leaving the technical aspects aside, it must be difficult for our bodies to keep up the various levels of energy and intensity that those fronts might bring about. For example, rain and dampness are known to have a debilitating or at least a disheartening, if not deflating, effect on many people. We are becoming increasingly aware of the consequences that changes in pressure, humidity and temperature have on human beings.

What were once considered old wives' tales are now being rehabilitated on a regular basis.

Ignoring the effects of the moon on the behaviour of human beings (whether it be on precipitating a delayed birth or giving rise to depressive phases or determining the right moment for picking fruit or grapes and so on), there is no doubt that the variations in temperature are particularly marked throughout the British Isles and that, as a result, our individual energy levels are influenced by a sort of tug-of-war. A sunny day or spell raises excitement, soon to be frustrated once the cloud cover reappears.

Admittedly not all individuals are affected in the same manner and to the same degree, but very often they are without even being aware of what is happening to them, or why.

Not to be discounted either as having an important effect on the health of the British people is the consideration that less sunlight reduces the amount of vitamin D available to the body. It is only in recent years that GPs have been dedicating greater attention to the effects of vitamin D deficiencies; as a matter of fact, vitamin D sprays and tablets are now available in most British pharmacies.

What is true is that people are conscious of the fact that their bodily functions slow down in cold weather and are reactivated by the appearance of warmth (whether of the real kind resulting from a rise in temperature or because of what one should term the psychological effect brought about by the presence of a blue sky or a sunny day). Most people know that they are more cheerful and more energetic when the sun is shining and they rush out in light clothing or short sleeves, to nibble sandwiches during their lunch hour in the park or elsewhere.

The effects of variations in air pressure, humidity, temperature and light have a marked, almost magnetic, effect on the body's hormones; blood circulation is often at the mercy of weather changes.

I have always thought that considerable weight must be attached to the unpredictable and possibly unique meteorological conditions prevailing in England as an explanation of the changes in mood and behaviour that come over English, and northern, people, as soon as they move even for short periods to warmer climates.

I would go further and suggest that the inevitable and rather stoic habituation to the particular weather conditions prevailing in the British Isles has had an exceptionally marked formative influence on the British national character and, furthermore, has contributed to the creation of a typical kind of humour which is of great help nationally in the acceptance of difficult or unusual circumstances.

The Gulf Stream does have a tendency to play strange tricks on this part of the world. Temperate our climate may well be, but one thing is certain: it is wholly unpredictable.

There is nothing new about this. I am not sure whether it was Tacitus or Julius Caesar, but it was remarked quite some time back by the Romans that Britain's skies were almost perpetually full of clouds. It is certainly a fact of life that one can have long periods in England when the sun is not visible.

The effects of that are to be seen all over. Some are related to building patterns. It has often been observed that one of the principal reasons why, at least until recently, the English preferred to build houses of at most two storeys, was not only related to their desire for seclusion, but was inspired by the need to receive as much light as possible.

Skyscrapers will not provide much daylight at the lower floors level.

One obviously does not have to go so far as some of the ancient people who thought that the sun was <u>the</u> god, but it suffices to notice how the face of some of the principal British cities changes completely on a sunny day. People become more extrovert, more loquacious, more inclined to smile, sit at outside tables at cafes or stand in groups on the street with their pints of beer or, more commonly, their white wines (nowadays, Pinot Grigio, extremely popular though not necessarily one of the best Italian whites... but that is a matter of opinion).

The pressures of work seem to become more bearable on a sunny day. But when it is cold and rainy, there is not much else to do and if one has to refrain from becoming too industrious, then possibly the only solace left is that of alcohol or drugs.

I am not saying that there is no sun in England. I don't go so far as Byron did when he remarked (in his Don Juan) about the English summer 'starting in July and ending in August'; but I am making the point, with conviction, that the temperament and the character of the English have been moulded to a great extent by what I would call a northern-type weather.

Such kind of weather has ensured that extremes of feeling do not often occur and when they do, they seem to last less than in hot climes.

Apart from the Civil War, revolutions of the French or South American kind are unknown in British history. Indeed, it is almost inappropriate to define what happened in 1688 as a 'Revolution', at least by continental or southern American standards.

This is all to the good. It makes the English more peaceful, more tolerant, more benevolent generally towards the foibles of other human beings. Even if on the negative side one of its effects on the psyche is introversion, it guarantees a certain disinterest in the activities of other human beings, which is one of the hallmarks of the social freedom that until the Swinging Sixties and the advent of unexpectedly violent manifestations (protests, riots, violence etc.) of extreme, partisan, un-Christian beliefs and behaviour, made England such a desirable country to live in.

A further point I should like to make, with less conviction since it is a highly debatable one; but I believe it is worth a mention.

I have often wondered whether it is because of the particular climate prevailing in our part of the world that the English are not gifted artistically, at least in the sense that painting (with a few notable exceptions) and sculpture have never thrived in England. The only truly national arts are literature and poetry. If one asks a foreigner how artistic the English people are, the answer is usually not too definite: in the main, the names that are cited are confined to Byron, Oscar Wilde and Shakespeare (I know, we also have Constable, Turner and the Pre-Raphaelites…).

It may be that different weather conditions and patterns of living, diet included, have contributed to this lesser artistic development in certain fields. Perhaps the English are reliant on a different kind of imagination; certainly they cannot be accused of not having any. The literary inventiveness that prompted the works of Shakespeare, let alone those of most other English writers and poets, must have been enormous, their feelings just as powerful. But it is almost as though these could be expressed only in words rather than in images.

The emotional 'constipation' of the English (if the noun seems inappropriate, let's replace it by a constitutional reluctance or a marked repression) openly or otherwise, to acknowledge the power of their emotions may well be a contributory factor to what I should like to describe as an inborn inability to give a graphic, visual representation of their inner thoughts, at least to a significantly high standard.

Perhaps the Latin races, treated to different influences, to a different light, have succeeded in doing just that; perhaps Greek architecture and sculpture have provided for them a more visual impact and a shapely, almost sensuous influence on the imagination, thus facilitating the development of a more body-centred expression of feelings and emotions. It is difficult to tell and I clearly do not claim to have provided an answer.

A difficult topic this. I think I should let it rest at this point... save to make two observations.

The first one is that I have little hesitation in stating that if our weather were more reliable, consistent, less subject to extreme temperature fluctuations and to long periods of cloud cover – in a word, more Mediterranean if not Caribbean in style – there would not be many English residents wishing to travel to the Continent for their summer holidays...

We tend to forget that England's countryside, coastlines and features of interest are quite worthwhile.

Let me conclude by observing that Oscar Wilde had remarked that conversation about the weather is the last refuge of the unimaginative...

A Classless Society

'You can be in the Horseguards, dear, and still be common'
– Terence Rattigan, 'Separate Tables', 1954

A British Prime Minister, John Major, is on the record as having said more than once that it was his wish to try to make Britain a 'classless society'. Understandable perhaps, since he certainly wasn't a typical Conservative minister or originated from a particular class in British society. In a sense, it might have been quite difficult for him to determine what exactly is meant by a class-bound society, although he must have seen for himself how important an education at Eton or Oxbridge was when choosing his colleagues, members of the diplomatic corps, high court judges and generally in identifying suitable candidates for what one might term higher posts[14].

He does not seem to have appreciated either that the impact of class in Britain is reducing, slowly, hence possibly his desire to pursue greater social equality, something which I do not believe he even remotely achieved.

It has always been difficult to determine what occurs within the various class divisions in Britain. Upper class, middle class, lower class are the fairly ordinary classifications and now, thanks to the much-criticised sociologist Charles Murray, we also have an underclass[15]. I believe we failed to understand the accuracy of Murray's description and may have been quite unfair to him when levelling the accusation that he was pushing history back a hundred years, by arguing that there are some people who are more deserving than others; but there are different shades and standards of distinction, or lack thereof, within each of these descriptions and they are accentuated by speech.

A certain identification with a particular class is manifested more often in England than in other countries by the manner in which both language and voice are used. Perhaps not so much a matter of the language itself, since that would be dependent on the type of education received

---

[14] *The elitism (and consequent advantages) of an education obtained as such three establishments is of itself a unique, typically English marker of class, deserving of a chapter to itself!*
[15] *Charles Murray, Underclass – Losing Ground, IEA, H&W Unit, London 1996*

and of knowledge acquired, rather a reliance on the accent of the person and, more particularly, on the mannerisms that very often form an adjunct to accent. Admittedly, there are some to whom both accent and mannerisms of speech come naturally, almost as a visceral manifestation; but they are not many. The remainder of those who are keen on accent and linguistic fads are on the phonetic make, trying to be what they are not and, above all, to impress. Of course, we have variations from university to university, from city to city, from England to Scotland, but there seem to be certain common traits in the way English is spoken in England.

Consider some of the following:

1. As far as I can tell, Britain is the only European country where there are so many establishments that offer elocution training; in other words, where people are taught admittedly how to speak, but above all how to change their accents in order to be able to utter sounds that are more acceptable (whether of the Queen's English, received pronunciation type or otherwise) in a manner which is more persuasive, abandoning (as though ashamed of them) whatever original inflections their home town dialect might have provided. I am not aware of similar establishments, let alone in such numbers, in, say, France, Italy or Spain. Even though I may be prepared to be corrected on this particular issue of numbers, I maintain that in these three countries, which I happen to know well, people do not go out of their way to hide the fact that they originate from one

region rather than the other: often, quite the reverse, since their local accent may indeed be an advantage from the electoral point of view. The way in which some English people try to speak never ceases to fascinate me, even leaving aside any question of the presence or otherwise of a local, more provincial accent.

2. But it is not merely a matter of teaching people to efface or refine their accents and, as perhaps an unwanted but inevitable result, even to some extent their individuality. It is the manner and their delivery of speech and, above all, the tone of voice. I have always enjoyed the study of languages and I am very interested in those English people of all religious and political affiliation who, at a certain level, try to use speech as a marker of class distinction. I leave aside particular instances of the use of vowels ('gaune' instead of the more ordinary 'gone', 'craws' instead of cross, 'awfen' instead of often etc.; the examples are legion and all British comedians have used and played upon them).

3. There is a type of delivery, soft, suave, with calculated cadences, occasional well-planned hesitations to show how much thought is going into words, to convince the listener that the speech comes from the heart. In reality, almost with the purpose of allowing the listener to become hypnotised by the sounds uttered without having to consider the substance of what is being said. There have been a number of what I would term 'classy' persons who have indulged in this practice but discretion prevents me from mentioning names; and in any event, the list would be too long.

I believe that the average Englishman tends, tolerantly perhaps, to overlook these attempts to hide one's personality or the substance of what one is saying behind a façade of suavity and pleasant sounds: a most unfortunate trait. Much better the strong Lancashire accent and positive, honest beliefs.

In my view, John Major's statement, recorded above, is much too optimistic. And it is clearly contradicted by Margaret Thatcher's assertion that there is 'no such thing as society' but merely a series of different classes. Admittedly, she said it in the context of her observations on the BBC, when she argued that there exist only a series of different classes, each of which qualifies for having particular types of programmes especially made to appeal to it.

Perhaps even more serious than an artificial accent is the deterioration in the use of the English language, under substantial pressure from technology and, much worse, American jargon and vulgarity. Dare I mention the current, offensive use of meaningless fillers like 'you know'...? Well, I am not alone.

'... the English language is now threatened less by foreign imports, often useful or stimulating, than from within, by slovenly chatmasters, ill-educated journalists, commercial fraudsters, literary pretenders with self-indulgent verbal inflation and self-appointed committees of public safety demanding political correctness. All share ignorance or contempt for the marvellous resources of English.'[16]

Lexicographers refer to the expressions 'you know' as 'meaningless fillers', as I have already observed. But the use is spreading incredibly fast and even those who might be expected to speak English more correctly and fluently are tempted to indulge in it.

These two irritating words are used almost repetitively, like a mantra. Admittedly, sometimes the abuse of 'you know' reflects a need to connect sentences which would otherwise appear disjointed and lack fluency, owing to the inability of the speaker either to manifest thoughts coherently or to use syntax properly. It seems to have the same repetitive drone as much modern music and, in my opinion, is without doubt the result of a desperate need to communicate with the person addressed making speech appear more personal and more intimate. In a strange sense, it is almost an attempt to indoctrinate one's interlocutor by convincing him or her of facts of which they may not be aware. 'You know this, you know that; I have no need to tell you, really, but I am informing you nevertheless.' It may be that it is used to cover hesitancy; it clearly is at times, but it is difficult to say how, where and when it all started.

---

[16] *Peter Vansittart 'In Memory of England – a Novelist's View of History', John Murray, London 1998*

It has certainly been around for more than a decade but, as far as I know, its source is indeterminate.

Cynically, I would suggest that it was the politicians who started it all in order that, when making fraudulent statements or at least statements which they knew full well not to be true, they could be more convincing for their audience!

One cannot run from it because it is everywhere.

There was published in 1997[17] a very interesting analysis of the class distinctions that still pertained, at least at that date, in Britain. Some excerpts may prove interesting. Page 165: 'Doctors from ethnic minority backgrounds are far less likely to be given consultant jobs than whites: after examining 418 in 45 NHS Trusts... the Commission for Racial Equality found that out of 147 consultant vacancies, 53% of applicants were from ethnic minorities, out of 130 senior registrar vacancies 37% of applicants were from ethnic minorities, representing only 17% of the appointments'.

Page 178: 'Equally important is the persistence, despite the existence of the NHS, of inequalities in access to health care'.

---

[17] *Andrew Adonis and Stephen Pollard, A Class Act – The Myth of Britain's Classless Society, Hamish Hamilton, London*

Page 179: '...the middle classes spend more time on average with their GP than those with working class backgrounds and are more likely to be referred to specialists by their GPs'.

On pages 225and 226, the authors refer to the inter-marriages and dynasties in the media and say in terms (page 225) '...it begins to seem as if every newspaper or TV station is linked through marriage'.

On page 227 dealing with tabloids and popular TV, they argue that 'even supposedly working-class papers, such as The Sun and The Star, are written by the same middle-class graduates whom one finds in the BBC, just as downmarket BBC programmes are produced by the very same people who script Newsnight and The Archers'.

They also observe on page 227 – but that is obvious in any event, even to a layman like me – that there is a strict class distinction when purchasing tickets for the Royal Opera House. For example, prices rose when Pavarotti or Domingo appeared, which prompts their remark that 'the taxpayer should not subsidise the ticket price of a wealthy merchant banker'. Perhaps I am belabouring the point but it is not an unfair observation to make, although obviously it is a natural result of what are known as market forces.

George Orwell was particularly scathing about class distinctions in the country. One must take what he wrote with a pinch of salt given his socialist programme and his vigorous campaigning for a socialist Britain; but he is on the record as saying that 'England is the most class-ridden country under the sun' and, perhaps because of his political principles, he added that 'there has been a decay of ability in the ruling class in Britain'. I believe that his observations are still valid today.

Nor should one forget that for centuries there has been in England a somewhat snobbish kind of disdain by the upper classes for those 'in trade'. I do find, however, that this has reduced somewhat and especially in the 21st Century it is probably less a marker of social distinction.
An appreciation of class in the general sense is also to be seen in the fact that as late as the beginning of 1939 Lord Rothermere was describing Hitler as 'a great gentleman', by way of endorsement of the previous campaign in the Beaverbrook press that there ought to be no war against Germany.

I would also suggest that there is very marked class significance in the use that the English make of the noun 'adventurer'; that, perhaps unwittingly, has also to do with a theoretical class distinction.

It is, in my view, quite interesting to consider the use that in English we make of such a description, which seems to convey the idea of a person who is a mixture of good and bad and is, in fact, a function of the nature of English class distinctions, especially since his type of personality does not fit easily into any of the class definitions.

For this reason, I trust I may be forgiven a digression to consider some of the characters who did not fall into any particular classification of class, did not fit into any box identifying a special character, but because of their conduct and their deeds were a significant part of English history, despite – or perhaps because – being, in common description, 'adventurers'.

The identification of out-of-the-ordinary behaviour with the description of that noun is not confined to people like Cecil Rhodes or Robert Clive, although there is probably some justification for calling Robert Clive an adventurer[18]. He landed in India, at Madras, in 1744 as a young man in the employment of the East India Company. In fact, he started out as a rogue trader and most of his early activities were certainly not related to the building of an empire. He went to India for adventure, sex (he was very fond of girls, local or otherwise) and alcohol (in fact, he shared his passion for alcohol with many other persons in the employment of the East India Company; not for nothing it was said that the drink 'punch' was created in India, as indeed has been suggested for the 'gin and tonic' beverage).

Purely in passing, I should mention that something else came over to England from India as a result of the activities of the East India Company, well apart from the creation of incredible wealth for certain members of British society. It

---

[18] *Clive is sometimes referred to as the 'Shropshire Lad' because he came from Market Drayton.*

is said that one of its officers brought back to the Malvern Hills the recipe of what became known as Worcester (originally Worcestershire) Sauce. Nothing could be more English than that, surely, developed in Elgar's beloved county just as he created what is probably the second British national anthem, namely 'Land of Hope and Glory'. But I mention this more as an item of gossip than anything else.

Clive ended up as Lord Clive of Plassey; not bad for an adventurer, although as a cynic I remark that to be ennobled using the name of a battle that, well apart from providing control of a larger part of India, also confirmed the monopoly of the British East India Company on the production and export of Indian opium, might not necessarily be something of which to be proud...

In passing, I observe that the East India Company proved to be one of the major factors in the establishment of the English Empire because of its activities, almost always successful, and its prosperity. It has been recorded that at one stage it had its own army of a quarter of a million people and ruled over a territory where at least 350 million people lived. On the whole, it did a lot of good but lost some of its honour when it neglected to take care of the famine that had spread over the territory of Bengal, which it then ruled.

It was initially a commercial enterprise. Of gigantic proportions and a source of great wealth for its shareholders, it gradually became, thanks to the efforts of Robert Clive, a political entity.

When Robert Clive landed in India, as stated above, apart from the activities already referred to, he behaved in a highly debatable manner prompted always by his personality and ambition. He certainly had no intention to build an empire. It is also said that he did no more than what many other Englishmen who went to India did or intended to do, mainly because of their love of adventure, sex and alcohol.

His administration may have been thoroughly corrupt, but by virtue of his victory (in a sense, by stealth) in 1757 over the forces of the Nawab of Bengal, he annexed the totality of that territory and effectively consolidated British rule in India. Nevertheless, he is still considered by his compatriots as an adventurer.

Perhaps at heart he was. But one ought to pause and consider what Clive achieved for Britain and it is probably unfair to comment repeatedly, as has been done, over the fact that he was a little too fond of alcohol.

After he became Lord Clive of Plassey, a parliamentary enquiry did find that his administration of India had been corrupt and, probably as a result, or maybe even because of a combination of drug-taking and depression, he committed suicide.

Along similar lines, there can be no doubt that Cecil Rhodes was also an adventurer but, as Clive had done for India, he laid down the foundations for Britain's empire in Africa.

Nevertheless, Cecil Rhodes was certainly a capable man with the makings of an Empire builder. The one episode in his life that is against him and must be questioned is his behaviour vis-à-vis the King of Matabeleland, Lobengula. His ambition was to conquer Matabeleland; and he did. In his honour it was named Rhodesia but as most people know, his means to achieve such result were somewhat questionable.

The Victorians did not like his close companion and friend, the former doctor Leander Jameson, and it would appear that both of them were addicted to drugs, although that is not certain. Perhaps for this reason Queen Victoria didn't like Rhodes at all and forced him to resign at the same time as Jameson was put on trial.

Again, a wrong judgement even by Queen Victoria because ultimately, after the defeat of the Boers in the Boer War, Jameson made it both to a title and to the Privy Council. Not bad for another adventurer.

Sir Walter Raleigh was a pirate or perhaps, more politely, a privateer. Queen Elizabeth I and England owe him; yet the average Englishman would consider him an adventurer rather than a pirate.

Thinking of piracy, I suppose I should record, as an another example of how England has always acknowledged the success of those who added to her power even though the means used may not necessarily have been 'proper', the position of the Welshman Harry Morgan. He too was a pirate, and a very successful one. He then decided to fight his former pirate friends and managed to gain control of the Caribbean for the Crown, essentially by raiding Gran Grenada in 1663.

In recognition of his looting but above all of the territory conquered, he was made Admiral of the Fleet and then ennobled.

It has in fact been suggested more than once that Henry Morgan's spectacular feat was the event that started up the creation of the British Empire; or, as one writer put it, the Empire came about 'in a maelstrom of seaborne violence and theft. It was not conceived by self-conscious imperialists aiming to establish English rule over foreign lands or colonists hoping to build a new life overseas'.[19]

Queen Elizabeth I had already turned a blind eye to the activity of English pirates who, over the years, became better at what they were doing than their predecessors and contemporaries, the Portuguese, the Spaniards and the Dutch.

---

[19] *Niall Ferguson, Empire –How Britain Made the Modern World, Penguin Books, London 2004, p1*

Morgan's performance was quite typical, inasmuch as it allowed England to pass from a phase of conduct which, if not unlawful in the technical sense, was really improper, to a set-up where political power predominated and, by changing the nature of the world map, allowed the initial piratical acts to be effectively forgotten. Conduct and conquests not entirely becoming and very often the fruit of violence and abuse were given the chrism and endorsement of political manoeuvring.

"In effect, the Crown licensed the pirates as privateers, legalising their operation in return for a share of the proceeds." Those proceeds were substantial and represented one of the principal elements in the accumulation of English wealth.

Not that the English themselves have ever been openly appreciative of the kind of behaviour that could be termed eccentric because of the label 'adventurer' applied to the individual. It is probably correct to say that those whom the English have defined as eccentric have quite often been considered as adventurers, even where it was not officially stated. I find that the noun adventurer is normally used by English people to describe those who have made a success of whatever they have embarked upon by being, in essence, either patently non-conforming or extravagantly enterprising. There is a derogatory note about the noun that is difficult to reconcile with the fact that, throughout its history, England has had to rely essentially on those who could only be described in current English language as adventurers, because they were eccentrics.

Is one too cynical if one observes that when we had a lot of eccentric personalities we had an Empire? But now we have no more such eccentrics and that's probably why we no longer have the Empire.

One can perhaps understand why Viscount Cranborne called Disraeli 'a political gamester'; that was to be expected and, in any event, I would argue that all politicians are gamesters. But he might have gone too far in terming him an 'adventurer', bearing in mind that some of the major social reforms and foreign policy ventures of 19th Century England are owed to this Christian of Italian/Jewish descent. Perhaps Viscount Cranborne did not like the fact that Disraeli married a wealthy widow. I am no historian but I don't see how, unless on the grounds of class distinction, one could apply the term adventurer to a person, Disraeli, whom Britannica describes as 'one of the most extraordinary figures to reach the pinnacle of British politics'.

Class apart, I think that the indiscriminate use of such noun is due to an inability to classify the personality and to identify the motivations of the person so described, whatever their religion, nationality or function in life. It is, in effect, a convenient term born out of the need to compensate for a failure of comprehension on the part of the person who applies it. Usually, there is a noticeable difference of success in such situations between the adventurer and the person who so describes him and I should like to suggest that in many cases the use of the noun is prompted by envy. The inability to understand those whom the English define as adventurers is a direct result of what I should term a national trait: that is, the need that English people have to classify human beings, to put them into pigeon holes. A person has to be this or that or something else; but the moment the features of a particular personality are not clear or blend one with the other or are possibly even exorbitant, the Englishman is in a difficulty. If the personality cannot be slotted into a clearly identifiable box, then there must be something wrong with it. By adopting such an attitude the English often develop blind spots about people.

One of the results is that, in some circumstances, one finds excessive praise derived from either an unbalanced assessment of the facts or a form of idolatry which is the result of short-sightedness. I have in mind in this context the hero worship by Rudyard Kipling of Cecil Rhodes, whom he went so far as to describe as the 'Colossus'.

Whichever way one looks at it, there is something in the make-up of the English which is both drawn to, and simultaneously repelled by, the kind of person to whom the term 'adventurer' is applied. That, in my view, is certainly a marker of an insistence on class distinctions.

Apologising for the rather lengthy digression and going back to the concept of class, I must confess that I have always found it somewhat difficult to understand, if not to appreciate, the subtleties of English class distinctions. I find class a very awkward topic.

We have so many nuances to consider, so many differences even regional to take into account, that one's judgement always seems somewhat lacking in definition and certainty.

I suppose that the easiest, if not the best, understanding of our class system is probably to be derived from Noel Coward's theatrical works...

Clubs

'Please accept my resignation. I don't want to belong to any club that would have me as a member' – Groucho Marx

One of the most obvious and, in a sense, typical characteristics of the English people as a whole is their gregariousness. When three or more Englishmen meet, the first thing they will do is to form a committee of two, if not of three. It is a natural development and a positive one: much work is done in England by committees and the sting is taken out of many a situation by participation, in the decision-making process, of representatives of those who might be affected.

It is a mode of operation consonant with what I would term generally a public school mentality and with a broadly tolerant approach to life which, until recently, has been the hallmark of England. It is, as George Macaulay Trevelyan put it in his social history of England by reference to parliament, the outcome of the tolerance and common sense of the people 'who have always preferred committees to dictators, elections to street fighting and talking shops to military tribunals'.

Such an approach to life finds its most notable manifestation in the 'clubbability' of the English. It was Dr Johnson who was recorded by Boswell as having called the English 'clubable' or 'clubbable' and it was Addison who remarked that clubs are 'the natural offshoot of men's gregarious nature'. The English clubs have always provided not merely meeting places where views on society and on politics could be voiced privately and exchanged freely; essentially, they have ensured conformity, of dress, of thought and of behaviour.

The dilution of individual traits resulting from club life has always been substantial and the blackballing system such as to ensure that nobody was admitted who, because of his schooling, background, family connection or general attitude would not make a jolly good fellow and not become one of the boys. Thus, there was derived the major source of strength of English society, namely its ability to provide uniformity, to absorb and permeate, to bind together, to re-enforce patriotic feeling and unity and, where necessary, to anglicise.

For centuries male bastions, they have now been stormed by women.

We are taught that, historically, English clubs followed on from the coffee houses that became established in the 17th Century in London; there were valid reasons why clubs should become so popular in England to the extent and in the manner that has lasted until the present day.

These reasons include the desire to be together with people of the same class and taste, or as an outlet for conversation, as a place to drink at any time of day, indeed, also as an escape from the female sex, for the reassurance provided by the continued presence of people of the same school and background whom one knew and trusted, the haven of tranquillity thus established, the ability to use smoking and billiard rooms, the need to belong to a group for company or support; a genuine liking for one's fellow men, a sense of loyalty and of camaraderie or sport and, where appropriate, the political affiliations that distinguished Whites from Brooks, or the identification with particular strata of society like the Athenaeum or the Garrick.

As a result, it was easy to establish clubs as a male preserve, since they not only provided meeting places where views on society and politics could be voiced privately and exchanged freely but, as I say, they also ensured conformity: of dress and of thought.

(The tendency for English males to 'club' together was also noticed by a number of foreign visitors in the practice prevailing at dinner parties when, after the meal was concluded, the ladies withdrew. The men were left to their port, cigars, gossip and also, 'evacuation' – by which I mean that one can still find nowadays, especially in country auction sales, remnants of the pieces of furniture, small commode-type, with one or two compartments lead-lined to hold bottles, decanters and glasses <u>and</u> the section containing a chamber pot clearly needed after the guests had imbibed so much liquid… But let's go back to clubs.) There were leaders, obviously, like Brummel for dress and Pitt for thought and politics; but the dilution of individual traits was great and the blackballing system was extremely effective.

Thus clubs represented one of the major sources of strength of English society.

There are however some drawbacks to this 'clubbability'. I need hardly mention how homosexuals have always prospered in England. Their prosperity has been fostered by a kind of fraternity, a secret society and mentality facilitated by the fact that such type of conduct was subject to the criminal law and ensured that, whilst individuals might have more or less disliked one another, they always banded together when one of them was under attack.

Where persons come together to protect one another against prosecution, as many homosexuals had most unfairly to do until very recent times, there is established inevitably a kind of mafia mentality with all that it entails, not only by its attempts to defeat the applicability of sanctions resulting from the criminal law but also, and much more dangerously, by favouritism in jobs and appointments to public places.

But clubs have changed. They have ceased to be havens of tranquillity where members all of the same social strata, all of the same scholastic background, all of equal tradition, attire and taste, could meet to discuss the political and social events of the day. I know of a major such establishment where, until recently, admission was denied to those who did not wear a tie and in any event most clubs are now run by committees whose assessment of candidates is, on the whole, reasonably superficial.

Provided there is a suitable introduction with adequate bank and other references it is unlikely that a respectable member of the community would be turned away: in most instances, and for most clubs, the days of blackballing have gone.

My Italian side ensures that I should record the debt owed to Italy by British clubland...

The first English club, Whites (still one of the most exclusive), was founded by an Italian called Francesco Bianco. Those of my readers who are in some doubt will be able to verify the fact by perusing the first 'History of Whites' compiled by the Honourable Algernon Bourke of 39 St James' Street London in 1892, a limited edition publication in two volumes (with betting book from 1743 to 1878 and a list of members from 1736 to 1892) published by Waterlow & Sons Ltd of London Wall, which is to be found in the library of Whites Club.

Odd, I know, but true...

Proverbs and Sayings

'Cleanliness is next to godliness.'

Reader, do not worry.   There will be no religious statements. Having mentioned that it would appear that the saying is to be attributed to Francis Bacon, who first used the expression in 1605, I shall proceed to... show off a little knowledge.

It is interesting to observe that although the water closet was invented in 1596 by an Englishman, Sir John Harington, it did not really come into use until much later dates. In fact, we have to wait until the second half of the 19th Century before certain even elementary features of civilised living were adopted in the major English cities, let alone London. Up to the end of the 19th Century one of the presently most distinguished parts of central London, namely the St James's area, was neither paved nor lit and its streets, which nowadays are much frequented by tourists (Jermyn Street, King Street, Pall Mall, and the famous St James' park), were in those days used mainly for whoredom and the park often enough for 'evacuation'.

There were, in fact, some who earned a living there by offering a kind of protective shield for privacy...[20]

Although the English shone amongst Europeans for their manners and smart attire as early as the 18th Century – I have already quoted the observation by Trevisano as to attire – it cannot be said that personal cleanliness was foremost in their minds in days gone by.

Indeed, cleanliness as a concept was rather suspect. Criticisms were often made about the effect on health and cleanliness of the ever-increasing tax that was imposed by the government on soap and other toiletries, which were considered luxuries. The tax was raised in 1711/12 during the reign of Queen Anne and continued to be unpopular until it was finally repealed in 1853 by Prime Minister Gladstone. For the whole period, complaints were voiced that English people did not wash quite so often as they ought to, simply because they wanted to save money.

Samuel Johnson is on the record as saying that he got 'no relish' from clean linen. His biographer James Boswell boasted that during his Grand Tour he had not taken his clothes off for a week.

There is an element of double standard in Boswell's approach to cleanliness; it is probably unfair that he should actually boast about something that he found offensive in

---

[20] *Royal St James's: Being a Story of Kings, Clubmen and Courtesans, E J Burford, London 1988*

others. For example, after his visit to Naples, he made fairly unpleasant remarks about the ill-dressed, dirty poor of Naples, known then, as now, as the 'lazzaroni'. His description of them is worth quoting: *'a shocking race; eaters of garlic and catchers of vermin'*[21].

English women of that period did not fare much better. One of the leading feminists of the 18th Century, Lady Mary Wortley Montague, is said to have replied to someone who was commenting on the dirty state of her hands: *'if you call that dirty, you should see my feet'*[22].

I was taught at an early age that proverbs, the sayings of our ancestors, represented the accumulated wisdom of generations and were the best information that my parents could impart to me, as they did.

Some are still valid today; many more are perhaps not so significant. Inasmuch as they reflect the thinking and the customs of a society at a particular moment in time (and many are the same in most languages), they could be found to be out of date or, perhaps, even scientifically inaccurate. Take the obvious 'red sky at night, shepherd's delight; red sky in the morning, shepherd's warning'. It may well have been true when I was young, but it is no longer a reliable guide now that our weather patterns have changed so dramatically.

---

[21] *See Boswell on the Grand Tour 1765-1766, edited by F Brady and F Pottle, London, 1955*
[22] *As cited in Christopher Hibbert's 'The English: A Social History 1066-1945', p335*

On the other hand, I always remember being taught by my mother that I should choose my wife from the same place where one would choose one's oxen! I did do that and am still happily married after 50 years: and so on.

Nevertheless, there are some respects in which a change in situation, thinking, habits or trends, causes sayings which one may have taken for granted at a certain moment in time to cease to have much significance.

I'll have a go at two or three, because they endorse my point that English society has changed quite a lot.

Take for example, *'the Englishman's home is his castle'*. I am certain that this was perfectly true in the past and the number of beautiful castles scattered throughout the British Isles provide a permanent and undoubted record of a different approach to one's home and to how it should be protected.

Nowadays, however, this saying is meaningless. I may own my home, but even if it is mortgage-free, I am subject to planning and building regulations that will ensure, without a shadow of a doubt, that I cannot do what I intend to do with it unless some bureaucrat gives me permission.

Speaking of bureaucrats, you may happily believe that you can stop anybody you like entering into your home, but that belief would be quite mistaken. There are no less than eleven categories of individuals and 252 different authorities which provide powers of entry to inspectors. This results in a total of 3887 persons entitled to enter private premises without a specific search warrant whether you wish them to or not and, as a result, may complain and have you prosecuted if you actually succeed in obstructing them in the execution of their 'duties'[23]. (I am ignoring the somewhat extreme powers granted to the police by the Prevention of Terrorism legislation, starting in 1974 after the Birmingham bombings and culminating in the Criminal Justice Act 2003.)

All right, you will say, but just let somebody try to enter my house to steal or molest my family and I shall show him. Well, that's not true either.

The law of self-defence in this country was for decades and until recently a clear example of how gutless a nation we have become. It sounds sensible: in defence of yourself and your family you are entitled to use reasonable force. Problems arise when lawyers start defining what 'reasonable force' is.

Regrettably, what is reasonable force will be judged <u>after</u> the event, presumably (though that's not sure) reasonably, by either a jury or a judge or a judge and jury. But the test that they will adopt will be a subjective one, since they were not there at the time. Someone who is woken up at two

---

[23] see Salmond & Heuston, *The Law of Torts*, London 1987 p.316 and 'An Inspector at the Door', London 1979

o'clock in the morning by an intruder who appears menacing, if he apprehends danger and can lay his hands on a shotgun or other weapons, will react instinctively, especially if he believes that himself or his wife or, above all, his children, are at risk. He will not go to the bookshelf and pick up Archbold's (the leading text book on the criminal law) or Moriarty's Police Law, to find out exactly how much force he is allowed lawfully to use. I would like to suggest that he might well be tempted to shoot the miscreant, because he cannot possibly believe that the intruder is a frustrated philosopher who is there to debate with him the principle of the immortality of the soul, or the finer points of Kant's Categorical Imperative, or that the poor fellow comes from a broken home and has arrived to seek reassurance and advice.

Quite the reverse, he will undoubtedly and correctly surmise that he's there to steal what he, the house owner, has worked hard to accumulate, or do harm to his wife, or molest his daughter, or hurt his children. He will react, as I have said, instinctively.

For this, he will undoubtedly be prosecuted and he may even end up in prison or, at least, with a conviction as a criminal, albeit perhaps with a suspended sentence, in the same way as the retired naval officer who, not too long ago, trying to defend himself from hooligans on the Underground, merely pulled out a stiletto from his walking stick (that he did not use), for which _gesture_ he was convicted and had his walking stick confiscated. He also got a criminal record…

It is all wrong. I might be going over the top, obviously, and I am sure I will be forgiven for that because essentially I consider the protection of my family a priority: but if anyone shot and killed an intruder in his home in the middle of the night, I would give him a decoration (an MBE or something like that, although nowadays they appear to be given to anybody) or, perhaps more profitably, exempt him from payment of income tax for the rest of his life. He will have saved the State a lot of money: the cost of the police investigation, the taking of statements, the trial, the conviction of the intruder as a thief if he is still alive, and the time he might spend in prison, as well as that of the house owner (someone who acted 'unreasonably' in the middle of the night). What utter nonsense the law of self-defence in this country was until recently.

And before you ask, no, my home has not been broken into, at least not yet; I've never had anything stolen from it; at least not yet, and not that I know of. True, I did surrender some time ago my shotgun and firearms certificates, because I have little doubt that I might have been tempted to use them in the circumstances to which I have adverted above, and absolute certainty that, if I had, I would have been prosecuted and possibly convicted. I did not relish the thought of going to prison for having behaved according to the dictates of my conscience and my instinct.

Furthermore, a major drawback of the present state of English law on self-defence is that it discourages self-help but above all, it often stops people from going to the help of others who might be in danger.

One frequently hears complaints that crimes happen on the street and passers-by do not go to help; alternatively, they claim that they have seen nothing and they walk on. Whilst it is true that in many cases such an attitude may be due either to cowardice or disinterest, it must be acknowledged that, in others, the consideration cannot be entirely absent that it is better to shut one's eyes and not get involved. By going to the rescue one runs the risk of either overreacting in protection of oneself or of going too far protecting others, of being taken to task afterwards and maybe even effectively punished for having yielded to the fairly natural instinctive reaction of wishing to help others.

Considerations such as these are never taken into account when judgments are passed on what are termed the excesses of self-defence. It is fairly obvious that the State must look askance upon any form of 'vigilante' activity on the part of its citizens; firstly, because its authority should not be undermined in any event and secondly, and maybe more importantly, because any such type of activity is nothing else but an acknowledgment that the public services provided by it, via the police or other bodies, are not available or inefficient or insufficient. As such, it is an admission of failure by the State.

One can see the logic and the usefulness of maintaining the prerogative of the State to protect the individual. The difficulty nowadays is that, at least in England, the police are often unable, or maybe even too understaffed, when it comes to safeguarding individual rights. Certainly, when dealing with violence on the streets, housebreaking or burglary, the citizen feels quite helpless and this feeling is compounded by the not-at-all uncommon reaction of the police who say that, in respect of minor cases of theft or burglary, they simply do not have the time or the staff to investigate. Hence the establishment of 'neighbourhood watch' arrangements, for what they might be worth.

Nowadays the position is further complicated by the fact that in England, very fortunately for its past social life in the broadest sense, things have been run for a long time on fairly easy-going lines which were developed and maintained at a time when British society was civilised, disciplined and tolerant and the country, as a whole, was fairly prosperous. All these features were so essential and so formative of the real England, the England of our youth, the country which gave hospitality to hundreds of thousands, the country of tolerance and fair play; but they are gradually disappearing since England is under considerable pressure not only because it has ceased to be so powerful or rich as it was, but also because of immigration, racial and religious dissent, political correctness and so on.

An analysis of these particular aspects of the problems that the country is experiencing I defer to another chapter. At this stage, I mention them here solely for completeness, because self-help is clearly overdue.

Let me consider another saying, namely *'the Englishman's word is his bond'*. May I point out immediately that this statement is politically incorrect; it should read 'the English person's word is his/her/its bond, or nowadays, ungrammatically, 'the English person's word is their bond'. I say so not because I wish to be politically correct, a stance that I abhor, but simply to make it clear that what was being said when this expression was formulated was that English people, whether men or women, kept their word.

I have no doubt that this statement was once perfectly true. It must have represented the basis of England's success as a world power and there are many of my English friends to whom, I am sure, the statement still applies in its entirety.

But again, things have changed and it will no longer stand. A few examples will suffice.

Let me consider divorce in the first place. At the moment, more than 50 percent of marriages that take place in the United Kingdom end up in divorce[24]. In 2013 there were 129,763 divorces. That means that at least 259,526 persons had given each other their word that they loved and

---

[24] *ONS (Office for National Statistics), 2013*

cherished each other and would live together. We no longer say until death might part them but the intention is quite clear, namely to the exclusion of other parties.

Slightly more than half of these people, let's say 51 percent, will have broken their word within no more than five years after the date of marriage, and have divorced.

Quite normal, you will say. I agree, quite normal for Great Britain: but they did give their word, did they not?

Of course, we must make allowances for human psychological frailty and for the individual's desperate search for happiness at all costs, even at that of breaking promises (but what about the poor children?).

Do we make similar allowances when it comes to money? Of course we do. Let me give you another example. It occurs in the field of property purchase.

The English system of buying and selling property, more commonly known as conveyancing, is fairly unique. It came about, historically, when the country was rich, stable, when people knew their places, and when, in truth, the Englishman's word was his bond. (Land registration in England commenced in 1925.)

Because of the complications of land tenure, matters were so arranged that when people struck a bargain to buy a property it was then recorded either by them, their estate agents, or their solicitors, or all of them, in a document which had appended to it the hallowed formula 'subject to contract'. That formula meant, as it still does, that the deal was clearly intended to go through but the parties were entitled to resile from it at any time! In practice, it meant that the solicitors had the opportunity to investigate the true legal position and the client to obtain a mortgage, but in the ordinary course of events the deal would fail to go ahead only if something really deleterious emerged: for example, a mortgage was refused, the property was about to be compulsorily acquired or to have a motorway either through or adjacent to it, or the vendor wasn't really entitled to sell or, as lawyers put it, could not make title to the property.

In practice, deals seldom fell through in the 'good old days' and when they did, it was usually the buyer who withdrew because he or she had changed intention or the solicitors had found something detrimental about the property or a mortgage was unavailable. There is no such system in any other country I know of, not in Scotland and certainly not in other Roman law countries: unorthodox it was and, to some extent, still is, but it worked; though only until the 1960s.

The explosion in prices and the complications of the property market in the early '70s and thereafter were such that both vendors and purchasers, but mainly vendors, withdrew at will from 'subject to contract' agreements when they got a better price than the one agreed upon. So much so, that there came into being the verb 'to gazump' and its formulations in the past tense, 'gazumped', present participle, 'gazumping' and even as a noun, the 'gazumps'. The verb is described in the dictionary as 'to go back on an agreement with a prospective purchaser of a property by raising a previously agreed price' (1); alternatively (and interestingly) 'to swindle' (2)! What it means, in effect, is that the bond that was supposed to be established between vendor and purchaser by the agreement reached, albeit subject to contract, goes by the board, and one or more parties are swindled.

The parties may have given their word, they may have shaken hands on the deal that was struck, but all to no avail: the deal is off. One party has gazumped the other.

Is the Englishman or woman sticking to his/her bond? Certainly not, and they are breaking their word so frequently that we've even had to import from the Yiddish a verb and a noun to express, and possibly dignify, this failure to honour contractual obligations.

You may well ask at this stage: but does all this matter? If we are all doing it, what is the harm, since it is obvious that things have changed? That, of course, depends on your point of view and I am not here to moralise, merely to observe.

I do not comment on what politicians say because they are all the same in whichever country one is: they never keep their word.

'If you cannot beat them, join them.' I have had some difficulty in finding an equivalent, in the language of other countries which I know, of this very English expression. The closest I could get to it is an old Neapolitan saying to the effect that if you want to succeed in life, you ought to mix with those who are better than yourself even if it costs you money to do so.

In respect of both these gems of proverbial knowledge, I find evidence of both defeatism and excessive humility.

Humility is rather surprising in the Neapolitan saying, given that people from that part of the world are strong individualists and consider themselves superior to everybody else! In respect of the English saying, the element of defeatism is also rather surprising, given that it is not a usual feature of the English temperament.

Why should a Neapolitan consider anybody else better than himself? Why should an Englishman suppose that he cannot defeat an opponent?

But, on closer consideration, both sayings contain one or two pearls of wisdom, based, as they both are, on substantial doses of realism.

If it is true that one is judged by the company one keeps, then it can only profit one to be seen mixing with one's 'betters'. If one wants a certain amount of peace and quiet, it is probably easier to compromise, or at least come to terms with one's enemy so that one can proceed to enjoy life. This principle explains, at least in part, why the English people are so fond of the understatement. In fact, they are often referred to as 'the masters of the understatement'. To say to a person who has told an untruth 'you are mistaken' is less controversial than to say 'you are lying'. Both statements may be correct and whilst the former lacks cogency, it is unlikely to provoke an aggressive response.

Realism apart, however, the English approach seems to me less likely to result in the upholding of principles and beliefs, once it is decided to join those whom one cannot beat. It may prove disadvantageous, if one is set in one's ways, to assert principle. This might explain both the success of British foreign policy throughout the centuries and the fact that others found an element of perfidiousness about it. Perfidious Albion was dubbed such because quite clearly the country was prepared to sacrifice its principles to achieve particular results: the English have always preferred practice to theory.

As an aside, it is worth noting that this aspect of the English genius is a well-known fact and has been acknowledged as such.

As Jeremy Paxman points out [25], quoting Ralph Waldo Emerson 'Collected Works, Volume 5, p.46 ('English Traits'), the English mind prefers utilitarian things to ideas. As

---

[25] *op. cit*

Emerson put it, 'they love the lever, the screw, the pulley, the Flanders draft horse, the waterfall, windmills, tide mills: the sea and the wind to bear their freight ships' and this is one of the reasons why the English have always produced many great scientists.

It is, no doubt, because of this approach that England was able to establish its Empire. I am not so sure that such an approach serves it so well in the personal and social context.

As I have observed, a strict application of this particular maxim may make for peace and quiet, but is essentially defeatist.

Live and let live.' I have always considered that this expression aptly crystallised the English approach to life until, shall I say, the 1960s. It encompasses so much that is moral behaviour, at least in the Christian sense, and as a rule of life it is highly praiseworthy. Not so all-embracing as the Ten Commandments, of course, but almost a synthetic equivalent of what, according to the Gospels, is the cardinal rule of life for a Christian, namely 'love thy neighbour as thyself'. Sadly, one seldom sees it applied in today's world. It goes hand in hand with a much less elegant but equally forceful English present participle that describes how we should all help one another, namely 'back-scratching'. There is just as little back-scratching in present-day English society as there is any desire to let others live.

To me, 'live and let live' means that we should never grasp more than we need, that we should not go out of our way to score points off our neighbours and that we should all try and get on. This is not what the present-day fragmentation of English society reflects.

'Heaven helps those who help themselves.' Go and tell that to all those who prefer to remain on state benefits.....

Writing in 1859 ('Self Help'[26]), Samuel Smiles reminded us of this maxim. He took it as the starting point of what he describes as the 'strong individuality and distinctive personal energy' of the Englishman. I have no doubt that it could properly be applied to the Victorians and there is no denying that even when, as is often the case, the Englishman becomes part of organisations and institutions, he has a tendency to retain his own social identity, relying on his freedom of thought and, above all, of speech.

But enough of this: I have already made the same point above.

It is a feature that has singled out Englishmen from the 16th to the early 20th Century; but it is certainly reducing in scope.

In the same manner as some proverbs, sayings or expressions appear to have lost their meaning either wholly

---

[26] *publ. John Murray, Edinburgh*

or in part because of changed circumstances, there are others which have either come to the fore or have acquired greater significance.

For example, I am thinking of the expression 'if you've got it, flaunt it'. The Greek philosopher Socrates taught his pupils that real knowledge consisted in hiding knowledge, the Romans used to say 'scientia est celare scientiam'; the English paraphrase that by saying that it is not good manners 'to blow one's own trumpet'. Apart from the logical inelegance of the expression (I have in mind that it is unlikely that one would wish to blow somebody else's trumpet) this would appear to contradict both Socratic teaching and the tendency of the English people not to go over the top. In fact, I am quite convinced that the English – as I have already observed – are indeed the masters of the understatement and all these notions are inculcated into them at school from a very early age.

How one reconciles the fact that one should not blow one's own trumpet with the opposite concept that one should flaunt what one has is something that I have not yet been able to determine.

'The Englishman is born free.' This was certainly true until, shall we say, the 1950s and 1960s but I am not so sure that it can any longer stand as a valid assertion of the Englishman's status.

To be born free essentially means, to me, that one will be brought up in a country free from interference by the State; a democratic country where things work simply because individuals have been taught to show both public spirit and a sense of responsibility, where they have respect for institutions, a feeling for honour and for sportsmanship generally. The English language uses expressions borrowed from the major English sport, cricket, which are general representations of this principle: we have expressions such as 'playing the game', 'fair play', 'a straight bat', 'it is not cricket', expressing not only what one could term an amateurish approach to sport but also almost a gentlemanly approach, which was a reflection of the individual's attitude in his private life.

That, I fear, is no longer true today, since many restrictions are imposed upon us in England.

As I have already observed earlier on, I recall with nostalgia the days when not many offices in central London had entry phones; practically no house or flat had a burglar alarm; one would hardly dream of locking one's car if one went into the pub for a drink; driving licences did not have photographs; if stopped by the police one was under no obligation to identify oneself; if arrested on suspicion of a crime one need not say anything – if one had an alibi one could keep it up one's sleeve; if charged with a crime, one could keep silent under interrogation; and I suppose if I thought more carefully about the matter I could find many other examples...

Much has changed since the '50s. A well-known English judge, Lord Devlin, could then describe the English system of criminal prosecution as a game of tennis where the prosecution and the defence were hitting balls at each other and the judge sat like an umpire to determine who scored the point...

The Police and Criminal Evidence Act 1984 had not yet come into force and the old provisions of the Magistrates Courts Act 1952 still applied to detention without trial, inasmuch as one had to be brought before a magistrate as soon as reasonably practicable.

The change that has taken place in the rights of the individual Englishman in less than two generations is quite dramatic and is not necessarily brought about by the need to protect the State from terrorism. Rather, it is the result of an avowed policy of strengthening the State to the detriment of the individual; it is as though those government representatives who had always wanted to keep things secret now at last have the opportunity of making the State supreme, nullifying the individual freedoms of which this country was always, and justly, proud.

It is trite to remind oneself of Thomas Paine's dictum that 'he that would make his own liberty secure must guard even his enemy from repression'. The statement has meaning and style but modern British governments do not seem to be interested in that. A succession over nearly two decades of illiberal Prime ministers (Thatcher and Blair) has left the country with the individual less and less protected against the State.

Of course, we must safeguard ourselves against terrorists: no sensible person could suggest otherwise.

But as Baroness Helena Kennedy argues[27], this justification, so often proffered when inroads are made into civil liberties, is spurious.

'Suspected terrorists can now be stripped of their citizenship and under the latest Criminal Justice Act 2003 police powers are being extended yet again so that people can be held for interrogation without charge for up to 14 days. The 'abolition' of the right to silence which entitled people to refuse to answer questions and which was opposed by Labour in opposition, has now been extended' (See Criminal Justice and Public Order Act 1994).

'It used to be inapplicable to children under 14 but even children can now have an adverse inference drawn from their failure to answer questions. Ministers who had been champions of civil liberties themselves fell silent on the subject once in office.' (op.cit. p.32)

It is not terrorism that has brought such harsh measures in its train: the erosion of civil liberties had occurred before

---

[27] *see 'Just Law' Chatto & Windus, London 2004*

September 11th 2001, marking the decline in the Englishman's much-fought-for freedoms.

I am ignoring – for the discussion would be too lengthy – any reference to the implications of the abuse of the Terrorism Act 2000, especially Schedule 7.

'Let bygones be bygones.' This is a wonderful rule of life and is a corollary of the saying *'If you cannot beat them, join them'*.

It identifies the Englishman with a broadly tolerant and non-vindictive approach to life that has served Britain in good stead throughout its history. Politically, it has taught it to negotiate with those who, starting out in life as terrorists, soften their attitude, at least formally, in order to achieve a specific aim or strengthen a political stance.

Socially, it has shortened people's memories and has made it easier not to bear rancour, but it is doubtful that such an expression has been able to retain its validity in the 20th Century.

Another saying which is representative of the English mentality is to the effect that one should keep a *'stiff upper lip'*. This is tied in with the requirement that one should not display too much emotion. Not a good thing to bottle up one's feelings, I am sure…

I should say, however, that we seem to have lost our stiff upper lip. I deal with this aspect of the matter in the chapter on 'hypocrisy'.

After the Second World War the rather narrow-minded approach of the trade unions in Britain was thought to be confirming the expression *I am all right, Jack*. This ended up by being the title of a successful film on trade union attitudes with Peter Sellers, which was very popular in its day. To me it highlights a feature which seems to have distinguished the English in times of peace – that is, the development of rather slow desires with a consequent slowing down of the reaction times. This feature had already been pointed out by H G Wells when, in his 'The Work, Wealth and Happiness of Mankind' (1931) he said that it was the custom of the English to allow sometimes 50 and possibly even 100 years to occur between 'the perception that something ought to be done and a serious attempt to do it'.

He was hypercritical of his fellow countrymen; but there is an element of truth in the observation as has happened, for example, in the nearly two decades that it took to realise after the Kings Cross Station fire that smoking should be banned on the Underground system. In a totally different, wholly political context, at least 30 years had to elapse from the first anti-apartheid protests of the early '50s to the dawning of the realisation in this country that the era of apartheid was over.

But there you are: the English are the English. God bless them!

Mad or Eccentric?

First Clown:	*...it was the very day that young Hamlet was born: he that was mad and sent into England.*
Hamlet:	*Ay, marry, why was he sent into England?*
First Clown:	*Why, because he was mad: he shall recover his wits there; or, if he do not, it's no great matter there.*
Hamlet:	*Why?*
First Clown:	*'Twill not be seen in him; there the men are as mad as he.'*

W Shakespeare, Hamlet, Prince of Denmark – Act V, Scene I

I know that it has now been, for many years, topical to 'challenge' Shakespeare either because, perhaps, it was really Marlow who wrote his plays, or even Sir Francis Bacon, or because the whole of his output is said to have been contributed by poets and other writers. I am certainly not qualified to comment on that. I merely observe that whoever he was, he has said so much which is true about human nature and so valuable about its emotions that to attack him, in a sense, is to attack the whole of the human race. He is to England as important an expression of national genius as Beethoven is to Germany, Molière to France, Cervantes to Spain and Leonardo to Italy. He is as unique as they were. Accordingly, I believe that one has to pay attention to what he says. If he is right, then the English are mad or at least as mad as Hamlet. Nor was Shakespeare the only one to make this observation. In 'The Five Nations' (1903), Rudyard Kipling went on record as saying '...for Allah created the English mad – the maddest of all mankind,' going much further than Shakespeare by using a superlative. I cannot say whether, having been born in India, Kipling was able to know better and to form a more detached and accurate view of his compatriots. Of course, it is rather extreme to accuse a whole people of insanity and I am not doing that. I am merely highlighting the fact that at least two Englishmen of importance considered their fellow countrymen to be a trifle odd.

On the other hand, while I do believe that the English are not quite mad, they can be mildly eccentric. There are oddities in their behaviour but, before tackling them, I make it perfectly clear that if, and in so far as, the English are mad, then the nationals of other countries are just as mad since it is a common trait, if not a privilege of the human race, regardless of nationality, to be rather inconsistent.

What is true however is that oddities appear more evident in England than elsewhere, perhaps because they are least expected. It cannot be a coincidence that we have the Yorkshire saying 'there is nowt so queer as folk'. I have found it difficult to find an exact equivalent in the languages of those other countries with which I am fairly conversant. I am not saying that there is no affirmation there of the unevenness of human beings, but merely that in England one remarks upon inconsistent patterns of behaviour because they are more obvious, given the other distinguishing features of its people.

I should like to mention four examples of eccentricity in the English people, which the average reader may ignore.

We have had an Army commander who held briefing sessions in the nude, apart from reminding his troops that bathing was unhealthy and that the best diet was total reliance on onions.

We have also had a titled lady who allowed herself to be photographed whilst performing acts which the Scottish trial judge in a divorce case described as 'disgusting sexual acts'.

Another titled person, who lived in Paris, liked his fellow creatures so little that his only concern in life were his twelve dogs. For them, a table was laid so that they might share lunch with their master every day. There was one servant to each of them and they wore napkins around their necks and boots on their paws.

Much to the disappointment of his friends who came to dinner, the menu never varied: potatoes and English boiled beef.

Finally, there was a well-known English naturalist who travelled with a porpoise, which he bottle-fed when in railway carriages. If that were not extravagant enough, he enjoyed sampling the flesh of most animals in his menagerie. He is said to have eaten crocodiles, a boa constrictor, rhinos, a panther, numerous giraffes and even sampled a kangaroo soup.

It is clear to me that these are examples of conduct obviously related to eccentricity, a fact of which the English have from time to time been willing either to boast or to complain, at least when they recognised it. What the average Englishman doesn't appreciate, however, is the consideration that the eccentricity of a race is, in an odd sense, a function of its resourcefulness, inventiveness and power. The problem at the moment is that it is rather difficult to identify too many eccentrics in the England of today: miscreants, showmen, clowns and crooks abound, of course: eccentrics do not (I am not including in the definition of eccentricity the various forms of unusual if not perverted sexual behaviour, with one exception). Whether this is because they are no longer so common or they have become fearful of expressing their true personality, I am not sure; I believe that it is not entirely a coincidence that when we had so many eccentrics we also had power and an empire. Now that there aren't so many left, we find ourselves with very little power and, of course, no empire at all. But there I go again: I am afraid I am repeating myself...

Other countries obviously have their own eccentrics and adventurers, but those who emanate from England seem to be both more noticeable and more interesting.

In a sense, it could be said that even an English king, Edward VII, was eccentric in his own private behaviour. His public figure was impeccable as were his conduct and the performance of his duties as king and for that he was extremely popular.

He was a lot more capable than his mother, Queen Victoria, ever believed and we owe to him the correct anticipation that sooner or later Great Britain would be at war with Germany. Because of this, he saw to it that the British Navy was strengthened so as to become the most powerful weapon of war in the world.

His private behaviour, on the other hand, could be defined as that of a libertine, especially coming after decades of Victorian prudery. One of the few English kings to do so, Edward VII spoke French fluently. He was fond of France and especially of Paris and of French prostitutes. There he regularly visited the well-known and luxurious brothel 'Le Chabanais' (much frequented by many other males of distinction whether artistic, literary or diplomatic).

He had a special room dedicated to him and a chair built to his design to accommodate sexual activity with two or possibly more persons. It was known then, as now, as his 'siège d'amour' (his being overweight would prove cumbersome and inconvenient for the ordinary position of intercourse).

But he knew his duties and the people loved him for it, as was demonstrated by the masses who attended his funeral.

There is, in fact, almost an element which could be hyperbolically described as schizophrenic in the attitude of the English people, who are quite capable of manifesting virtues and vices in different spheres of their lives. This is not, in my view, quite the same as a hypocritical stance; there was no hypocrisy as such in the conduct of Edward VII because nothing was hidden. The essence of hypocrisy, with which I shall be dealing separately, is the hiding of conduct; but conduct can be open for all to see and yet consist of attitudes that are contradictory.

There was an element of adventure certainly, but even more of eccentricity, about those wealthy Englishmen who could afford to go on a 'Grand Tour' with their personal staff and their 'cicerone'. At least in the sense that in many cases it was an exercise in showing off, in its inception at any rate, it was a form of keeping up with the Joneses by the wealthy English gentry. Maybe crossing the Alps made them look more eccentric, since the novelty in the weather and the landscape undoubtedly brought about a change in their behaviour. The Englishmen on the 'Grand Tour' became suddenly more extrovert and, since they took the view that the people with whom they were consorting were so completely different in every respect, they felt no need to maintain any longer the strict standards of thought and behaviour imposed upon them by the society that they were leaving, albeit temporarily. Their newly gained freedom made them behave in a manner which to locals must have seemed eccentric.

For example, foreigners would undoubtedly consider eccentric the behaviour of the enterprising English women who either scaled mountains or walked deserts or explored Africa alone, save perhaps, where appropriate, in the company of one or more guides.

I suppose it could be said that, despite all his merits in the fields of engineering and aviation, even Noel Pemberton Billing was a little eccentric in his conviction that, during the First World War, English society was tainted by the presence of '47,000 highly placed perverts' who were blackmailed by the German espionage system because of their latent homosexuality. He maintained that their names were to be found in the 'Berlin Black Book', the contents of which revealed that the Germans intended to exterminate the manhood of Britain. From the standpoint of the early 21st Century his beliefs and attitudes do smack of eccentricity; but then, it depends...

Our eccentrics of today are somewhat different: homosexuals in extravagant clothes, sportsmen with fancy haircuts, members of parliament with quaint if not offensive forms of behaviour. They are, in fact, possibly fewer, but certainly less interesting and much less useful.

It is also to be observed that there seems to be a tendency in England to confuse eccentricity with misanthropy. We appear to have a noticeable number of misanthropes in our country, but they are not necessarily eccentrics. On the whole, at least according to dictionary definitions, a misanthrope doesn't like his fellow human beings or steers clear of them, is not too keen on social intercourse and prefers to be alone. In a sense, one could argue that he doesn't really love life. This doesn't apply to eccentrics who, generally speaking, do not mind or perhaps even enjoy the company of their fellow men (and women if appropriate) and could be said to be quite fond of life; fond in their own way, fond of doing things somewhat differently from the normal expectation of ordinary social conduct.

The eccentricity of the English emerges in the most unusual set-ups and has been commented upon by foreigners.

Take, for example, the attitude of English parents towards their children. It is not merely a matter of the children not being allowed until recent times to set foot inside a pub so that their parents could drink more freely. The observation goes back somewhat further, as the following extract will show:

> *The want of affection in the English is strongly manifested towards their children, an Italian visitor to England noted. For after having kept them at home till they arrive at the age of seven or nine years at the utmost, they put them out, both*

males and females, to hard service in the houses of other people... And few are born who are exempted from this fate, for every one however rich he may be, sends away his children into the houses of others, whilst he, in return, receives those of strangers into his own. And on enquiring the reason for the severity, they answered that they did it in order that their children might learn better manners. But I, for my part, believe that they do it because they like to enjoy all their comfort themselves.[28]

This is of course arguable: my views on the point have already been set out above.

The writer A J P Taylor has described the English as 'a peaceful and civilised people, tolerant, patient and generous'. This is perfectly true and is proven by the fact that they have been quite successful until recently at blending into Englishness the immigrant populations, with great benefit to the country.[29]

And profit we did, especially in industrialised Victorian England, from what foreigners have done. For example, Henry Bessemer was born in France, as was Isambard Kingdom Brunel.

---

[28] *Italian Relations of England, Camden Society 1847.24. With acknowledgements to Christopher Hibbert 'The English: A Social History 1066-1945', Grafton Books, London, 1987, p112*
[29] *See Peter Vansittart's 'In Memory of England: A Novelist's View of History', John Murray, London, 1998*

Pugin, who appears to be so popular at the moment, was the son of a French émigré and both Oscar Wilde and John Betjeman had Dutch forebears. Sickert's father was Danish and Alfred Milner was of German stock. The Rossettis were originally Italians.

Disraeli's grandparents and great-grandparents were born in Italy, arriving in England from Venice in 1748 (though he claimed throughout his life that he was a Sephardic Jew of Iberian descent).

But was it eccentricity or cruelty that gave rise in the 16th, 17th and 18th Centuries to cock-throwing, cock-fighting, bull-baiting, to the Stamford bull running, to bear- and badger-baiting, to ratting with terriers, to fox-hunting and indiscriminate shooting? The popularity of the dancing bears, of dog-fighting and of prizefighting may not necessarily be ascribed to eccentricity but rather to an appreciation of physical prowess.

Between 1832 and 1845 a number of Acts of Parliament were passed making cruelty to animals, and sports which involved the baiting of animals, illegal, the last of such Acts occurring in 1845 when cock-fighting was officially forbidden.

I should not wish to go so far as John Stuart Mill when he said that 'the amount of eccentricity in a society has generally been proportionate to the amount of genius, mental vigour, and moral courage which it contained' – also because I cannot profess to be one of his admirers. He himself was, in a sense, an eccentric, especially since he never really succeeded in loosening his ties to Mrs Harriet Taylor's apron, as evidenced in particular by the fact that he believed she was a better poet than Shelley and a greater thinker than Carlyle.

But there were always in England other forms of behaviour that qualify as eccentricity of sorts. It is strange that in such a peace-loving country as ours, manifestations of violence are quite common. Leaving aside the football hooligans with whose misdeeds all of us have become quite so well acquainted that we tend to take them for granted (although, happily, in recent years the examples of violence on the terraces have in fact reduced) it is as though, when it comes to violence, the English manifest what I would call an atavistic regression, if not provoked then at least facilitated by their attitude when it comes to alcohol. I use the term advisedly because the violent behaviour of the English was recorded quite a long time ago; a conduct that was not quite in keeping, truly off-centre.

An Italian friar, Salimbene di Adam (well known for his 'Cronica' – Chronicle – covering the years 1167-1287, which he began in 1282; he travelled extensively), writing about England in 1285 stated in terms that 'the English delight in drink and make it their business to drain full goblets'. He further observed and commented on a feature that has continued to this day, namely that when an Englishman is drinking, his attitude to his companion/s is that they should drink as much as he does[30].

I remark in passing that this particular trait has remained fairly constant throughout English history. Speaking from personal experience, I can say that what was noted, as above recorded, in the 13th Century is still true today. There is clearly a tendency on the part of English people who are, so to say, out drinking or even drinking at table to try to ensure that those in their company, unless they are teetotal... (or nowadays, intend to drive a car), drink as much as the host. It is almost as though this is the result of a certain type of insecurity. The person encouraging his companions to drink does not only wish to ensure that they are having fun as he is, but also that they accept that he might perhaps say things that he would not when he was sober. There is an unexpected form of gregariousness in such exercises that makes for sociability and enjoyment. I consider it a rather typical feature of the English, which should be viewed together with the unwritten rule that what is said over drinks or particularly at table should not really be reported outside the confines of the other guests.

Various older writers remarked on how common fornication was in England. It was reasonably widespread and tolerated and by no means a subject for criticism. Indeed, there is almost unanimity, amongst foreign writers, that the three most essential features they observed in

---

[30] *As quoted in Christopher Hibbert's 'The English: A Social History 1066-1945', Grafton Books, London, 1987, p11*

England were drunkenness, sexual addiction and violence generally.

It is certainly not my intention in trying to establish a kind of profile of the English people to consider, discuss or analyse in any shape or form their sexual behaviour and tendencies, at least not in this work[31]: I should certainly wish to avoid pruriency... Furthermore, decency and discretion exonerate me from mentioning the recent spate of enquiries into unlawful sexual conduct by public figures going back decades; almost, it is said, to the 1950s; I can only wonder whether the existence of such disgraceful conduct can, in some form or other, be related to what I shall be referring to as the barbarism in English society.

However, I should not omit to mention, as a form of sexual eccentricity, the behaviour of a group that had a great impact on our sexual customs and on our society generally in the 20th Century: 'the Bloomsbury Set'. The description is almost pleasant, conjuring pictures of a fairly respectable and easy-going group of people in a civilised London district (the British Museum was and still is there) so that the reader who knows nothing about the characters who composed this particular group might think that they were generous artists, pleasant painters, sensible intellectuals, probably with Cambridge degrees, who had a positive contribution to make to the well-being of the country. Some of the names have become quite familiar but the

---

[31] *See R Goodall, The English and Sex – The Shadow of Hypocrisy, Amazon, 2013*

truth is that one might not be too harsh if they were described as a fairly rotten bunch, Bernard Shaw possibly excepted. Picking at random, Lytton Strachey objected violently to Britain's stance during the 1914-18 War. He was a conscientious objector who believed that the war was the result of our Victorian influences and that the values of the Victorian society would, in due course, lead civilisation to slaughter. He went on the record saying that he didn't much care about England coming out of it victorious.

The writer of 'A Passage to India', E M Forster, had always made it quite clear that he would sooner betray his country than his friends and, like Strachey, was a homosexual. Forster's lack of patriotism was well known and he too openly and violently criticised Victorian values, showing an utter disregard of family and other concepts like patriotism, loyalty and duty that had given Britain the opportunity of establishing an Empire.

If all these people had lived privately and quietly in Bloomsbury it wouldn't have mattered very much; but they were quite keen on advertising their views and their behaviour and the effect on our country cannot have been too good. Indeed, a writer[32] has claimed – though one cannot go so far as to say that his argument is convincing – that the Bloomsbury Set's attitudes to Germany and to Russia may have seriously contributed to the Second World War. Negative eccentricity, I should call it. If one wished to

---

[32] *Andrew Roberts in 'The Eminent Churchillians', Phoenix, 1995*

moralise, one could say that the concepts that its members propounded, of the greatest freedom for the individual in matters sexual and the irrelevance of any kind of morality, have resulted in a hedonistic view of behaviour which is a marked feature of present-day English society and which could be said not to bode too well for our future. But that is a separate issue, of course.

However, I cannot refrain from adverting to an aspect of such behaviour which has been classified as a 'sexual deviation' (clearly, in my view, off-centre...), established ages ago and specifically associated with the English.

Flagellation, namely the use of violence, often extreme, whether self-inflicted or inflicted by others, with a sexual connotation, became quite famous round about the year 1800 on premises where the particular activity took place, so much so that it was termed 'the English disease' (or as the continentals put it, 'Le Vice Anglais'). Evil wagging tongues even suggested that, when Crown Prince, George IV claimed that he had visited some of these London establishments.

Whether this can be related back to the use of flogging in English schools must be a matter of debate; but there is no doubt that flogging was quite common and even in high-ranking and long-established scholastic premises such as Eton it was exceptionally severe, especially in the 19th

Century.   As has been observed [33], Eton birches were 'grotesque instruments consisting of three feet of handle and two of a thick bunch of birch twigs'. Birching at Eton always took place in public and the poet Swinburne was affected to such an extent that, in grown-up life, he 'liked to patronise Seven Circus Road in Regent's Park, a lovely little villa presided over by a well-educated lady, well versed in the birchen mysteries'[34].

Have things changed much since his days? I wonder...

[33] A N Wilson, 'God's Funeral', John Murray, London 1999, p208
[34] op.cit, p209

Swinging Sixties

'If a woman is going to leap into the bedroom waving a sex manual and demanding her right to have 15 orgasms every five minutes, men are going to lose their pride and confidence. Do that to a man and he is finished.' – Barbara Cartland, The Guardian, 2000

I find it quite interesting to observe that in England we should have chosen this description for what was to prove one of the most important decades in British social history (plus or minus two years).

It is not at all clear who first coined the expression but the internet dictionary definitions of the verb/noun 'swing' include
- (a) To be lively, trendy and exciting
- (b) To engage freely in promiscuous sex
- (c) To exchange sex partners (used especially of married couples)
- (d) To have a sexual orientation toward one or both sexes
- (e) To hang

Similar definitions for the swinging sixties remind us of all the events, catastrophes and changes that took place throughout the world in that decade.

I should like to suggest that the two sets of descriptions should be unified for my stated purpose of trying to understand what went on at that time in British society and how that may have been influenced by what was happening in the rest of the world.

I am not at all certain whether the decade that marked the successful rebellion by women to the slavery of the unwanted result of sexual intercourse – the creation of new life – was a coincidence with the fact that during the same period there were other types of protest throughout the world and, indeed, a number of wars, some particularly vicious (e.g. Vietnam); nobody can tell, nobody will ever know. But I cannot resist the temptation of mentioning that, perhaps, protests in one sphere of human activity can by contagion provoke or accelerate belligerent and aggressive attitudes in others.

Only out by one year, since it started in 1959, the Vietnam War is a classic as punishment for imperialistic tendencies and short-sighted policies. But there were a number of other events in the world in the period 1960-1970 that are certainly worthy of note, for example, the Bay of Pigs invasion in 1961, the commencement of building the Berlin Wall that same year, the start of the Portuguese Colonial War, again in 1961 (ending in 1975) and, a year later, the Cuban Missile Crisis that proved more significant than the American failure in the Bay of Pigs.

The world was not really at peace for very long because the Pakistan/India conflicts started in 1965 and, more importantly for us, the Northern Ireland problems that same year.

In other parts of the world, with which perhaps we are less concerned, there were equal difficulties. For example, the Six-Day Israel/Egypt/Jordan/Syria War of 1967, the Nigerian Civil War of that same year, and the rise of a military dictatorship in Greece also in 1967.

The upheavals in China the previous year might not have been too important for us but the student uprisings in France in 1968 got greater attention, at least in the British press.

The year 1968 was anything but uneventful. It saw the assassination of Robert Kennedy at the Ambassador Hotel in Los Angeles by a 24-year-old Palestinian. The assassination of Martin Luther King Jr in Memphis, Tennessee. The Prague Revolution. The Vietnam offensive. I suppose the only redeeming feature for the year was the three American astronauts' successful trip into space, apart from which 1968 was a time of bloodshed.

Marginally important for the British were the Manson murders in 1969 but it is correct to say that one of the most significant 'revolutions' to affect us were the increasingly popular anti-war movements which in our country became more prominent throughout the whole of the sixties.

The decade also saw Britain's adventure in Europe by rather belatedly joining the new political and economic union set up by the Treaty of Rome.

The situations that arose in England during the years 1959-1971 and, more particularly, the legislation passed during that period, were to prove much more important for us than the problem in the Bay of Pigs, since they resulted in a period of extreme sexual permissiveness, the consequence of which was a challenge on all fronts to the long-established role of British women in society and the passing of legislation nominally aimed at liberalisation but, ultimately, causing a number of highly significant social problems.

Much of what occurred in that decade was either promoted or endorsed by the then Home Secretary Roy Jenkins (who presided over the Home Office between 1965 and 1967). A discussed figure, whose private life — as it emerged much later — was perhaps somewhat debatable. His avowed aim was to obtain what was termed at the time a more 'civilised' society. Under his stewardship, capital punishment was abolished, as was theatre censorship, and birching. The reader might recall his endorsement of the relaxing of divorce laws and the legalisation of abortion.

I suggest that the expression 'civilised society' is probably a mis-description because the measures adopted could perhaps be considered as progressive but were not necessarily that civilised, especially since, in my view, progress and civilisation are by no means coincident. In any event, I feel bound to record the fact that many – and not only myself – thought even at the time that his 'liberality' was somewhat misplaced.

The decade saw the repeated publication of material which 20 years earlier would not have been available to the general public: for example, Henry Miller's works ('Tropic of Cancer', 'Tropic of Capricorn', 'The Rosy Crucifixion' – 'Sexus', 'Plexus' and 'Nexus').

It also saw renewed attempts to challenge the unfortunate definition of obscenity that had become available as a result of the passing of the Obscene Publications Act 1959.

That Act endeavoured to bring up to date and more in keeping with the mood of the country the definition of obscenity which had caused heartache to the prosecuting authorities and, above all, to the Courts ever since the end of the Second World War. It was decided that a publication was to be deemed obscene if it had 'a tendency to deprave and corrupt...', a definition which gave rise to as many difficulties as it endeavoured to solve.

But the reality, as I see it, is that a lot more was at stake than legal interpretation and definition, since the swinging sixties saw a determined attempt to open the windows of England on to what was believed to be 'a new world', a world freed from the shackles of Puritanism, imperialism and sexual hypocrisy. A combination of political fervour and social restlessness combined in that period to change the face of England and, eventually, its soul.

This is certainly what people at the time thought they were doing; but several generations later the assessment may not be quite the same.

It is worth considering in more detail some of the events and the laws that came about in our country in the 12 years from 1959 to 1971.

In the first place, what has been termed by some – myself included – 'a sexual Hiroshima'[35], the contraceptive pill became available in the UK in January 1961. The Sexual Offences Act, that gave effect to the recommendations of the Wolfenden Report referred to elsewhere in this booklet, was passed in 1967.

The availability of a means to control fertility and births altered whatever balance of power might have existed between men and women. It transferred a control that, until then, had been precarious and at times dangerous and allowed women to ensure (technically at least) that no child was born who was not wanted. Thus a woman was, as she still is, able to frustrate her husband's or partner's desire to have children.

---

[35] v. R Goodall, *The English and Sex – The Shadow of Hypocrisy, Amazon 2013*

Like someone who has been starving and sees a table full of goodies, or a pauper who wins a major prize on a lottery, woman suddenly found herself freed from the risks of pregnancy and able to indulge her sexual desires or whims with the same abandon that men had displayed through millennia.

That ability, that control and ultimately, that incredible power gave her the possibility of behaving sexually in the same manner and with the same irresponsibility as men, thus strengthening the hand of all those women who had always felt that they were like men and, accordingly, should be allowed to behave like them.

Hence the sexual freedom of the decade (promiscuity, wife-swapping and so on) which marked liberated woman. Hence the endorsement of feminist beliefs and the call for parity, not merely in the workplace but in life generally.

The passing of the Sexual Offences Act 1967 resulted in the decriminalisation of male homosexual activity, which was long overdue, England lagging well behind a number of other European countries which had always adopted a much more tolerant attitude towards it (female homosexuality was never a crime in Britain).

That, in turn, brought into the open all those who had been in hiding and who, as the expression went, were at last allowed to 'come out'. In the same way as women's voices for equal treatment grew louder once the balance of power in the reproductive cycle was transferred from man, so male homosexuals claimed equal rights: rights to recognition, to equal treatment, to endorsement of cohabitation and 'marriage'.

A new philosophy had to be established to justify the new claims (one could call them the 'swinging sixties' claims) of both men and women. The individual had to get used to the idea that things had changed; the State had to be brought in to provide official recognition to freedom of sexual orientation.

It is hardly a coincidence that the decade was termed 'the Swinging Sixties', since woman's inhibitions were swung right, left and centre. The liberalisation which occurred, considered at first shocking by a number of people, established itself so quickly that one cannot help wondering how strong British women's feelings of sexual repression and psychological enslavement must have been throughout the previous one thousand years. At the same time, political correctness English-style was born.

One should not forget that Lady Chatterley's Lover, the book by D H Lawrence which was published in hardback in March 1960, in paperback in May of that year, was prosecuted also in 1960, its acquittal following on 2nd November, again in 1960.

In 1959, at the same time as the Obscene Publications Act 1959, the Sexual Offences Act (already mentioned for its liberalisation of homosexuality) was passed, consequent on the recommendation of the Wolfenden Report, in an attempt, which quite clearly has failed, to drive prostitutes off the streets.

In the same decade, there occurred the great shock to the public provided by the nude photographs of the Duchess of Argyle in her divorce case (especially that of the so-called 'headless' man...); the Profumo Affair with Christine Keeler; the almost incredible success of the 'Carry On' type of films, which projected onto the large screen much that could not be published; the Family Planning Act 1967, which provided unlimited contraception also to the unmarried; David Steele's Abortion Act of that same year; the abolition of theatre censorship in 1968 with the resulting open display of nudity and vulgarity on the stage; the introduction of basic sex education in schools in 1969; the Divorce Reform Act of that same year, which made available for the first time divorce on demand and which resulted, in my view at least, in the destruction of the family unit as traditionally understood.

On October 26th 1963 there was published 'The Denning Report' into the Profumo scandal, the suicide of Stephen Ward and the frolics of Christine Keeler and Mandy Rice-Davies. The judge's main concerns were the alleged activities of a cabinet minister (John Profumo) who was supposed to be attending sexual orgies wearing only a small apron; and the identity of the so-called 'headless' man.

The report was shocking in some of its conclusions, or at least it was so considered by the majority of its readers; others thought it was a whitewash. Whichever way one looks at it, it created a number of shock waves in the country, especially in its finding of the existence of 'perverted sex orgies' and 'other sexual activities of a vile and revolting nature'.

The gravity of the conduct unearthed by the Report is underlined by the circumstance that, despite the passage of time, some sections of the report have not yet been made available to the public.

The so-called Profumo affair, which shocked the country, is in fact one of the biggest scandals in British political life. It is, in a sense, one of the more significant manifestations of what I would term the English disease of trying to keep under wraps what is going on in the sexual sphere. It was easy to try to minimise its significance by identifying a scapegoat; nevertheless, there is no doubt that the prosecution (persecution?) of Stephen Ward does little credit to those in authority at the time (I observe in passing that things have not improved, as the Savile saga and other more recent cases have shown).

The 1960s also saw the emergence and incredible success of The Beatles and of Mary Quant and her creation of what has been described as the defining fashion of the 1960s, namely the mini-skirt.

If one considers that the package-tour industry (that made travelling for sun and sex a much desired development, which continued for decades as being extremely popular) started in 1971, it is easy to realise that in just over a decade the moral and social face of England was altered dramatically.

During the same period the Office of the Lord Chamberlain, who controlled what happened on stage, was abolished, as was the death penalty.

It was undoubtedly fair that the jury in the Lady Chatterley's Lover case should consider that the charge of obscenity against it could not stand; but one wonders to what extent John Mortimer, who defended Penguin Books, must subsequently have looked back from time to time and considered whether his capable arguments were clearly taken out of context now that we have, as a matter of routine, displayed under the banner of literary freedom, representations of acts, events and conduct that are repugnant to a number of people. It has always been a fact that absolute freedom ultimately results in selfishness and chaos, since egoism replaces altruism, intolerance breeds misunderstanding and the clamour of minority groups and interests, of whatever nature, drowns common sense in a raucous chorus of inelegant abuse.

Furthermore, although the subject is considered separately, one should record at this stage that when the seeds of extreme feminism were sown in the '60s, they fell on a soil that was unusually receptive, having been fertilised by so-called liberal thinkers and by an ever-increasing acceptance of the vulgar and absurdly extreme beliefs that were reaching Britain from the USA.

The contempt that started to be felt for all kinds of authority, or at least 'moral' tenets of any description (which became the subject of ridicule), has stayed with us.

As an aside, I should observe that the general rejoicing felt by British society at the liberalisation of sexual conduct, which resulted from the introduction of the Pill and the spread of particular kinds of behaviour during the Swinging Sixties, did not last very long. The subsequent decade, 'the Seventies', became one of the worst periods in our social history because of tensions, political mistakes and class fights that resulted in what became known as the 'Winter of Discontent' that paved the way for Margaret Thatcher.

If the campaign of denigration of established values (I was almost tempted to say, the values of the 'establishment') had run its course as most natural phenomena do, the damage done to Britain and to western society generally might have been less serious or at least better contained. It persisted however since any voice of dissent was promptly and effectively silenced (I am reminded of Edmund Burke's statement that 'all it takes for evil to exist is for good men to do nothing').
The silence strengthened the determination of 'liberal' thinkers and, above all, of those minority groups (women,

feminists, lesbians, homosexuals, drug takers, etc.) whose views still hold sway over our country, also because during the intervening years they have become part of news-making and, very often, of political establishments, which carry increasingly considerable weight with our society. More importantly, what they have achieved is the giving of an air of normality, if not of respectability, to forms of belief and behaviour which would cause our forefathers to cringe.

To ascribe entirely to the Swinging Sixties what occurred in the 12 years from 1959 to 1971, and has been defined as the moral corruption of Britain is, of course, unfair since other possibly more insidious forces were and are at work as a result; however, there is little doubt that, just as we were swinging happily in the '60s, so the country's morality is now swinging from the scaffold[36].

A further consideration of our hypocritical stance is the fact that, as some have suggested, the hatred and persecution for James Joyce's Ulysses was not so much brought about by the British public's sense of decency being offended by his description of Molly's orgasms, but rather by the fact that he would not enlist to fight during the First World War.

Some have also argued that this applies to D H Lawrence's persecution, since he was notoriously against the War and in 1915 he actually published his anti-war novel by the title 'The Rainbow'.

---

[36] *For more in a related vein, please look at the Appendix.*

Clearly, something is badly wrong somewhere in our British society.

The mood of liberalisation that prevailed over the decade of the '60s was aimed at eliminating repression, bigotry and moral intolerance; little did its proponents, and especially Roy Jenkins, realise that freedom was being confused with licence and that moral permissiveness, coupled with the collapse of respect for social institutions that had served the country well over centuries, was going to set the tone for the following 50 years. The cultural revolution that was propounded struck at the core of British society and was aimed at subverting its traditions and morality. In fact, perhaps we should call the decade the period of our history when the privatisation of morality resulted in the sanctification of selfishness and the glorification of a free-for-all, uninhibited sexual behaviour.

It is pertinent to record that, in a sense, this had already been anticipated by more than one writer. However, I have always considered the most interesting observation about this aspect of sexual behaviour in the British Isles to be that of a popular writer in matters sexual and a feminist, namely Mary Carmichael Stopes. Two years before her death, in 1956, she began, for the first time, to voice her disillusionment. In the preface to the 29th edition of 'Married Love' she says in terms: 'alas, today, over emphasis on sex has become one of the features of the less serious newspaper press...; nowadays the normal does not supply the necessary 'spiciness' for flare-head articles in the popular press. And we suffer today a popularisation of over-emphasised sex verging on, if not actually, abnormal and unpleasant.'

Divorce and Marriage

*'Love and marriage go together like a horse and carriage'
– lyrics by Sammy Cahn, music by Jimmy Van Heusen.*

So goes the song popularised by Frank Sinatra, but I doubt that the statement is correct today.

The reader may think that the heading is mistaken, since logically marriage should be put before divorce: you can divorce only if you've been married. But the priority here given to the noun 'divorce' is meant to underline the fact that in Great Britain at the moment (and in other parts of the world as well) divorce has become much more important than marriage, particularly because nowadays people get married convinced that if it should not work out, they could divorce...

Furthermore, it is becoming increasingly obvious that, nowadays, more money is to be made, at least by some, out of divorce than out of marriage. There are many (mainly women, I regret to say) who get married solely in order that sooner or later they might divorce and obtain a substantial financial settlement that will set them up for life. But we must not be too unkind!

As already observed, it is a sad fact of modern relationships that most couples who nowadays tie the knot do so secretly thinking that, if the relationship will not work, it will be terminated. In a sense, it is like going into a competition knowing that you are going to lose...

Divorce is undoubtedly an excellent idea as far as the parties themselves are concerned, but the worst possible solution where there are children. However, the separation of the parties has acquired much greater importance than their coming together especially since, in the third millennium, increasing doubts are being voiced as to the significance of the word 'marriage' which has begun to acquire several meanings, particularly in England. In its concrete form, it identifies the ceremony that takes place when a man and a woman decide to join in an intimate and stable union, sanctified by religion, recognised by the State, or both. In its abstract sense, it means the union itself between a man and a woman that, theoretically, is aimed at a physical and spiritual integration of two personalities so that, if the parties so intend, it will provide some kind of satisfaction of their sexual instincts and possibly allow for the perpetuation of the species.

In the Christian, and more particularly in the Roman Catholic marriage service, it is all these things; but marriage also has as its primary object the procreation of children for whom the parents must undertake responsibility. Indeed, for Catholics, it is a sacrament; for Christians, it ought to be; for some it is but a game, whereas for others it is merely a state that is entered into simply because it is expected of them.

My choice of words shows how old-fashioned I am, since nowadays (2014) it is said that marriage is no longer a communion between man and woman but is capable of being extended to persons of the same sex.

For those who consider that marriages are made in heaven, they are indissoluble and thus, in the words of some marriage services, the parties are united for better or for worse, whether or not they get rich, are or are not fit, until their mortal spoils are abandoned; not too long ago a rather cynical American lawyer expressed the idea that marriage is such only 'until death or the laws of the domicile us do part'.

For most English people, marriage is no more than a simple contractual relationship between the parties who are allowed by law to get out of it at will.

Things were not always so. Even though the Romans recognised that divorce should be available in certain circumstances, they claimed that marriage had a religious and sacred value, since they respected the family unit which Cicero considered the principal force of the State (in fact, he is on the record as expressing satisfaction when he saw a married friend of his emerging from a brothel, voicing the thought that by the visit he was less likely to molest sexually a friend's wife). Accordingly, although divorce was allowed in certain circumstances, it was discouraged, if of a casual nature, by financial penalties and by limiting the power of remarriage for the sake of the children. Indeed, the philosopher Seneca spoke with distaste of those noble women who counted their age not by the number of consuls but by the number of husbands.

After Constantine had acknowledged the Catholic religion as an acceptable form of worship for the Roman Empire, that is to say from the beginning of the 4th Century up to the time of Justinian (early 6th Century) there was a formal reaction against divorce owing to the influence of the Catholic church, but mainly because of the abuses of the system that coincided with the ever-increasing corruption of Roman society.

Over the years, especially as a result of the preaching of Ambrose (c. 340-97) and Augustine (354-430), the concept of the indissolubility of marriage became firmly established and sometime later Thomas Aquinas reinforced the idea by laying down Catholic theories and beliefs in systematic form.

As we all know, Henry VIII (1491-1547) was not happy with the Church's teaching on the subject of divorce and the consequences are well recorded. Nevertheless, the Christian view of marriages made in heaven continued to prevail in England and was adopted by the Canon Law, which recognised only the nullity of marriage and not divorce. As a result, it was extremely difficult for English parties to divorce; decrees of judicial separation were available in the English Ecclesiastical Courts from about the 13th Century onwards, mainly for desertion and cruelty and what were then termed unnatural offences. There were anomalies, there was dissatisfaction especially because of the criticism by the Protestant reformers of 16th Century who, for these purposes, could be termed the forerunners of present-day feminists, at least as far as divorce was concerned.

As usual, money prevailed, since those who could afford to do so had the right to promote a private Act of Parliament and get divorced that way. This procedure was expensive and was also fairly rare since only ten private Acts of Parliament were passed before 1714 and from 1714 to 1856, a most significant date for divorce in England as we shall see, there were only 307 private Acts of Parliament dealing with divorce. And so it went on, until May 1856 when the first 'Divorce Bill' was introduced into Parliament by Lord Cranworth. After much debate and extensive transformation it became law as the Divorce Act 1857 and thus opened the door onto what was to become, just over a century later, the pathway to unrestricted divorce and to the destruction of the family unit.

There was furore in Parliament. Many argued that the proposed Bill, once it became law, would make divorce available at will. One of the Bill's principal opponents, Lord Redesdale, a Conservative, anticipated such a development in his powerful dissenting judgment of which it might be useful to quote part to show the precise words used:

> *'These divorces will thus be opened to another and numerous class, but a still more numerous class will*

be equally excluded as at present. Once created, an appetite for such licence by the proposed change and the demand to be permitted to satisfy it will become irresistible. The cry for cheap law has, of late, been universally attended to... and must ultimately lead to extreme facility in obtaining such divorces.'

Historically, the situation was awkward. One of the avowed aims of the government at the time was to bring divorce to the door of the poorer classes, thus trying to reduce the privileges of the upper class. Its stated intention was to make divorce easier and cheaper, also for the middle classes. What was not stated openly, however, was that the government in reality intended to keep both divorce and judicial separation 'wholly inaccessible to the lower middle class and the poor'. In any event, Lord Redesdale saw the future correctly and, despite the efforts of Gladstone and others who opposed the passing of a law that, in their view, would facilitate divorce, the scheme went ahead.

The 1857 legislation was passed to give effect to the decision of Queen Victoria to appoint a 'commission into the state of the law of divorce in England'. Interestingly, perhaps, the report was completed in 1853 but was not published until 1856.

Until that date, English law had solved the problem of the unhappy marriage in a very practical way: namely, the husband could actually sell his wife; wife-selling being a rather typical aspect of English culture.

The practice of wife sales at market fairs is said to have originated in Anglo-Saxon times and to have become a custom of the Realm.

The reader with a literary bent would no doubt recall Thomas Hardy's 'The Mayor of Casterbridge' (a fictitious hamlet, of course, which he based on the village of Wheyhill, just off the A303 a few miles from Andover in Hampshire, where the famous Fayre was held at which wife sales would occur).

There seems to have been no legislation at any time officially sanctioning the sale of one's wife, but it did take place especially amongst the lower classes and, more particularly, in rural communities. Even though churchmen attacked the practice, it carried on for a very long time indeed and one had to wait until the first decade of the 19th Century before the issue of wife-selling and its legality began to be considered by both civil and church authorities. Indeed, as has been observed[37], 'wife-selling retained a popular legitimacy until the 1880s'.

Nevertheless, whilst historically significant, the number of cases of wife-selling was really small. Peter Vansittart records that "Thompson is suggesting that the number of

---

[37] *'British Society 1680-1880', Richard Price, Cambridge University Press, 1991, p316*

wife sales between 1760 and 1880 was 218 and that the practice 'performed the function of ritual divorce both more available and more civilised than anything the polite culture could offer'"[38].

The 1857 legislation changed the practice that had lasted for centuries.

It should not be forgotten that, in England, the basic approach of the old Canon law had prevailed ever since Christianity was brought to the British Isles. This meant that once a marriage was valid, there could be no divorce; on the other hand, a marriage could sometimes be found to be not wholly valid. In those cases, church lawyers would argue on one or more of the grounds of Canon law that the marriage should be declared null and void.

The situation that prevailed in England from, say, the 4th until the 19th Century did not really present too many problems for a number of reasons. Firstly, decrees of judicial separation were available in the English Ecclesiastical courts from about the 13th Century onwards, mainly for desertion, cruelty and, what were then termed, unnatural offences. Inevitably, there were anomalies in the same way as some that occasionally manifest themselves in proceedings before the Catholic Church courts in Rome. These did give rise to stringent criticisms by the Protestant reformers of the 16th Century, as already observed above.

---

[38] *'In Memory of England: A Novelist's View of History', John Murray, London, 1998, p157*

Whatever the principle may have been, economics determined which way the parties' future would develop, since the cost of proceedings in the Ecclesiastical courts was considerable and only the wealthiest could afford them. Time, amongst other factors, contributed to the costs. It has been calculated that an undefended decree of judicial separation would take between six and eight weeks to obtain if both parties agreed, but if the parties were at loggerheads and one or the other defended the proceedings, it might take two or three years, with a relative expenditure of thousands of pounds.

These impediments did not seem to bother the British people too much. Extramarital sexual activity was the norm, at least in 17th Century England and the lower classes relied much more upon 'de facto' cohabitation than upon any legal requirement. In reality, it can be said that they tried to avoid getting embroiled in technicalities concerning marriage and accepted that a permanent consensual union was just as good. Very often marriages took place merely by the man kissing the woman before witnesses and by presenting her with gifts, a ring or something else, which of itself was considered to constitute a binding marriage. It was only in 1753 that the Marriage Act determined what was and was not a real legal marriage ceremony and decreed that, from that date onwards, the only marriages that were to count were properly constituted church ones.

Whilst divorce was not permitted save in the somewhat rare circumstances mentioned above, other forms of disposal of a spouse, mainly of the wife because the man had greater freedom in those days, came to the fore. The obvious one was bigamy, which was not necessarily prosecuted, and the more common one was the ritual 'wife sale', mentioned by Thomas Hardy and referred to above, which dispelled the notion that it was only a drunken husband who sold his wife for a pittance and then lived to regret it. In the normal course of events, the husband had thought the matter over quite well and the sale of his wife was a ceremony that, if properly performed, in the presence of witnesses, was considered by the people at large as divorce. This generally took place where a number of persons congregated, usually at markets or at fairs, and much has been made of the humiliation of the woman being paraded like a cow at auction with a halter round her neck. This was mere show because, in the normal course of events, the sale had been prearranged and in all likelihood the buyer was the woman's lover in any case.

How widespread the practice was, nobody can now tell. It may well be that, at a much later date, newspapers advertised it because of its sensational nature rather than because of its frequency; but the point must remain controversial.

The system for obtaining divorce based on the fault or guilt of either of the parties lasted in England, to the great joy of divorce lawyers and private investigators, until the Divorce

Reform Act 1969 superseded it. That Act established the principle that marriage was no longer indissoluble.

The 1857 legislation had provided for the first time that divorce could be obtained only if one of the parties was at fault. The grounds for divorce were the same as remained until 1969 – namely: adultery, cruelty, desertion, unsoundness of mind, sodomy, bestiality and rape. Put differently, fault or guilt was the basis for obtaining a divorce. Subject to a substantial number of limitations (such as passage of time from date of marriage, connivance, condonation and collusion) the parties, whilst technically not entirely free to bring their marriage to an end, could achieve the same result if either was guilty, or could be made to appear to the Court to have been guilty, of any one of the said offences. The door to unrestricted divorce, which the Christian tradition had kept more or less shut and bolted, was opened halfway.

In 1951 there was another Royal Commission on divorce to make that step somewhat easier, resulting in the Matrimonial Causes Act 1957, and in 1969 the Divorce Reform Act turned the whole situation round. Whilst the hypocrisy of the legislation was insufficient to enable it clearly to state that just as the parties had decided to marry, so they should be free if so-minded to terminate the marriage, 'irretrievable breakdown' of the marital relationship was the criterion by which the lasting nature of marriage was now to be determined. The objective standard proposed of a 'misbehaviour' by the type of conduct referred to above and established by the Court, was replaced with the subjective decision of the spouses that the marriage could not continue as it was. Where the parties claimed that the marriage had irretrievably broken down, then they would obtain a divorce. To all intents and purposes we now, in England, have divorce by consent. It is true that the Court still has to endorse what the parties have agreed but that is mere rubber-stamping, since its intervention is not too different from that which takes place in the Probate Division on a death in order to 'prove' a will.

The factual situation of the breakdown of the marriage cannot be changed. It must be repeated (and I am sorry! I am boring): the divorce courts merely rubber-stamp what husband and wife have already decided about their future. It must be pointed out, repeatedly, 'ad nauseam': divorce can now be obtained formally because of what the law terms the 'irretrievable breakdown of the marriage' but the formulation is quite clear: the objective finding of the fact of fault has now been replaced by the subjective decision of the parties who have decided that the marriage has irretrievably broken down. No one else is in a position to decide that for them.

In earlier times, hypocritical though it was, we at least had the face-saving device of the court being asked to determine whether one or other of the parties had been guilty of a matrimonial offence (adultery, cruelty, etc.). The principle was stated to be that one had 'to preserve a balance between the binding sanctity of marriage and the considerations of public policy' which determined that whenever a marriage had come to an end, this ought to be officially stated. In theory, the court could find that none of the factors that were claimed to amount to a matrimonial offence had been proved, so that the parties were not entitled to a divorce; but this happened rarely.

Now it is solely up to the parties to decide whether the marriage has or has not irretrievably broken down. The main consequence of this principle being established is that the motivation for saving the marriage has gone. Given that the marriage can, in fact, be dissolved, it will never be retrieved.

Furthermore, it has become increasingly common for people to remarry after divorce, often more than once. Monogamy seems no longer fashionable, so much so that it was reported many years ago that a 14-year-old student, when asked by his teacher to explain what monogamy was, said that he thought it was some kind of wood...

The conclusion of this short historical exploration is that whereas, say, in the case of Henry VIII (which is a classic), divorce was used for dynastic and political reasons, in our present- day society divorce has become a social tool. The State has in reality actively encouraged divorce and when one hears politicians and judges speaking of the binding sanctity of marriage or of the need to uphold family traditions and values, one is forced reluctantly to the conclusion that they are all either stupid or liars – or both.

The consequences of the Divorce Reform Act 1969 are there for all of us to see, if we felt like looking at them: regrettably, we don't. In my view, this Act has sounded the death knell for the traditional English family that is gradually being replaced by the State: a most unsettling circumstance in our society.

A major contributor to this destruction, I hope unwittingly, was the Labour MP Barbara Castle, a highly controversial figure in her time (the Minister of Transport to whom we owe the introduction of the breathalyser, the permanent 70-mile-per-hour speed limit and seatbelts, even though she did not have a driving licence...).

She fought hard to give women benefits and pension rights but probably failed to realise that by continuing to use the expression 'single-parent family' without any statutory authority, she established a situation now normal in the British Isles where in 2012 (see Jan 2012 Office for National Statistics) we can claim to have two million, the highest number, in Europe, of children brought up in single-parent families and three million children living in a single-parent household representing 26% of all dependent children. Should I comment on this? Better not.

Most politicians in the United Kingdom (and indeed, even elsewhere) pay lip service to the family but are reluctant to acknowledge that divorce is becoming more and more common. In fact, at least 51% of marriages taking place in our country end in divorce. About a quarter of all divorces are in respect of marriages that have lasted less than five years, one in 11 couples splits up before a child of the marriage is five years old, and 63% of all UK divorces occur where there are children. Furthermore, 50% of children can now expect their parents to separate or divorce by the time they are 16.

Expressed as a 'divorce rate', that is to say the rate of divorce per one thousand members of the population, the United Kingdom's rose from 2.6 in 1985 to 2.9 in 1990; but in December 2012 reverted to 2.6. These figures may not mean much to the reader but a reminder is appropriate that the figure of 2.6 is the second highest in Europe where we are beaten only by the Czech Republic with a divorce rate of 3.0 (it is also the fourth highest in the world, the leader being Russia with a rate of 4.5 followed closely by the USA with a rate of 3.6).

These facts should not be understated. In his book 'Brave New World'[39], Aldous Huxley had correctly anticipated the current situation when he wrote that in not too many years divorces would be '...equal to the number of marriages. In a few years, no doubt, marriage licences will be sold like dog licences, good for a period of 12 months, with no law against changing dogs or keeping more than one animal at a time. As political and economic freedom diminishes, sexual freedom tends compensatingly to increase'. The

---

[39] *Harper and Row, New York, 1946*

language may be considered by some to be over the top, but both developments expressed by these words, namely the number of divorces and the sexual freedom, were quite correctly forecast.

The major, inevitable consequence of the accuracy of Huxley's forecast we see today in our society, namely the ever-reducing significance of the importance of marriage itself. It is a fact that throughout the western world and the USA probably more people cohabit than get married. Despite the spurious and totally inappropriate white gown at marriage ceremonies, it seems to me that people prefer to live together rather than undertake the more formal obligations of marriage. Whether this is the result of female emancipation or of greater sexual freedom or of the reluctance of the modern male to take on formal commitments is a moot point.

It is interesting that the situation is not too different, when it comes to this aspect of human relations, in the USA, from what it is in Great Britain. There, the so-called nuclear family households have dropped from 45 to 23.5 percent since the 1970s. Whether there were children or not, in 1930 married couples accounted for approximately 84% of all American households. The most recent figure shows that this percentage has now reduced to just under 50. At the same time, the number of couples who are cohabiting without being married has increased from about 500,000, as it was in 1970, to more than five million in 2008.

The situation in our country is hardly reassuring. The number of opposite sex cohabiting (unmarried) couples has increased from 1.5 million in 1996 to 2.9 million in 2012; the number of dependent children living with such couples has doubled from 0.9 million to 1.8 million in the same period.

There are 12.2 million married couple families in the UK; the trend shows a decrease since 1970 in the number of marriages.[40]

Interestingly, 66% of us think there is little social difference between being married and living together and 48% believe that living with a partner shows just as much commitment as getting married.[41]
I have to confess my surprise, constant it is, that the English have taken in their stride, if I can put it that way, the fact that as a result of the 1969 legislation the family unit, as traditionally understood, is being gradually demolished.

When statements of this kind are made, politicians and sociologists run to the rescue and say that it is not the traditional family unit that is being demolished but merely that new, different and better types of families are coming into being. The so-called 'nuclear family', consisting of two parents of different sexes and its appendage of the extended family of grandparents, uncles, aunts, in-laws, etc., is no more valuable, so modern arguments run, than other 'families' that might be established by two male

---

[40] *Office for National Statistics, November 1st 2012.*
[41] *British Social Attitudes Report, 2007/8*

homosexuals, two lesbians, a single father and/or a single mother. Concepts such as the new ones have been bandied about in the western world, and not only in England, for over 20 years and it is not pleasant to admit that any voices that may be raised contradicting them are weak, in falsetto and are easily drowned by the shrill tones of belligerent homosexuals, lesbians, pseudo-libertarians and, above all, impotent sociologists and politicians.

But there you are. I must stop moralising. I should not wish to turn myself, unwittingly I can assure the reader, into a modern Colonel Blimp...

The English in Europe
(more correctly, perhaps, The Englishman Abroad?)

'Mad dogs and Englishmen go out in the midday sun' – Noel Coward, 'The Third Little Show', 1931.

No, this is not a political chapter, although I cannot help saying a few words about how interesting it is to consider why Great Britain became part of the European Community.

It is my firm conviction that Ted Heath, he who was unfairly nicknamed 'The Grocer', was fully cognisant of the fact that Napoleon was in the right when he described the English as a 'nation of shopkeepers'. Heath must have struggled to decide how he could sell the idea of Europe to his countrymen. Ultimately, however, he focussed on an easy solution. He explained to the people that this was going to be an economic union, that we could export a lot more of our goods to Europe if we joined the EEC and that, as a result, we would all make better and bigger profits, be wealthier and presumably happier. Indeed, it was almost too easy for him to focus on the trade features of the EEC rather than on the 'political' ones; was it not called the 'European Economic Community'?

I credit him with sufficient intelligence to have realised that he was being less than honest, because he must have known that Europe would end up by being primarily a political union and that joining it would have meant becoming subject to laws passed by a parliament on the Continent, laws which, as Lord Denning so aptly put it[42], would be like a tide coming up the English creeks and affecting everything and everybody; out of office he would certainly have gone if this is what he had told the country. And from this mis-selling of the idea of Europe have stemmed a lot of the problems that England has had to face in its relations with its European brethren; but that is another story, although it is worth recording that Heath got there somewhat late, Britain having failed to join the Common Market when it was first set up and paid the price ever since. Indeed, the well-known English intellectual, Noel Annan, has described that failure as 'the most ruinous

---

[42] *H P Bulmer Ltd and Showerings Ltd v. J Bollinger SA (1974), p.418*

diplomatic decision' taken after the Second World War. This may be ascribed to the fact that, even though Britain had in the meantime, with dignity, commendable speed and very little bloodshed, disposed of its Empire, its imperialist, if not xenophobic, mentality still remains.

No, it is not politics I am interested in but rather the attitude of the English when they go abroad, mainly to Europe: a brief look at history before I turn to the present-day position.

It is commonly said that the tourist activities of the British in Europe, especially in France, Switzerland, Italy and Greece, started with the Grand Tour. This is partly true: the English men, and women, who could afford to go on the Grand Tour were usually those with some money and probably class distinction. They travelled more or less in comfort at least until the advent of the railways, in the 19th Century, in a carriage with one or more servants, one or more guides and a tutor. Their excuse was that they wanted to go and imbibe the culture of different countries, especially of the Mediterranean. The dictum of Dr Johnson has already been quoted in the Introduction. And undoubtedly, there were some who went almost exclusively to visit antiquities and museums, thus profiting in the fields of architectural design, interior decorating, building, gardening and so on.

But the majority of them went for what one could term in a very general sense personal reasons, namely to escape, from the strictures on behaviour imposed by a puritanical society, to countries where, firstly, because they were away from their own environment and, secondly, because of the customs of the locals, they could be much more relaxed.

They also went to learn about other sexual tendencies and activities. Whether it was to the carnivals in Venice and to frequent the well-known Venetian courtesans, or to visit the nobility in Turin or Florence, or be carried away by the sensuousness and the lustful feelings of Naples and its surrounding area, it was especially when they got to Italy that their true sexual proclivities were allowed a free rein.

Those who, like John Addington Symonds, maybe even having been married with four children but had other tendencies, were at last able to indulge much more freely in homosexual activities.

Those who had been more restrained in heterosexual behaviour at last found that they had a lot to learn from the local girls or waitresses or prostitutes.

And even those whom we now term bisexual, whatever that expression means, could let themselves go with 'one or the other', as the French put it.

This also applied to people who, though they had money, were not necessarily famous, but more especially to those who, for one reason or the other, did become famous.

That tradition has continued. The number of Englishmen who have travelled to the Continent to indulge their sexual proclivities has been very substantial. Amongst the heterosexuals, James Boswell, Cyril Connolly, Anthony Burgess, Alec Waugh.

Amongst the homosexuals, A E Houseman, Edward Carpenter, E M Forster, John Lehmann, Christopher Isherwood, Oscar Wilde, Wystan H Auden, Joe Orton, Kenneth Williams and Kenneth Halliwell. We shouldn't forget either the alleged bisexuals such as Lord Byron and Rupert Brooke.

What they all realised was that they were acquiring knowledge and techniques which, in the normal course of events, were unavailable to them in England. One cannot help wondering whether E M Forster's statement that 'the Mediterranean is the norm' was cultural or sexual in overtone; perhaps both.

Whichever way one looks at it, it is undeniable that during the 17th and 18th Centuries, but particularly during the Victorian era, the Grand Tour was part of the English gentleman's education.

John Dennis went there to look at the gardens, Sir Thomas Isham (who stayed quite a while, two and a half years) and the Earl of Exeter to collect antiques, Bishop Burnet to appreciate the landscape. The well-known names who followed this particular itinerary are legion: Gray, Walpole,

Manby, Lascelles, Bromley, Addison, Lord Shaftesbury, Richardson, Bishop Berkley, the Earls of Leicester and Warwick, Smollett, John Ealing, John Brown and John Wilkes, and the women – the Ladies Hertford and Miller and many others.

John Kent and Lord Burlington learnt about house building, Sir Henry Wootton went for business purposes, others for botanical purposes or to improve their classical reputation or knowledge or to study politics. Some stayed a few months, most a year, others many more, like John Evelyn, who was away in France and Italy for nearly four years. But what they all had in common is that, ultimately, they were the upper classes in England, the nobility of title and of education. What they all also had in common was that as soon as they crossed the Alps their lives changed. They suddenly became more extrovert, they felt that since the people with whom they were mixing were so completely different in every respect (tradition, culture, appearance, eating habits, social customs and so on) they need no longer maintain those strict standards of thought and behaviour imposed upon them by the society that they were leaving, albeit temporarily. In other words, they suddenly felt free, in counties where they were probably unknown.

It wasn't only the English, of course: all northerners feel that way as soon as they cross the Alps, where even the sky looks different; it is as though they are escaping from the cage in which their societies keep them and they are at last free to behave in accordance with their instincts. And behave in accordance with their instincts, some of them quite base, is exactly what they all did.

Some liked the locals and others didn't. Ruskin hated the Italians. But they all felt feelings welling up in them that they had never experienced before, especially at the sexual level.

I trust I may be allowed, at this stage, a small digression. I have always considered Ruskin's attitude to the Italians to be typical of the approach of many Victorians and, to a lesser degree, also of some Englishmen of today. The following is, I suggest, fairly typical (extracted from John Ruskin's 'Works', Vol.36, p48, Letters to his Parents, October 23rd 1845 and Ruskin in Italy, editor Shapiro, Clarendon Press, 1972):

'Take them all in all, I detest these Italians beyond measure... they are Yorick's skull with the worms in it, nothing of humanity left but the smell.'

'...the ordinary Italian is 'lazy, lousy, scurrilous, cheating, lying, thieving, hypocritical, brutal, blasphemous, obscene, cowardly, earthly, sensual, devilish...'

Italian postillions, *douaniers* and country people 'appear knaves of the first and most rapacious water' (p50); Italian people 'seem bad enough for anything' (p51); 'Beggars, mosquitoes, customs officers, priests even, were a great nuisance, evil, smelling, and vile' (pp86 & 160). Compared to the Swiss, Italians grumbled and swore: 'they were very barbarous, uncaring about art and about anything that was good' (p114).

'If I were the devil, I wouldn't buy these Italians to roast at a farthing a pound – they smell so abominably already' (p154); elsewhere: 'I am quite sick of Italy – the people are too much for me – it is like travelling among a nation of malignant idiots, with just brains enough to make them responsible for their vices – they have taken the whole feeling of the country away from me' (p194).

'Now, if I could put these Italians in a water-butt with the top on, or roast them in sulphur a little, or wash them in steepdown gulfs of liquid fire, or in any other way convey to them a delicate expression of opinion, it would do my heart good, but as it is I am so sick that I believe I shall have to give up art altogether.'

All he could see around were 'ugliness, meanness, vice, folly, idleness, infidelity, filth, misery, desecration, dissipated youth, wicked manhood and withered, sickly hopeless age' (p51).

However, he did have some enthusiasm for northern Italian art and architecture but his contempt for southern Italy, especially Naples, is shown in another one of his statements, namely when he described the city as 'the most loathsome nest of human caterpillars I was ever forced to stay in', adding that, in his view, Naples was certainly 'the most disgusting place in Europe'. A bit much, don't you think...?

A contradictory character, John Ruskin (probably because he was impotent), since altogether he travelled to Italy a total of 15 times... as a matter of fact, if it hadn't been for the Italian culture which he imbibed, he would not have become so well known...

How things have changed in the third millennium! Many more Englishmen now travel abroad and many have bought second homes there or actually have moved residence.

In my view, the Englishmen who nowadays live in Italy, or have second homes there, or travel to Italy for holidays, can be divided into three broad classes.

The first consists of those who, whether as members of a diplomatic corps or a trade mission, or as part of their job, take up residence there. These are numerous and multi-faceted but obviously represent a very small percentage of the population of the British Islands.

The second class consists of those possibly wealthier but definitely better educated and more refined Englishmen who are rather like some of their ancestors in the 17th and 18th Centuries who started off on the Grand Tour of Europe with plenty of money, some culture which they hoped to build on and possibly one or more servants. These are all the English people who have taken up residence permanently or temporarily in continental countries, especially France, Italy and Spain.

Whether in Normandy, the Dordogne, the Côte d'Azur, 'Chiantishire', Umbria and the Neapolitan coast, the Costa Brava, the Costa Blanca, southern Spain or elsewhere, these are all individuals who, for one reason or the other, do not create too many problems, do not misbehave (I am ignoring the criminals on the Costa del Sol) try to absorb as much as they can of local customs, folklore and especially gastronomy, of which they are badly in need, ending up being what they would probably have been at home, namely respectable and maybe even respected members of their local communities. The people just mentioned will no longer be referred to in this section because, as I have remarked, they do not give rise to problems.

But there is another class of Englishman on the continent that is not only the most numerous but also the most offensive, intellectually, aesthetically and practically. Cynically, one should suggest that all the English (and the Scots and the Welsh, but that's by the by) who belong to this class, created by the ease of communications of the 20th Century and encouraged by the package tour, should never be allowed to leave their own country. Especially not for destinations associated with good food and good wine, namely the Mediterranean: more specifically France, Greece, Italy and Spain.

This is because the Englishman, like the northerner generally, is under extreme pressure when he reaches the Mediterranean. In olden times, the period of adaptation was longer; a trek through France, a crossing of the Alps, perhaps stops on the route to admire art and antiquities: it might have taken as long as two or three months before sun and sea were reached and started to have an impact[43].

Nowadays one can begin to experience different climates and places often in about two hours by air from the UK and a good percentage of all the English people in the third category have imbibed sufficiently on the aeroplane for it to be said that, by the time they reach their destination, they are already half drunk. The weather, the food and the drink that they find there intoxicate them completely. They change their outlook, they alter their behaviour.

This may sound like an exaggeration but regrettably is a true statement: some of the English people on holiday in Greece, Italy and Spain or France are a disgrace. Chauvinist travel journalists never stop and ask the local barkeepers, hoteliers, bus or taxi drivers, what their opinion is of the Englishmen they meet. An arrogant, drunken, noisy lot, instantly recognisable in public places or restaurants at any time of day and especially at night; with no respect for local

---

[43] *The following is mainly concerned with the Englishman who can profit from the comparatively inexpensive cost of holidays abroad and whose type came into being in the 1970s. It would be too long to list the successes of the English abroad often prior to the Second World War. I have in mind the development of places like Nice and Cannes, of Florence and its surrounding countryside, the construction undertaken of villas in parts of France, Italy and, to a lesser degree, Spain, which have rejuvenated decaying villages and at times even towns. For that, of course, and for related benefits to foreign countries full credit is due to the English; but within the general framework of this booklet such achievements must be taken for granted.*

traditions or customs (and I am not thinking only of football hooligans).

In fact, they repeat abroad the kind of behaviour in which they indulge in their own country on Friday and Saturday nights.

Nor is the rather loutish behaviour of the English abroad a recent development brought about by mass tourism to the Costas, and elsewhere, and the congregation of football fans/hooligans.

In one of the stories published in 1882 by the title 'Correspondance' the French writer Guy de Maupassant remarks as follows: *Je dois cependant ajouter, pour la justification de la politesse française, que nos compatriotes sont en voyage des modèles de savoir-vivre en comparaison des abominables anglais, qui semblent avoir été élevées par des valets d'écurie, tant il prennent soin de ne se gêner en rien et de toujours gêner leurs voisins.'* That, freely rendered, reads as follows: *'I should, however, point out in justification of French manners that our compatriots, when travelling abroad, are models of good manners when compared to the abominable English, who seem to have been brought up by stable lads to the extent that they're careful never to inconvenience themselves in any way and always to inconvenience their neighbours.'*

Obviously he was exaggerating… and, as we all know, the relationship between England and France has always been one of love/hatred.

What is particularly noticeable is the level of noise that is created today by Englishmen of the third group in any restaurant or bar. After no more than a couple of drinks, laughter, back-slapping, f-ing expressions of one kind or the other, 'another plate of spaghetti', 'another sangria', 'more brandy'.

As I have remarked, there is no doubt that the northerner of any kind (but here we're considering only the English) is under extreme pressure when he gets to the Mediterranean. When, very many years ago, I first started considering this phenomenon I thought that it could be ascribed to the free and cheap availability of alcohol: I am no longer sure this is the true answer.

An Italian writer[44] (in describing the reaction of the Eighth Army during World War II when it reached the road that runs from Salerno to Naples, undoubtedly one of the most beautiful coastlines in the world) said that the soldiers stood gaping 'breathless', struck by a beauty which was completely alien to them and the likes of which they had never seen before. But these were disciplined soldiers who had seen the horrors of the war and who, on the whole, knew how to behave.

---

[44] *Giuseppe Marotta, 'L'Oro di Napoli', Bompiani, Milan, 1956*

They were drunk, of course, but with the beauty of what they saw and which they tried to understand; a modern package-tour Englishman abroad is drunk: full-stop. No question of beauty, understanding, appreciation. Before the arrival of the Euro, sometimes a favourable rate of exchange with local currency made these tourists feel as though they were small emperors lording it over the local populace. There was no question of 'Pax Britannica', merely of 'Britannica Ebrietas'. Now that we have the Euro, exchange is not so favourable but the cheapness of the air fare has compensated.

It is sad. I have often felt ashamed when finding myself speaking English in a restaurant in the company of such delightful travel companions (they were not of my party, of course...!)

Like hooligans at football matches, these Englishmen (and women, regrettably) project an image of their country that is not only untrue, but also hopelessly unfair.

And yet, the hordes keep coming. They are the Mongols of the tourist trade, a loud, tattooed, vulgar, inept, ignorant, violent, inconsiderate, drunken lot, who would thoroughly deserve the fate that might befall them at the hands of the local police but for the tireless and tactful efforts of British consular officials.

The reader will have gathered by now that I have no sympathy whatsoever for Englishmen belonging to the third group that I've tried to describe.

If I had felt, for one moment, that despite all the damage they cause to themselves and to the reputation of this country, they stood to learn something by which they could profit when they returned home, I might have used much less strong language because I am conscious of the fact that we're all inclined to deviate, every now and then, from the norm: common humanity ensures that. As the Romans used to put it, 'you are allowed to be mad once a year'[45]!

But I have lived in England long enough and frequent the Continent often enough to realise that this does not happen. At most, the particular Englishman will come back home, put a dish of lasagne in the microwave, uncork a bottle of inexpensive supermarket red plonk and dream that he is in the Mediterranean. It is only a dream: he cannot understand what he has seen, the local spirit escapes him, the civilisation that could inspire him is meaningless to him.

It might be objected to this analysis that mass tourism creates travel zombies even out of other nationals. Of course that is true and the masses of Japanese who flock to different parts of the world may, for all I know, fall into the same category. The fundamental difference is that, as a

---

[45] *Semel in anno licet insanire*, attributed to Seneca.

rule, they do not get drunk, they're always impeccably behaved and they try to appreciate what they see in the hope of understanding the spirit and the motivation of the peoples and the places they visit. I have never heard any complaint of drunken behaviour abroad by Japanese; the French and the Spaniards in England don't, as a rule, make noises in restaurants. The Greeks try to see what it is of their ancient civilisation that was exported all over the world, or more particularly stolen; one seldom meets an Italian tourist getting off any plane in a drunken state.

This weakness for alcohol is quite clearly a feature of northern people generally and, in a sense, the English vie with the Scots (save that perhaps the Scots appear to be on the whole slightly better behaved when abroad; but there is not much in it).

One must therefore ask oneself why situations as described occur.

As I've said, it is far too easy to attribute such behaviour to cheap alcohol: on the whole, some inexpensive wine can be found in England as well, if one looks for it.

Is the arrogance due to the fact that the Englishman feels like the boxer, Mohammed Ali, that he is the greatest, having established the biggest empire that the world has so far ever known; that he is king? That he was born to rule in the same way as Britannia used to rule the waves and, accordingly, that the citizens of the host country are there at his beck and call, especially since he is paying (not too handsomely) for the privilege of behaving in this fashion?

These are very difficult questions and it is not always easy to provide an unequivocal answer to them. I believe that one of the principal reasons is the fact that, as soon as this modern type of Englishman leaves his country, he wants to shake himself free of the shackles (the discipline, the tolerance, the order, the fairness, the good behaviour, the overall constraints imposed by a civilised society of long-standing) and desperately desires to escape; in this, he is like the Victorians on the Grand Tour. He feels that the locals are freer than he could ever be at home: therefore, he wishes to be like them. Since they spend time in the open, they eat well, they drink wine, he believes that, by doing so himself, he will end up by behaving in as carefree a manner as he thinks they do. In other words, at this level, despite his traditions, he suffers from some peculiar kind of inferiority complex for which he tries to compensate by his arrogance.

In some cases, though not many, if we are dealing with the third class of Englishmen abroad, there is a rather more subtle reason. This may be related to the fact that some amongst these package-tour visitors might have studied a little history and may be aware that the English Empire is the only modern empire that could compare with that of the Romans, so that perhaps they feel that the English are the true political successors of ancient Rome. When, for example, they arrive in Italy, they cannot really equate present-day 'Romans' to those who ruled the world two thousand years ago. A country apparently incapable of national unity, harassed by the proliferation of political parties and unsteady governments, and open to criticism on a number of points; or so he thinks; and yet, the locals are amongst some of the people who are enjoying themselves wining and dining. Why can't he be more like that?

Furthermore, what annoys him intensely is the disregard by the locals of their antiquities that he has travelled so far to inspect. Dirt, neglect, the buildings at Pompeii collapsing, the Colosseum closed to tourists because of a strike or similar occurrences, the disinterest manifested by the very same locals who stand to make a profit out of the arrival of foreign tourists and who seem quite incapable of understanding that by neglecting their antiquities they are, in a sense, cutting their noses off to spite their faces.

All these criticisms and sensations that the tourist experiences quite often in Italy are genuine and correct. The problem arises because there is too much to be seen and the local inhabitants are surrounded by too much beauty and too many antiquities[46], so that in the same manner as manufacturers of chocolates probably are not greedy and wine producers do not get drunk (the examples can be multiplied), when one has too much of something one tends to attach little significance to it.

---

[46] *In fact, Italy is said to have about 80% of the whole artistic patrimony of the world.*

All this is perfectly true: the locals lack discipline, organisation and pride in their history.

There may be a further reason, probably more debatable and less acceptable, but I believe it to be entirely apposite. The sexual drive of this particular type of Englishman is, in all likelihood, impaired, hence his need to assert his personality. He finds himself in a country where he knows, from what he has heard and seen, that his fellowmen, being Latins, operate in a different, more carefree and less inhibited sexual environment. He would like to feel that he can imitate them and that the intake of alcohol will help him free himself of his inhibitions. He then finds that, in reality, things don't work out that way at all and that is why he has to make a fuss. Put differently, his drunkenness and misbehaviour are in direct inverse proportion to his sexual prowess and success. I have no doubt that this will prove a most unpopular notion amongst my readers; but it is what I proffer, and I add, by way of both consolation and reassurance, that the reader might be surprised to learn that this view is very commonly held by Greeks, Italians, and Spaniards. I don't know the French quite so well as to be able to say that they also feel in the same manner; furthermore, I've learnt from experience that nobody ever knows what the French really feel for the foreigner!

It is not too clear, however, that the 'misbehaviour' of this particular type of Englishman is the same in France, as it is in Greece, Italy and Spain. The reason may well be a different one, namely that exception made for Provence and the south eastern parts of the country, France is an Atlantic country and not a Mediterranean one. But this is probably a more controversial aspect of the matter.

It is not being suggested here, of course, that all the English people who go abroad behave in the manner that has just been described. That would be tantamount to the kind of generalisation that one is trying very hard to avoid. But very many of them do. Determining how many is not at all easy; but the numbers are sufficiently great to be noticeable. This must be so, because of the views formed by the locals. If we were dealing with isolated occurrences, it would be impossible for, say, a Greek to maintain that 'all' English people misbehave, because they drink too much 'ouzo' or 'retzina', or 'Metaxa' brandy.

If this were a guessing game, one might say that about 20 percent of the Englishmen abroad who belong to the third category that has just been described are a disgrace to their country. Obviously, this is speculation.

Furthermore, one should not ignore the English woman who goes abroad. In the 17th, 18th and 19th Centuries a number of enterprising women made history. Amongst them Margaret Fuller, Jane Digby, Emily Keen, Mary Wortley-Montague.

But they were quite different from their modern counterparts. It is often stated that modern liberated English women of today who go to African countries where they can pick and choose young men with whom to have relations are said to be exercising their feminist's spirit of independence. It is an attempt on their part to subjugate man, the local penniless man, by paying him for his sexual services.

This is a feminist psychological justification which I do not accept. What these women want is the sexual attention that they lack at home: nothing else, no psychology, no domination, no assertion of one's power, merely sex.

One cannot, of course, compare the tourists of today with the English who went on the Grand Tour in the 17th, 18th and even part of the 19th Centuries. They tended to band together and remain in their own company, even though they were in a different country. Their respectability did not prevent them from either buggering or being buggered by the locals, but it did preclude, save in very rare cases, more intimate and stable social relations. It was as though they were concerned that their own social and cultural standards might be attacked and be found wanting. Ultimately, the locals were basically hostile to them, or so they thought.

Ruskin's attitude I have already set out. There is some of this mentality still left in the modern English tourists who flock to the Mediterranean; but the resistance to the impact of local culture is less marked and occurs, I believe, with lesser conviction with the passage of time. Obviously, this is all to the good for international relations but, more particularly as far as the English are concerned, it is allowing them to manifest feelings and traits which were previously kept under control and, whilst in many situations, as I have pointed out, these are thoroughly objectionable manifestations, simply because they are over the top, in others they do allow the English to develop a more intimate knowledge of the locals.

It can be said that the development by the English of a better knowledge of their European brethren can only be to the good. It is obvious that although England is legally part of Europe, it is difficult to see the English as suddenly becoming part of the Mediterranean, even assuming that they would wish to do so.

But there is a fact that I cannot ignore.

I have always thought that the roots of England's imperialistic grandeur lay in the Grand Tour that started in the early 17th Century. Of course, there was nothing war-like about this kind of travel throughout Europe, which was aimed essentially at acquiring knowledge. But as soon as our compatriots got to the Mediterranean, as Doctor Johnson had pointed out in the remarks made in the preface to this booklet, they began to realise that all that was historically valuable, beautiful, artistically exciting, sensuously provoking did come, in fact, from the Mediterranean, whether it be France, Greece or Italy.

That gave the British visitor his first taste of what beauty and life were about. All the beautiful things he saw – architecture, sculpture, painting – whether inherited from the Greeks or developed locally, struck him in a way which was inebriating. As I have remarked elsewhere, the visitor was soon drunk, not on wine but on the beauty of life and art.

From this followed the desire to possess, to own a piece of such beauty of which the locals were so neglectful, to become part of a civilisation which was as novel as it was striking and exciting.

Here was born what I have referred to elsewhere as the almost natural acquisitiveness of the English.

Here too was born the Englishman's feeling for an Empire. He may not have owned the Venus de Milo – he didn't, of course: the French got to the small Greek island of Melos first...; as a result, he learnt to acquire many other important pieces of antiquity and the acquisitiveness of the British people started to extend to territories beyond the reach of the average inhabitant of the British Isles.

It may sound far-fetched to ascribe the creation of the British Empire to the Grand Tour, but I truly believe that this is a concept that should not be discarded that easily.

At the same time, there was developed a feeling that there was nothing that an Englishman couldn't do. Just as he had acquired bits and pieces, some exceptionally valuable, of civilisation going back at times 2,000 years, so he felt that he was lord and master of the new territories which by his thrift, discipline and ingenuity he had managed to conquer. That created what has often been referred to as the imperialist mentality of the British people.

As an aside, I should also mention that the Victorians were avid collectors. From butterflies to shells, from porcelain to silver, from paintings to statuary, they were very keen to establish museums throughout the country where their collections could be displayed.

Although the impact of such mentality has reduced over the past 50 years as a result of our having ceased to be masters of large chunks of the world, so something had to take its place. What succeeded the imperialist mentality is, in my humble opinion, the culture of the superlative.

Let me explain. The British feel, often quite correctly, that they are the greatest. As a result, when they have to describe their own activities or structures or developments or discoveries, they do not use ordinary adjectives. All the adjectives are in the superlative. Thus we have the best army, the most efficient navy, the most dutiful monarchy, the first this, the longest that; and so it goes on.

There is almost an elemental naïveté in these descriptions, which often are perfectly apt and true, but just as often are a figment of the imagination.

In a sense, it is this kind of almost childish enthusiasm that makes the British people at times loveable for, carried away by what can be their excitement and love of country, they sometimes do not see the reality of their society and of the world around them. Charming innocence!

Perfidious Albion or Imperial England[47]?

'Led during the War by a master of rhetoric, Britain now became the victim of her own rhetoric. She fondly imagined she had won the war. She had not. America and Russia had won the war. Britain had, in her finest hour, not lost it.' – Noel Annan, 'Our Age, Portrait of a Generation', Weidenfeld & Nicholson, London 1990 page 358.

'England expects every man to do his duty' (Nelson's message before Trafalgar) and there is no doubt that most Englishmen have always done their duty, whether losing their lives in great numbers on the Somme during the First World War or sheltering in underground tunnels during the German bombardments of London in the 1940s.

It is my firm opinion that the patriotic and military traditions in England are the oldest and strongest in the world. Suffice it to stop and think of all the wars on which the English, mostly though not always successfully, have embarked; wars of expansion maybe, wars of defence and even occasionally, wars of aggression[48].

---

[47] *The French equivalent of the adjective 'perfidious' was, it is believed, first used in the 17th century by the French writer and bishop Jacques-Benigne Bossuet when in one of his 'poems' he referred to 'la perfide Angleterre'.*

[48] *For present purposes I shall ignore the English Civil War/s in the 17th century (a misnomer in any event, since the war/s involved also the Scots and the Irish). A major historical event, when it is said that over 250,000 people lost their lives.*

As a matter of record, the reader might like to know that since the year 1700 British forces, or forces with a British mandate, have invaded, had some control or fought conflicts in 171 of the world's 193 countries that are currently United Nation member states; in other words, nine out of ten of all such countries. England, as distinct from the United Kingdom, was involved in 42 wars (excluding the total of 11 for our own local civil wars[49]).

I find it difficult to consider that any other countries can beat that record, if I may call it such. Fortunately, England was mostly successful although there were some unfortunate occurrences. A classic disaster in World War I was the Gallipoli 'adventure', which resulted in over 180,000 allied troops dead, of which at least 120,000 were British.

An equally unfortunate event was the evacuation from Dunkerque in World War II, which Churchill described as 'a colossal military disaster'[50].

One should not forget that, on and off, England fought the French for about 300 years.

During the long reign of Queen Victoria alone there have been recorded 72 separate British military campaigns.

---

[49] *Some of the battles have become almost household names for the British people (eg. Balaclava, Khartoum and Mafeking).*
[50] *More about that later.*

It does not seem to matter in which type of war the English were involved, its people have, until recently, always stood behind their leaders in moments of crisis in a spirit of allegiance, patriotism and solidarity for which it is difficult to find comparisons.

I can think of no other people for whom the saying 'my country right or wrong' is so well known and so appropriate. Nor would I go so far as to say that the English people are warfaring: they are probably not warmongers. But there are moments in the country's history when the peaceful image seems to dissolve exceptionally quickly, moments when the people are ready to forget their traditions of individuality, freedom and independence and when legislation is passed restricting individual rights in circumstances which would be quite unacceptable in peacetime.

There is a logic in this. As an island nation, England had first of all to learn how to protect its shores. Queen Elizabeth I started on the road towards ensuring such a result both building up the fleet and pretending not to know about acts of piracy by her subjects[51]. It is a matter of fact that the development of the British Empire can be traced back to the English attitude of not complaining too much about the acts of piracy that usually resulted in substantial wealth accruing to the country, but more particularly by her grant of a

---

[51] *To her we owe both the establishment of Protestantism and the creation of that 'Englishness' which since the 16th Century has distinguished the country.*

monopoly to what became known as the East India Company. The first step was clearly the establishment on the Indian continent of a trading post initially on a beach at Madras, which eventually was developed into a major defensive stone complex controlled by Fort St George.

Another example was the passing, starting in the 17th Century, of the Navigation Acts, which ensured that goods coming to the country could only be carried in British ships. Such legislation served England in very good stead and only started to be abolished in 1849, after fairly substantial criticism based on the fact that the Acts gave British ships a monopoly of trade with the colonies.

A decision of considerable importance was taken in 1714, when the government passed a law offering prizes for the development of a system that would aid the navigational ability of British ships (well apart from helping them not to be shipwrecked...) in determining latitude by reference to the stars.

This gave John Harrison the opportunity of inventing the marine chronometer that added dramatically to the safety with which English ships could roam the seas. In effect, it could be said that it contributed to the development of the British Empire, especially since, by the year 1760, this country had practical control of the seas.

England survived in the war against Napoleon because it had a strong fleet and its reliance on sea power is evidenced by the fact that three of the major events in British history, in my view at least, all occurred at sea: the Battle of Trafalgar, the Battle of Jutland and the resistance to U-boats in the Second World War.

This powerful reliance on their Navy (which started with Henry VIII and continued under Elizabeth) and Army (and more recently their air force) is acknowledged by the people with events dating back to its earliest history: leaving aside the impressive statue of Queen Boadicea on the Embankment, one may note that the principal monument in Trafalgar Square is that to Nelson.

At this point, I must confess to the reader that my sense of humour is rather odd. Hardly had I dictated the above few lines than the word 'Nelson' revived memories of a jingle which some 60 years ago was displayed in the carriages of the Metropolitan line of the London Underground.

It was promoted by a consortium for the protection of English woollens (I cannot now remember exactly the name) and it struck me that the younger readers in particular might find it moderately humorous...

It ran more or less like this:
Lord Nelson was an Admiral bold
Who beat the French, the storms, the cold;
'Cause in fleecy wool he clad
Each jolly pig-tailed sailor lad.

And if one tar as much as coughed
He had this signal run aloft;
Remember, men, the Navy's rule
There is no substitute for wool.

I think the jingle has a significance which goes beyond its humour. Let me explain. Lord Nelson is a much loved English figure, a national hero, a saviour of the nation. It is the mark of a strong people, an almost ruthless trait, that they can poke fun at such an important personage without fear of being labelled offensive or unpatriotic.

I observe in passing that there is another facet of the English personality, namely what appeared in different, striking form when it caused the people to allow Clement Attlee to succeed another saviour of the nation, Winston Churchill, on the occasion of the first General Election after the end of the Second World War.

But back to the text.

Those who have defended and/or died for their country are by no means forgotten. Witness military tattoos, the Royal British Legion Festival of Remembrance, the celebration of the poppy which now goes back 90 years or more, the sub-mariners' service in Westminster Abbey during the first week of November, the sea cadets and all the memorials to the dead in countless villages and churches throughout the country, let alone the Norman castles that show the country's resistance to Saxons and Vikings.

In particular, the castle came to represent both the Englishman's individuality and his ability to cope with war-like situations: from there we derived the saying that 'an Englishman's home is his castle' (that is no longer true, as I have endeavoured to show).

Furthermore, in times of emergency England has always thrown up its leaders: Wellington, Nelson, and, most effectively in the Second World War, we had Churchill, a typical example of a war-like commander, and his establishment of the War Cabinet.

Consider too his speeches on blood, sweat and tears and the resistance that would take place on the English beaches. Anyone who has read English history is well aware that the British are a warrior race with incredible reserves of valour, tenacity and pride, sometimes in circumstances which may be less than praiseworthy (the Crimean War, the Boer War, Iraq, Afghanistan).

In 2001 Lawrence James wrote 'Warrior Race – A History of the British at War'.[52] He makes the valid point there that 'of all the elements of our past, war is perhaps the most pervasive.   Conflicts and their results, intended or otherwise, have shaped Britain, its values and the view we have of ourselves and our place in the world'.

---

[52] *Edwin Lawrence James, Warrior Race: A History of the British at War, Abacus, 2001/2*

The same concept is borne out by the fact that there exist in England at least two national organisations to care for war memorials: the first one is the National Inventory of War Memorials and the second, The Friends of War Memorials. There is no doubt that this endorses the importance attributed to the memory and the honour of those who died in wars. And quite rightly so; the memory and the respect afforded to those who died fighting for their country continue to be evidenced by the ceremony on Remembrance Sunday and the continued success of the sale of poppies.

In fact, England has been at war practically throughout its history. It was officially at war with France from 1707 (the year of the Act of Union) until 1815 when it defeated it at Waterloo. A war of this kind reflected the Catholic and Protestant conflicts within the country, which only found a satisfactory outlet in the Reform Act 1832; it was a conflict which also coloured the view that the British formed of Catholic countries generally and had already contributed to much misunderstanding way back in the 18th Century. One can say that it kept getting worse until the Second World War ended.

This might have been as a result of the association of Protestantism with wealth and of Catholicism with poverty. It was the rich Englishmen who went on the 'Grand Tour' who first remarked on the poverty of the people in Europe and only after that, they acknowledged the arts of the locals.

It has been suggested[53] that the reason why Canaletto's paintings were so popular in England was because they pictured Venice as the commercial power that England was trying to be, a thriving power with wonderful buildings (as indeed England had) and 'yet securely controlled by an oligarchy', all neat and tidy, everything clear cut and well-defined.

In a similar way the English spoke of the Scots, namely with contempt throughout the 18th Century simply because Scotland was poor by comparison. John Wilkes bears witness to this.

In a strange sense, one could say that the only true exception to the conflict in the 18th Century between Britain and Scotland was the very close friendship between Boswell and Johnson.

This attitude however contributed to the forging of the English character because, even though at the time England consisted of very disparate people, the government tried to unite them in the war against the French. The French were threatening invasion and that, particularly for the poorer people of England, created a bond with the more privileged and led to the establishment of a national identity; whether one calls it patriotism or self-preservation in fighting a common enemy does not really matter.

---

[53] J G Links, 'Venice for Pleasure', 2000

It is a fact of history that the need to unite against a common enemy results in the attribution to that enemy of characteristics, whether national or individual, that are normally the opposite of one's own. If the French were Catholics, then the English were Protestants, if the French king was an absolute ruler, Britain had a democracy and so on. Normally the vilification of one country is the glorification of one's own...

(I shall revert to this aspect of 'vilification' in the chapter on Political Correctness).

Although it would appear that the figure of Britannia dates from the time when Britain was a Roman province, it seems to have first appeared on English coins in 1655, acquiring the familiar trident only in 1797 in the wake of the succession of naval victories against the French. In 1821 Britannia became an even more martial icon since she was equipped with a helmet.

The unity of the British people in times of war is remarkable. Let me quote just three very modern examples:

Thatcher was an unpopular prime minister until the Falklands War was won. The change in her standing within the Cabinet was particularly noticeable after that.

In keeping with its military traditions, England backed wholeheartedly Churchill's decision to continue with the war against Hitler. As is well known, Hitler had made or caused to be made a number of overtures of peace. His theory was that Germany and Britain should partition the then-known world, the British Empire representing, as he saw it, an element of stability.

Of course, nobody trusted him; but it is interesting to speculate what the future would have held if, in fact, Britain had acceded to Hitler's suggestions. One of the possible consequences might have been a slowing down of the influence, both military and political, of the USA on the rest of the world. If peace had been made, it is possible that the Japanese would not have bombed Pearl Harbour, the Americans may not have joined the war and they would have found it not so easy to display their hegemony, as they could over a defeated and hungry Europe and now, as a result, on the rest of world.

On the other hand, there was perhaps a historical inevitability in the Second World War. Certainly the personalities of Hitler and Churchill were so opposite that they could never be reconciled. After all, Churchill had a family and a capable wife; Hitler merely had his sexual frustrations and impotence.

Of course, it was not their different personalities that led to the Second World War... the more fundamental, historical and political reasons for such a conflagration, however, were in a sense compounded by their dramatically opposing characters.

The country was disunited about joining the USA in invading Iraq, there can be no doubt about that: but once the exercise started it rallied behind its Prime Minister, Tony Blair, even when very many thought that the action was misguided.

Support for action in Afghanistan was not quite so unanimous. From a historical perspective, suggestions are now being made that both interventions were strategic failures; a polite description for major blunders...

This approach has been a source of incredible strength. The English have endorsed in practice the old Latin saying that 'inter armas leges silent'; in more acceptable jargon, perhaps, that law makers should keep quiet in times of war. Quite right too: to succeed in emergencies one does not need committees but 'dictators'.

However, there is no doubt that in times of war, the British can, in a certain way, go over the top.

One need hardly recall at the outbreak of the Second World War the infamous Regulation 18B Defence (General Regulations), which allowed the arrest and internment without trial of anybody whom the Home Secretary considered as an enemy of the State or an enemy alien.
(Lord Atkin was the only judge who, in the House of Lords (see Liversidge v Anderson, a 1940 case) dissented from the majority who felt that they were powerless to intervene to quash the decision to give extraordinary powers to the

government. His words are often quoted: 'In England, amongst the clash of armour, the laws are not silent'.)

In the former category fell Oswald Mosley, who was detained for nearly three and a half years; in the latter, a number of resident and sometimes even long-resident Italians and Germans, who were picked up in the early hours of the morning from their homes (as a result of Churchill's statement of policy to 'collar the lot' – a most unfortunate, if not contemptuous, directive), sometimes quite at random and depending on the recommendation of the local bobby, and taken to internment camps on the Isle of Man. Amongst those thus interned were some 'enemy aliens' who were later to become well known in England: I can think of at least one such, Lord Forte[54].

Very many, however, in breach of international law, were transhipped from the Isle of Man to Canada and 680 lost their lives[55] when one of the ships carrying them, the 'Arandora Star' – a former cruise liner –, was sunk on July 2nd 1940 by a German U-boat that mistook it for a troop carrier, because it had been painted grey and displayed no red cross flag. It had no escort.

But that is history, though of a kind that was repeated recently with the emergency legislation against the IRA and, still more recently, against terrorism generally.

---

[54] *Unfortunately, no distinction whatsoever was made between fascists – declared or perceived – and non-fascists or long-standing residents.*
[55] *As well as 161 British soldiers, mariners and others.*

The State has to defend itself, as the Romans knew only too well, when they decreed that 'the safety of the State shall be the supreme law'[56]: and in times of emergency, it is as though the British are constantly reminded of the biblical saying that one should fear the wrath of the just.

But the drawback to this is that often the country has lost its sense of justice and fairness.

Unfortunately, it must be admitted that extreme measures taken in emergency situations might have been necessary. The trouble is that, as is happening nowadays, with terrorism (see in particular the Terrorism Act 2000 Schedule 7), not only did they result, as they still do, in strengthening the hand of the government generally, and weakening at the same time that of the judiciary, but also they have created a frame of mind which has brought about a number of miscarriages of justice.

There is no doubt that terrorism is a threat; but do we defend ourselves from it by trying to cope with the symptoms rather than by endeavouring to identify and eliminating its causes? But politics is not really a topic I intend to expand.

More important, however, in my view is the inability to explain the aberrant forms of behaviour that occur in

---

[56] *Salus rei publicae suprema lex esto.*

England when it is thought that the nation's interests are at risk.

The performance of the English during the Boer War is not one that could endear a whole people. In fact, it made us most unpopular at the time throughout the world, especially in Europe, despite the unfailing support for the Boers by our own prime minister, David Lloyd George.

The practice of razing to the ground the homes of the Boers and piling them up in establishments, which, in effect, was the first example of the concentration camps that in a different sphere became so fashionable during the Second World War, was very much criticised by the whole world even at the time; and yet, these were the same tolerant, forbearing, reasonably forgetful and forgiving Englishmen who had, throughout their history, given and continue to give generous hospitality to all those persecuted for either political or religious beliefs. These are the same people who will often be heard to remark 'let bygones be bygones': a most sensible policy, I observe in passing that makes for compromise, acceptance and forgiveness. (Not for nothing do we have in England the saying 'if you can't beat them, join them' or, as an alternative, 'if you can't beat them, get them to join you'... No question here of long vendettas.)

A Christian approach undoubtedly in keeping with the general softness and the overall kind-hearted mood of the English people which prevailed at least until the Second World War. Nowadays there appears to be a cauldron of resentment because many compromise choices and explosions do occur, so that such an attitude is much more understandable in a war situation than in peacetime. Nevertheless, the 'war-like' British temperament did allow the country to create the greatest geographical empire that the world has known since Roman days (it is conceivable that the Americans have now established a much greater, and more insidious, political/economic empire: but that is not something for me to deal with).

A feature of the English national character, which might, in an odd sense, form part of the British approach to life and which may in fact have contributed to the creation of its Empire – which in fact is often underestimated – is the reluctance of the people to admit defeat and their determination to turn it into something like a victory.

Nowhere was this more apparent than in May and June 1940 (on the occasion of the successful evacuation from the beaches of Dunkerque of 338,226 soldiers, members of the British Expeditionary Force to France, and others).

What was obviously a 'disaster', that Churchill warned should not be considered a victory, became almost a legendary feat which, despite its tactical drawbacks, is still looked upon by the majority of the British people as a victory, rather than as a defeat.

On a numerically smaller, but no less significant in social terms, occasion, the same spirit was displayed in more recent times. Let me explain.

In '84 and '85 there occurred a major event in British social history, the miners' strike. This too resulted in a related 'victory' display, although perhaps not so often underlined.

The miners lost their battle. The campaigning, almost demagogic spirit of Arthur Scargill clashed with the obduracy of Margaret Thatcher and, as Scargill had correctly anticipated and feared, the majority of the coal pits were closed.

When the strike was at an end, the miners did not retreat to the pubs to drown their sorrow in alcohol. They wholeheartedly organised what became known as the 'Loyalty Parades', namely marches through the streets, behind their bands and displaying their banners, as if, instead of shedding tears over what would prove for them and their families a social tragedy, they had emerged victorious. They were unbowed. They marched almost celebrating a major event, a victory, as I have observed above, even though the palm of 'success' was presented to the Government of the time.

Not for them any admission of defeat, despite the factual evidence of the failure of a protracted, bitter and socially destructive campaign.

To the establishment of the Empire I shall dedicate the next few pages recording the fact that I am by no means a political creature and am quite ignorant of the finer points of the art of government; but the subject is significant in the formation of the English character and I should say a few 'Italian' words about it.

Before I do that, however, I should record that one of the major difficulties of the English people nowadays is reconciling themselves to the fact that we are no longer an imperial power.

Every now and then situations arise in which we become involved where it is felt, especially at government level, that it would be nice if we could send a gunboat, as we used to do in the 19th Century, to sort out a local problem in other parts of the world.

That, of course, is no longer possible. The hankering after lost authority often creates difficult psychological imbalances, which are detrimental to sound decision making.

This is a well-established weakness of which we do try to rid ourselves, though not always successfully.

Luckily for us, perhaps, the Americans have taken over the mantle of imperialism and have developed similar traits to ours, at least in the sense that they quite frequently consider other people as inferior. From such a view it often follows that if and in so far as the Americans might realise that they are not liked, they overcome the difficulty by convincing themselves that the problem lies elsewhere than with them...!

I have already remarked on the manner in which the English developed what one should term an arrogant frame of mind as soon as they established an Empire, such arrogance persisting to this day. It is a chicken and egg situation whether particular characteristics in the personality of the English people have resulted from the fact that for many decades the areas coloured pink were prevalent on world political maps[57] (as I have said arrogance, but there are others which are less objectionable and, indeed, much more valuable traits, namely organisational ability, civil service structure, discipline, common sense and, ultimately, that most outdated commodity of modern times, patriotism) or whether they were, in fact, the consequences of such an assumption of power over great areas of the world, or finally were characteristics that were already there, in the people, as part of their genetic make-up.

Unfortunately, I have been unable to find anyone who could give an answer to these particular questions: neither historians nor psychologists. I certainly cannot, but what I must do is to accept the fact that the English were right in considering themselves as the successors of the Romans. The English displayed the same strong sense of discipline

---

[57] *It is a matter of record that, at the peak of her reign, Queen Victoria was monarch to well over 350 million people, one quarter of the total population of the globe.*

and patriotism which had allowed the Romans to conquer the then-known world. The English were tough, but fair. Like the Romans, they extended British nationality to all those they came to dominate.

I shall not be drawn into any kind of racial argument as to whether the grant of such nationality was not, in retrospect, a good idea, save to observe that historically it was an inevitable occurrence, which endorsed the English belief that <u>they</u> are the true successors of the Romans and not the Romans (the inhabitants of Rome) of today.

The Roman impact on Britain is quite noticeable. Apart from the civilisation that it brought to the British Isles, the legacy of Rome is visible to this day in the many prominent English towns which date back to the Roman occupation, in Hadrian's Wall, and in the continuous finding of coins and ruins, as well as mosaics; furthermore, the contribution of Roman Law to English law cannot, by any means, be discounted and has formed the subject of more than one learned tome. Nor is it merely a matter of our being reminded of Rome whenever we see names of towns, large and small, ending in 'cester', or similar, such as Colchester, Gloucester, Cirencester, Winchester.

There is no doubt that England's rule over its colonies was inspired by 'Roman' public spirit, and just as the Romans had extended their civilisation to the countries they conquered, so England brought to them its own judicial system, railways, hospitals, let alone the Christian religion.

Admittedly, the French were not happy when England conquered Canada, but the French there were treated fairly. In other countries, for example India, internecine squabbles and wars were brought to an end, as was slavery. Trade prospered and, insofar as such a result could be achieved, barbaric customs were halted. One thinks of the efforts (inevitably not too successful) of the British Colonial Service (particularly the campaigns by Macaulay and Lord Bentinck) to stop female infanticide, the Indian practice of the burning of widows (sati) and infibulation.

The dawn of the 19th Century saw the greatest empire in history being established, thus consolidating the policies and the dreams of William Pitt the Elder. Undoubtedly Britain gained financially because of the openings that were provided for trade; but in a strange sense, profit was almost a sideline (a very useful one, in fact, because it allowed quite a lot of people who traded or started business in the 'Colonies' to set aside large sums of money, part of which were employed in purchasing furniture, works of art, etc. to make more magnificent the numerous country houses which their riches allowed them to build in the first place).

One thing that the establishment of an empire certainly achieved was the strengthening of the English frame of mind, the 'Englishness' which has become an identifying mark of the nation and, to some extent, has contributed to the formation of the English personality and character. As an imperialist power, England was less arrogant than Spain, though perhaps less capable of blending in with the local population than either the French or the Dutch. But the English were fair, and even though one could not avoid the odd episode of mal-administration, or even cruelty, the English did have an imperialist conscience which was occasionally capable of being touched.

One can debate this matter at length. Some have suggested that there are 'particular' psychological reasons why the British established an empire (the men wanted to escape from their wives.....; they felt the need to lord it over poor savages; and so on). In my view, psychologists have no contribution to make to this topic. Historians have put forward many reasons to explain the success of the inhabitants of a comparatively small northern island, then not so densely populated as other countries of the world, in gaining an empire which was not only disproportionate in area to its own, but also so far-flung over the globe.

Some have gone along with Cromwell's saying that a man goes further when he does not know where he is going, or words to that effect, and have argued that the Empire happened by chance, since the English are not cast in an imperialist mould. The theory here is that they woke up one morning to conquer the world or part of it; alternatively, they didn't wake up at all and they did it in their sleep. That is obviously too far-fetched for criticism.

Others have said that the English did it for economic reasons, since their capitalist beliefs urged them further and further in the acquisition of wealth and trade. There have been those who have maintained that the reason was a totally different one, namely that the Empire was the result of the adventurous spirit of those, interestingly, perhaps, commonly referred to as 'adventurers' (Drake, Raleigh, Clive, Rhodes and so on) who, for either dynastic or personal reasons, felt they could not make a success at home and went looking for it abroad, which is tantamount to saying that we owe the success of Australia as a nation to the convicts who were sent there.

Historians who have looked at it more critically have argued either for a strategic view, namely the safeguarding of essential sea routes to India, one via the Cape of Good Hope and the other through the Suez Canal, or that the English intervened in Africa because local governments there were collapsing.

A further thought occurs to me. That the numerous British conquests contributed to the development in the British people of a feeling of superiority, if not arrogance, cannot be denied. Ultimately, all conquerors, of any nationality, have a feeling more of superiority and contempt than of understanding and sympathy for those whom they have defeated. The basis on which they can take from the conquered people whatever they want, is that they are and feel greater than the vanquished who, in turn, become an object of contempt. This contempt may arise because of their social structure, which is considered primitive, or of their political organisation, which is considered inferior, or because they may look upon their antiquities with neglect, not care for them and leave them abandoned amidst ruins, lichens, moss and capers.

This attitude encourages the conqueror to take from the vanquished on the basis that greater care will be given, say, to antiquities in the conqueror's country than elsewhere. Not for a moment the thought in the conqueror's mind that this might amount to theft because it is looked upon essentially as a good deed. This attitude, for example, is still adopted by Britain towards the Elgin Marbles.

I am not being too critical, since it must be admitted that there is a lot of truth in such an approach. One cannot help observing, however, that very often it stems from cultural – I was about to say imperialist – conceit and not necessarily from true artistic sensitivity or appreciation. One could maintain that leaving works of art amidst ruins is more in keeping with their history than to remove them to museums, just as leaving animals in their natural habitat is more consistent with nature than keeping them in zoos. But that is another argument.

Nor are the British alone in this. We know that Hitler did the same in Italy and elsewhere and if he had won the war, he would have appropriated even more from conquered territories to realise his dream of having a centre of artistic excellence of all kinds in Linz. Regrettably, this is a fact of life that only people who have been vanquished can understand.

But there is another respect in which the English developed a superiority complex and it is historical. If one reads Macaulay, one cannot help feeling that his admiration for Ancient Rome is so indiscriminate as to amount to veneration. He, like Kipling, strongly believed that all the virtues that he attributed to the Romans (strength, discipline, respect for authority, patriotism, etc.) were the very same that made the Victorians great. It was obvious to him and many others that the English were, in political terms, the successors of the Romans.

The English had, in fact, created an empire which could compare with that of Rome; as Rome had done, they had extended their citizenship to all those who lived under the British flag and they had created respect for that citizenship.
All this is perfectly true. To that extent the English are (were…..) the true political successors of Ancient Rome; just as Rome fell through the corruption of its body politic, so the British Empire crumbled away, not because of corruption, but rather since Britain had fulfilled its historical function.

Despite all these declarations I still do not profess to know why the British established an empire and, at the end of the day, I don't believe it is nowadays any longer relevant to enquire into the causes of such an occurrence.

It is a fact of history, it made the English the natural successors to the Romans, it established London at least by the beginning of the 20th Century as the political and indeed, the financial, centre of the world, and it showed that the Industrial Revolution which gave Britain pre-eminence in certain fields was not limited to this small island. The mentality it established is reflected in the horror manifested by Churchill in a speech at the House of Commons in November 1942. On that occasion he was arguing against Roosevelt's theory that the British colonies should be put under international control and undoubtedly Churchill was reflecting the views of the British government and the Foreign Office, which were quite clearly in favour of retaining the Empire. A decade or more later, Prime Minister Macmillan, who presided over the dissolution of the Empire, had probably forgotten Churchill's exact words, namely: 'We mean to hold our own. I have not become the king's first minister in order to preside over the liquidation of the British Empire'.

I have already remarked on the impossibility of determining whether the English were great and, therefore, established an empire or whether, having established it, they then became great. I think these are philosophical dissertations that serve no real purpose. We established an empire, without too much difficulty; we ran it competently and efficiently; and when the time came, we gave it up without too much fuss. I remark that this is worthy of praise, no matter what other criticisms can be levelled at Britain.

Quite clearly, it is the British Empire and not the English one, since one cannot decry the contribution made to it by the

Welsh and the Scots. Here, the country was at its greatest. In fact, after the Roman Empire, there is no 'imperial' example that shines more than the British; modern American imperialism, as recent events have shown, is not quite so universally acceptable, being based almost exclusively on money and brute force, rather than on any civilising influence.

Much criticism has been levelled at the exploitation by the British of Indian, African and other peoples; but I firmly believe that, in the overall historical picture, England does not come out of it that badly. The Empire has been much maligned but one can say with conviction that it is the greatest single contribution that England has made to history[58].

It cannot be denied that, in the general sense, many peoples have gained from British dominance, just as many have claimed that one of the most solid inheritances of the empire is the Common Law. Personally, I am inclined to doubt that, but this might be due to the fact that I find it rather humorous to see how certain legal customs (robes, wigs and so on) survive in some African countries. Still, no one can deny that civilisation was brought by the British Empire to many parts of the world, and for that full praise must be given.

---

[58] *It should not be forgotten that quite a few British people lost their lives in the process of creating an Empire. It has been calculated that some 72 million (although this figure is controversial) of our people have actually been buried in India alone and quite a few lost their lives fighting there for about 20 years against Tippu Sultan.*

There are, however, a few episodes in Britain's colonial history of which we ought to be ashamed. One of these was known as the Anglo-Chinese Wars of the 19th Century, better described as the 'Opium Wars'.

The attitude adopted by the country at the time showed, in a sense, the same mercenary nature as that resulting from the sale of armaments made by the UK after the Second World War, and continuing.

The governmental endorsement of the policy of the East India Company to supply China with immense quantities of opium produced in Bengal gave rise to what is probably one of the most undignified events in British history, particularly bearing in mind that the East India Company had a monopoly on the production and export of Indian opium. Nor should we forget that it was the Europeans who gave the Chinese the idea of mixing opium with tobacco.

There was little point in the missionary Walter Henry Medhurst denouncing the tragedies caused amongst the local Chinese population, particularly to its poorer sections, by the importation of opium, especially since he was also appointed Consul and was a supporter of 'gunboat diplomacy'. It is estimated that in 1830 the number of opium smokers in China exceeded ten million and it was almost inevitable that, when the 20,000 cases of opium belonging to the East India Company were dumped in the harbour at Canton, war would follow, despite governmental pronouncements that the State wasn't involved in the sale of the drug. It was sheer hypocrisy to recite (see the Treaty of Nanking) that the opium trade was 'officially' banned, especially since it has been estimated that in 1856 the mere contraband of opium in China exceeded five million kilos.

A difficult episode this of the Opium Wars, especially since Britain itself at the time was experiencing the spread of alcoholism. Nor should we forget the thousands who were killed during the first Opium War; they were not killed in the name of money, of course, but in that of free trade.

Perhaps the Royal Commission on opium, which sat between 1884 and 1896, is to blame for its finding that 'a habitual and moderate use of opium does not produce serious harm to health and well-being'. But, quite clearly, the abuse of gin in our own country may have precipitated Parliament in deciding, in 1890, that large-scale trafficking in opium was a 'morally unjustifiable' undertaking; after all, it was Parliament that had decided in 1838 that the country wasn't prepared to renounce the substantial income derived from the opium trade.

Not a joyful occurrence in our history, which prompted the historian Niall Ferguson to observe[59] that 'it is indeed one of the richer ironies of the Victorian value-system that the same Navy that was deployed to abolish the slave trade was also active in expanding the narcotics trade'. Quite clearly

---

[59] *Niall Ferguson, 'Empire: How Britain Made the Modern World', Allen Lane, Penguin Books, London 2003*

the narcotics trade was excused on the basis that Britain was introducing free trade to the oriental world.

This situation is one of those that gave rise to the conflict between the citizens of the UK who support the Empire and those who think that it was a waste of money.

Need I mention slavery? Not a happy phase in our history, particularly if we recall that it has been calculated that no less than 3.5million (although this figure is much debated, the estimates varying from 9 to 13 million; but not all were transported in British ships) slaves were transported on British ships from Africa to work in the American plantations. Admittedly the country redeemed itself when it abolished the slave trade (though not slavery itself) in 1807 but memories still remain along the coast of West Africa. The destruction by fire carried out by British troops on the city of Kumasi, in the Ashanti region of what is now Ghana, is another matter of which we cannot really be too proud. Clearly our concern to take over the Gold Coast overrode our basic humanitarian feelings. But then, there are episodes of cruelty in the history of most countries.

Another aspect of English behaviour which may be criticised – or at least, is worth recording – is the disregard of a circumstance which was attendant upon the abolition of slavery.

Students are taught about Lord Mansfield's judgement in the Somersett's case in which he declared that English Law did not recognise slavery. It took some time for these words to sink in, since it was only in 1807 that the Slave Trade Act was passed. Interestingly, perhaps, it applied only to the <u>trade</u> in slaves and not to the ownership of slaves.

Thanks mainly to William Wilberforce, a lot was said and done to change English thinking on slavery. But again, we were quite slow at it and had to wait until 1831, when a large scale revolt by slaves took place in Jamaica, the ruthlessness of the repression of which had quite an impact on our social conscience.

It was mainly because of this Jamaican revolt that the 1833 Abolition of Slavery Act was passed. In order to obtain the required majority the government had to agree to pay compensation to the slave owners, of which there were quite a few. It was calculated that 46,000 slave owners were paid compensation of whom at least 3,000 were resident in the UK. Not a penny was paid to the slaves, of course...

The amount paid in compensation for the 800,000 slaves who were freed was quite staggering, representing, as was calculated by the government itself, 40% of its total expenditure in 1834.

The sum finally disbursed was £20million. It doesn't sound like a lot save that, converted into present day currency, it amounts to no less than £17billion!

A lot of Englishmen made money. Well-known names in English society have ancestors who grew rich as a result of having owned slaves and subsequently having received compensation. It is beyond my scope to publicise these names, but I cannot help observing that the wealth and, to some extent, the fortunes of England as a nation received a major boost by the existence of the slave trade and the numerous English owners of slaves.

Certainly, coupled with the sugar trade originating in the Caribbean colonies, Guyana, Barbados etc., the trade in human flesh was quite profitable...

This does not detract in any sense from the work of Wilberforce and like-minded people: it is merely a matter of record.

On the other hand, we can take pride in the fact that we contributed to the abolition of slavery in British territories in 1833 (1834), an operation that was an open contradiction of the support provided by the country to the opium trade.

Against that, one could put both the cruel behaviour of British troops during the 1857 Indian mutiny, clearly encouraged by missionary zeal; as well as the ill-treatment of Australian aboriginal people, although it is probably true to say that the English were much more restrained towards the Aborigines than the Americans towards the Indians.

Probably, one of the worst instances of British imperialist 'misconduct' is what went on in the East African colony of Kenya in the 1950s.

The exploitation of the local Kikuyu population by British settlers there had reached such peaks by the early '50s that it gave rise to what was called initially the Mau Mau uprising.

The Mau Mau insurgents fought hard for many years. What was initially perhaps a local trouble turned into a real war where both parties almost vied with each other in cruel behaviour.

The British too fought back hard, determined to quell the insurrection; but the resultant war-like activities caused a number of victims, the total of which has been variously estimated at between 150 and 300 thousand.

Many Mau Mau were in fact tortured and thousands were held in dire conditions in concentration camps which almost brought back memories of what we did to the Boers.

Kenya finally obtained its independence in 1963.

To its credit, although there were examples of cruelty on both sides, Britain has recently apologised to the Kenyan nation for its behaviour during the Mau Mau war.

Another example of unwarranted cruelty was the practical annihilation of the native troop of the Khedive at the Battle of Omdurman, when the newly developed repeater Maxim gun was used with great effectiveness.

The imperial mentality seems to have gone out of fashion once the Commonwealth replaced the Empire. One cannot help wondering, therefore, whether the ever-decreasing importance attached to the concept might not be another manifestation of, or reduction in, patriotism by the British people or, at least, the inhabitants of England and, to that extent, a corollary of Britain's decline. It seems to me that the mood of self-denigration that has prevailed over the past twenty years or so in England, and that has resulted in completely ignoring the saying 'my country right or wrong' (I observe in passing that I cannot find an equivalent of this expression in any other language that I know) has occurred not because the English have come to realise that there might be some truth in G K Chesterton's saying that 'patriotism is the last refuge of a scoundrel', but rather because the country has lost its sense of direction.

The problem is exceptionally difficult, but one thing is certain: the fact that patriotism does not appear any longer to carry the same weight as previously in the mind of the average Englishman is not due to a philosophical, historical or literary rationalisation; most unfortunately, it is, in my view at least, to be ascribed to the fact that the country has lost its sense of history, the appreciation of its past and, indeed, its common sense: in other words, it has exhausted its historical function.

This is an acknowledgment that most English people at the moment are very reluctant to make, unwilling to ignore 400 years of display of power, and when the opportunity arises, they sometimes remember that the country was great, as witness the recent politically inspired jingoistic appeals to patriotism made both by Margaret Thatcher (the Falklands War) and by Tony Blair (the Afghan and Iraqi conflict): no real disagreement between the major political parties on this issue either.

These recent events bring to mind one of the many sayings of the Spanish writer and historian George Santayana to the effect that 'those who fail to learn the lessons of history are doomed to repeat them'. And maybe we will.

It seems to me, however, that the Second World War was England's greatest and most glorious effort, but it has sapped the energies of its people.

I see one further disadvantage resulting from our reducing importance in world history. When we had the Empire, we had a cause to fight for, to live for. Now that it is probably true to say that the fires which lit up our imperialist spirit are gradually being extinguished (the last spark – to date – was Margaret Thatcher's action over The Falklands, underlined by her coming out of 10 Downing Street on May 2nd 1982 asking the people to 'rejoice' at the sinking of the destroyer Belgrano with the loss of 323 Argentinean lives), we are reluctant to acknowledge the fact that our imperialist fancies are incapable of realisation.

We think we are still a world power and, as a result, have to manifest our ability to fight wars, as we have done recently by supporting the USA in Iraq, Afghanistan and elsewhere. But we do so, in a sense, lacking conviction and merely because it is expected of us, or so we think. This is an absolute fantasy, because nobody really believes that Britain is still the world power it once was. They may like us, some of them may even love us, but they know that the sceptre of world domination and authority has passed on from us to others. That upsets us psychologically. In a sense, we are like a man who has retired early and has nothing to do...

As the American Secretary of State, Dean Acheson, put it in 1962, 'Great Britain has lost an Empire and has not yet found a role'.

Nevertheless, in the overall picture England doesn't come out of it too badly and some might argue that it even derives a significant amount of impact on world history from its achievement in the establishment of the Empire. At least, that is my opinion...

Hypocrisy

'Keep up appearances, there lies the test: the world will give thee credit for the rest. Outward be fair, however foul within; sin if thou wilt, but then in secret sin.' – Charles Churchill, 'Night', 1761.

'We are the first race in the world, and the more of the world we inhabit, the better it is for the human race.' – Cecil Rhodes, (words used by him in his will).

Most Mediterranean people are wont to remark that the English are hypocrites. Is this true? Of course it is: the English are hypocrites. But then, so are most other people in the world. It simply is unfair to say that the English are hypocrites without more, because hypocrisy is to be found everywhere. I can think of some respects in which I myself am a hypocrite and so are most of the people I know. It really depends on what we mean when we use terms such as these.

Although I cannot refrain at this point from reminding myself of what the French writer Balzac said about this particular topic, namely that 'manners are the hypocrisy of a nation'. If I am correct in stating, as I shall, that the manners of the English have deteriorated somewhat over the past 20 years or so, and if – big words these ifs – Balzac is right in what he says, then the conclusion could be drawn that the English have become less hypocritical. Difficult to know... But let me continue.

As a generalisation, one may say that there are three types of hypocrisy. In the first place, there is what I would term the hypocrisy of manners. In the second, the hypocrisy of behaviour. In the third, the hypocrisy of conviction.

These are broad classifications and there is no doubt that much interaction exists between the various types I have set out. Certainly that between the hypocrisies of behaviour and of conviction is very marked indeed, but this need not be a situation that pertains all the time.

Let me amplify what I mean. By hypocrisy of manners I mean the ability to dissimulate one's true feelings or reactions for the benefit of the interlocutor. 'How well you look today', is a statement that one often makes to people who look anything but well, but whom one does not wish to hurt. 'Well played', is often said when one is really thinking that perhaps it would have been better if so and so had not gone in to bat. And how do we describe, except possibly just as a good chap, the husband who congratulates his wife on her hair every time she has had a perm, whilst thinking that she looked better before she spent the money...? There are many formulations such as these where one is trying to be nice in the general sense, not to offend, to make people feel good. One is saying the opposite of what one is thinking and to that extent, one is being hypocritical. But it is harmless hypocrisy, even assuming that one could define it as such rather than as pleasantness, consideration or good manners.

In this, the English excel since, being by nature kindly, they have no wish to injure more than strictly necessary. Foreigners often misconstrue the Englishman's reaction in situations of this type. Perhaps they would prefer him (or her) to be more open, more blunt: but there is merit in the Englishman's desire not to be openly offensive, especially with those whom he does not know so well. In my view, this first type of hypocrisy has an end, which is quite positive; it makes for good and avoids confrontation.

Its results are as satisfactory as the look of appreciation that a man might give an attractive woman. If she is the type of woman who enjoys being admired, that look will make her feel wanted and feminine, justifying all the trouble she has taken about her appearance and her attire.

Indeed, it will provide the inner satisfaction that transfers to her face and to her limbs, causing a glow to develop on her cheeks, a jauntier step, a shrug of the head and the mane to come about. The look may not even be that convinced, but it will make her day. (I appreciate that what I have just written may be anathema to many of today's women...)

All these forms of 'hypocritical' behaviour are common to most well-mannered people. In this, the English are no different from other nationalities, but their manners are usually superior to those of others, at least as a generalisation and ignoring, of course, the football and other hooligans whom we all know about; although, as I have already observed, the manners of the English have deteriorated, particularly those of the youth of the country. This is undoubtedly due to the lack of direction and discipline resulting from the disintegration of the unity of the traditional English family. But that is a separate issue.

It is not in this context that foreigners, and Mediterraneans in particular, say that the English are hypocrites, even though they may often misunderstand the situation.

It is when it comes to the hypocrisy of behaviour and of conviction that I should like to examine more closely how the English behave.

As I said, the second type of hypocrisy is expressed by behaviour and by apparent belief.

Certainly, it is a pretence manifested by the keeping up of appearances. The premise is that if one displays and promotes a particular kind of behaviour, people will end up believing that such behaviour corresponds to a genuinely held thought and will give credit even where it is not due. No matter how evil one's beliefs might be, if we speak words of consideration and fairness, the outside world will reach the conclusion that one is considerate and fair: politicians do this all the time. As the old saying goes, if you keep repeating a lie often enough, you will end up by being believed.

Within this framework, one can sin quite blissfully, provided one is not found out. One is, in fact, being schizophrenic, leading a double life. Not the double life to which Oscar Wilde referred in 'The Importance of Being Earnest', when he got one of his characters to say 'I hope that you have not been leading a double life, pretending to be wicked and being really good all the time. That would be hypocrisy'. No doubt he said it with 'tongue in cheek'.

On the scale of hypocrisy of behaviour, I am very sorry to have to say that the English rate quite high. It is easier to level such an accusation than to try to understand the cause of such particular form of behaviour. I have reached the conclusion that it is, if I may put it this way, genetic. What I mean is that it is an inborn characteristic of the people as a whole, possibly attributable to latitude and weather, but definitely fostered by a type of education and of society that looks askance on spontaneity, emotion, sentiment and extroversion: it is coupled with an extreme desire to conform, ensuring a pattern and a continuity of development and of manners which can and does have a very positive effect upon social intercourse. However, it also allows the English to maintain with conviction, though quite wrongly, that one should distinguish clearly between public and private behaviour and morality. It is easier for an English person to maintain such an unfortunate argument than for a Latin, because the Englishman accepts that, in a sense, he has a dual personality, namely that his private behaviour is one thing and the way he projects it to the world at large is a completely different issue. Hence the repeated but unsuccessful attempts at stifling information, photography and news about the private lives of public figures.

This fixation, because such it is, in wishing to keep one's private life secret, is highly damaging to the country. It can easily be tested this way: if I have a bookkeeper who appears to be the most honest man in the world, I should certainly be interested in knowing whether, once he leaves the office, he goes to bet on horses or visits a gambling casino; similarly, if one is the leader of a boy scout pack, we ought to know whether, when he gets home, he feeds on child pornography or is a member of a paedophile ring; if they wish to promote me to chairman of the Meat Marketing Board, they should first enquire whether I am, in fact, a vegetarian; by parity of reasoning, you wouldn't put someone who cannot even drive a car in charge of the Ministry of Transport (however, the reader may wish to be reminded that our Minister of Transport in the period December 1965 to April 1968, Barbara Castle, could not drive...). The examples are legion, and I for one am grateful to 'Private Eye' that keeps reminding us of them.

This schizophrenic desire to present an outward image that does not, in most situations, correspond to inward thought, usually forces the Englishman to impose constraints on his facial expressions, so that he acquires an appearance of sternness which does not always reflect his personality.

Within the confines imposed by such a desire to refuse to manifest facially any kind of emotion, it is not easy to find an Englishman who will smile naturally. This is not to say that an Englishman does not smile; it is to say, however, that his initial facial expression is usually fairly serious.

This is quite evident in the Englishman's (or Englishwoman's for that matter) approach to feelings.

E M Forster had already pointed out [60] the distinction between the feelings that Englishmen have and their fear of expressing them. He blamed it, of course, on the public schools where the boys were taught that feeling is bad form and that facial features must not convey either too much of the inward emotions, or any emotion at all.

This fairly constant, apparent sternness leads people, foreigners in particular, to the conclusion that the Englishman is a cold fish, that he is emotionally constrained, repressed. That is not true. It is not right to say that simply because the Englishman is not inclined to allow his face to betray his emotions, he has none. Quite the reverse is true: in many respects, he is quite a sensitive creature, but it is not easy for him to manifest his feelings, since he is repressed. That is the reason why he finds, as do most northern people, that alcohol provides the outlet that maybe will enable him to view and manifest his emotions in a truer light.

---

[60] *'Abinger Harvest'* 1936

In this, he clearly distinguishes himself from his Latin and Mediterranean counterparts. The partaking of alcohol as a social relaxant and almost as an individual need, especially in large quantities, is a feature common to northern people in any event and marks them out from their southern European brothers. The latter drink to heighten their enjoyment of life and of whatever they are doing, and especially of food; the former, on the contrary, drink to forget those features of their personality and of their life that they consider a brake to their self-expression.

It may be a counter to this statement to observe that manifestations of sentiment and emotion, sometimes even taken to excesses, are not uncommon in England. One may think of the outpouring of rejoicing in the streets of London at the official end of the Second World War, the sadness displayed at the death of Princess Diana, the singing and excitement at football matches and other sporting events. It is interesting to note, however, that these are all occasions when the Englishman is not on his own; he is part of a mass of other human beings by whose feelings he is carried away almost on a wave of hysteria and to whose behaviour he, in turn, wants to conform. He is comforted by their presence and he knows that if everybody is shouting the praises of a particular footballer, it is only right that he should do likewise.

I remark at this point that there are other situations where an Englishman can successfully give vent to his emotions, genuine or not: the classic is acting.

I have always thought that English actors are the best in the world; whether on television, in films, or at the theatre, they are, in my view, in a class of their own. I believe that there is a fundamental reason for this, namely that the actor does not have to be himself: he is merely playing a part. It may well be that some of the feelings expressed by him he can understand or share, but as regards those who are watching him, he is not the one who is speaking the lines but a different person; the character he is representing, the emotions that are expressed by him are laid down by the author.

I also think there is an additional reason why the Englishman is so successful when acting. It is that, in a strange sense, he can at last be free, manifest feelings – admittedly laid down by the author – which maybe are also part of his own personality and temperament or, at least, which he can understand; feelings which he has not been able to manifest directly himself in his personal life. Assuming the clothes of an actor, playing a part, allows him to do and say things which would be otherwise, so to say, forbidden to him in the world in which he normally lives.

There is, of course, merit in this as far as society is concerned: the blank expression on the face of the person who has been taught or has decided not to manifest any emotion, cannot possibly give rise to any kind of animosity, or reaction, favourable or unfavourable. In terms of social intercourse, it may even be beneficial; in terms of personal relations, however, it does have a tendency to stifle enthusiasm and extroversion.

In the same way, inevitably, it is not considered good form to cry in public, although custom and inhibitions were thrown to the wind in the days following the death of Diana, Princess of Wales. Then, a combination of overindulgence, excessive sentimentalism of a totally un-English type and, effectively, mass hysteria, encouraged, if not whipped up by the media, proved beyond a shadow of a doubt that generalisations are very dangerous indeed. On that occasion we saw the English, the British, if one prefers, giving vent to feelings of mourning and mass grief that were quite unpredicted. In fact, it could be said that millions of inhabitants of the British Isles were, as Ian Robinson reminds us[61] quoting D. H. Lawrence's definition, 'working off on themselves feelings they didn't really have'.

The case of Diana is exceptional. Again, I am not saying that English people do not cry in public, merely that this is something, for the English, which is to be avoided. Nor am I criticising in any way: but the observation I believe holds good and is often formulated by Mediterraneans who are, perhaps, more inclined to let their emotions filter through to their facial muscles.

---

[61] *'Faking It, The Sentimentalisation of Modern Society', Social Affairs Unit, London 1998 (p.121)*

Writing in 1872[62] Charles Darwin – comparing the situation that prevailed in certain parts of the Continent – had observed that 'Englishmen rarely cry, except under the pressure of the acutest grief'. Whatever may have been the position at the time of Darwin, things are clearly changing nowadays, given the frequency of English men crying in public. Indeed, the 2012 Olympics with their protracted manifestations of emotion expressed in tears, in public, especially on TV screens, by athletes (winners and losers), sports writers and TV interviewers are proof of the changes that are occurring in our society (interestingly, perhaps, many more men were pictured in tears than women; which goes to prove – if confirmation were really needed – that women are the stronger sex!).

There is one exception in my mind to this approach, and it occurs when even a minor quantity of alcohol is imbibed: then, smiles abound. But this is a fairly standard occurrence amongst people generally.

It is almost as if there was a reluctance to let oneself go, even though the fact that I smile does not mean that I am inwardly at ease, any more than it means that the smile is genuine. Most of the crooks I have come across in life, of whatever nationality, had a most pleasant facial appearance and, indeed, general deportment, and that is exactly how they fooled the rest of the world. But because of this restriction imposed upon outward manifestations of

---

[62] *'The Expressions of the Emotions in Man and Animals'*

feelings, English people very often are incapable of assessing their fellow citizens: that can sometimes be a handicap in negotiations.

There thus often comes about a complete failure to choose the right people for particular jobs.

I am, of course, distinguishing quite sharply between smile and laughter. In an unusual sense, I find that the Englishman is more likely to be provoked into laughter than into smiling; but perhaps this is personal experience. Furthermore, it certainly appears that the Englishman is more inclined to laugh when he is in company than when he is alone. Laughter comes very easily to the Englishman in groups when watching television, for instance, quiz shows, interviews, or listening to comedians or when in pubs, or (now no longer) going to the movies to watch the 'Carry On' style films; but it is a kind of institutionalised laughter and, in my view, it is very much influenced by what I can only term a marked leaning towards rudeness and vulgarity. Whether they believe it or not, the English have always liked rude things: there is a stream of rudeness that runs from Chaucer to the 'Carry On' films[63], and is reflected not only on screen and on television, but also on stage. One need think only of Kenneth Tynan's 'The Romans in Britain' or the more recent 'Mother Clap's Molly House' drawing on the history of 19th Century homosexual brothels. It is almost as though swearing and sexual references are an

---

[63] *Not to be forgotten in this context is the continued popularity of saucy seaside postcards…*

essential part of what the English enjoy and there is no doubt that the recent relaxation in censorship rules, both in films and on television, accords with what the average English viewer appreciates. To that extent one could say that the modern Englishman's behaviour is less hypocritical.

This is odd, because it is a clear contradiction in terms of the duality between inner thoughts and behaviour to which repeated references have been made. For example, as far as the Englishman is concerned, I don't believe it is because he has read Lord Chesterfield's letters to his son, in one of which the statement appears 'in my mind there is nothing so illiberal and so ill-bred as audible laughter'.

Before him, William Congreve went on the record as saying [64] 'there is nothing more unbecoming a man of quality than to laugh'.

However, even this second form of hypocrisy is not quite so serious as the last one that I have selected because the private behaviour of people, at least if they are in the public eye, can usually be ascertained or got at.
I now turn to what I shall try to define as a third type of hypocrisy and that is ultimately the most significant of the three. It is usually related in one form or the other to sexual activity, in the main; but not exclusively so. May I give a few examples in both spheres?

---

[64] *'The Double Dealer', 1694*

In the non-sexual sphere, it is my firm belief that the most noticeable hypocritical behaviour of the English is related to money. As I have already observed above, it was Napoleon who is on record as defining the English as 'a nation of shopkeepers' (or 'boutiquières', as he put it). I am sure that what he meant to say was not that he believed that there were only small shops in England, but rather that he felt, rightly or wrongly, that very often the English display a smallness of mentality when it came to money matters. I think he was right. My experience is that the English value money excessively: of course, we all of us value money and none of us do what we do only 'for the beer'. I should be the first to rejoice if I were rich: I am not decrying the acquisition of wealth as such.

But the Englishman is aware that the acquisition of money is something that one ought not necessarily to be proud of, so he does not advertise the fact; it is almost as though, in an odd sense, he were ashamed of it. (Our predecessors in the 18th century were, however, much more open about, and adopted a very practical attitude to, financial matters. Proof of this was the publication in 1742 of 'The Widower and Bachelor's Directory' which contained, amongst other things, an alphabetical list of eligible young or not so young spinsters, indicating both the estimated value of their capital and their annual income...) But whenever it comes to having to take a decision on any matter, in my experience, the Englishman will put money first and other considerations later.

In fact, the Englishman's approach to taxation has for one reason or the other had a great impact on the country's history.

For example, taxes were one of the principal causes of Civil Wars.

It was the imposition of indiscriminate taxation which caused the American John Adams to cry out for 'no taxation without consent' (or, as is more commonly said, 'no taxation without representation') for the colonials. Historically, if the British government had had a different approach to money, its decision to charge stamp duty would not have resulted in the Boston Tea Party and the consequent seven years of war for American independence.

Indeed, there may not even have been such a strong demand for independence from Britain...

The concern I am highlighting is particularly evident as a form of hypocrisy in the distinction that exists in the law between tax evasion, which is a crime, and tax avoidance, which is lawful. Put differently, one is proud to maintain that it is perfectly proper so to arrange one's tax affairs as to minimise the incidence of tax. This is considered by the English as being fair enough as a concept, save that it gives rise to fantastic schemes of tax avoidance, sometimes even encouraged by either the Inland Revenue or the Government, to the joy of commercial lawyers and, above all, accountancy firms, especially the larger ones. Tax scams are evolved on a regular basis, mainly for the benefit of big businesses and big corporate organisations, whether they are in the chemical or the tobacco, munitions, internet or other fields.

One can see the importance of big business to the economy of the country, but for the Inland Revenue to publish a report entitled 'Review of Links with Business', containing a great number of recommendations, the effect of which would be 'to strengthen the influence of big businessmen in assessing their own tax liabilities', as 'Private Eye' put it in its 1047 edition of 8th February 2002, seems excessive.

If the levying of taxes is essential for the maintenance of public services of one kind or the other, and if, as it should, it accrues to the benefit of the country as a whole, taxes should not be avoided any more than they should be evaded: they should simply be paid. It is sheer hypocrisy to maintain otherwise.

At the cost of being repetitive, I believe that from the philosophical point of view it is right that tax evasion should be illegal but it is equally true that tax avoidance is, in fact, immoral and if morality rather than money were to prevail, all the complicated schemes to avoid payment of tax that have come to the fore recently and have been much criticised (especially in the case of big companies such as Amazon, Google, HSBC, Vodafone, Starbucks and Tesco), would not only be unlawful but would also allow the State to gain billions in unpaid tax.

Some might dissent and say that perhaps one should term such attitude as 'sophistry' rather than hypocrisy; but it seems to me that the two terms are practically coincident.

Furthermore, I should repeat that a well-known characteristic of the English is their acquisitiveness. When on the Grand Tour, anything that was worth purchasing, as far as art was concerned was, in fact, acquired and taken back to England. The English country houses are, to this day, still full of items which the rich Englishmen and noblemen purchased or 'salvaged' on their trips to the continent, sometimes in France, but mainly in Italy and Greece.

Public authorities were no more self-restrained than individuals. The British Museum organised the first fully documented tomb robbery in Egypt, when they asked Giovanni Belzoni to bring back to England what he 'discovered' in Egypt. In fact, it can be said that what is best in the Egyptian galleries of the British Museum (the Young Memnon, the Pharaoh's Queen from Abu Simbel, the Figures of Sekhmet, the Head of Thothmes the Third and the statues of Ramses the First) were all stolen from Egypt by Belzoni[65].

The connection between England and Egyptian studies is confirmed if one visits the Sir John Soane Museum in

---

[65] *v. Stanley Mayes, 'The Great Belzoni', Putman, London,*

Lincoln's Inn Fields, London. One need hardly mention the Elgin Marbles, of course, brought back to England by another Italian, Gianbattista Lusieri.

This acquisitiveness is the result of what I would term cultural conceit and only occasionally of true artistic sensitivity or appreciation. I should not be misunderstood. I am not saying that all that has ended up in English art galleries or country houses only got there because the English are conceited. That would be foolish. What I am suggesting, however, is that the motivation, which need not have been profit, was much less noble than one may think. In the final analysis the Englishman who, in the 17th and 18th Centuries, was determined that he should bring back to England works of art or of historical interest which he found on the continent, was merely acting because of a desperate psychological need to do just that.

The need arose out of comparative scarcity in the particular commodity which the Englishman felt should be preserved for posterity. In the case of people with money, it may have been the result of a whim or fancy; the attitude is, in fact, persisted in and with the passage of time it is much more difficult to justify, as witness the retention of the Elgin Marbles. That was certainly so in the 17th, 18th and perhaps even the 19th Centuries. In the 20th Century, however, the appreciation of antiques and works of art is prompted more by venal than aesthetic considerations: it is the rarity of the item that provokes the desire to possess it in the first place, with an eye to profit.

It is strange: those who have little of a particular artistic commodity are probably the least well equipped to appreciate the true nature of its intrinsic value, as distinct from the market value.

Turning to the 'sexual' sphere, the hypocrisy becomes more patent, simply because the Englishman cannot make up his mind about the conflicts engendered by his own sexuality when related to what he feels; and especially in the light of the Christian morality that until recently has distinguished the nation. In fact, I am firmly convinced that one of his major difficulties is an appreciation of the difference between love and lust; but that is a more controversial aspect of the Englishman's character.

It was Lord Macaulay who remarked (see Thomas Moore's 'Life of Byron'; 1843): 'we know of no spectacle so ridiculous as the British public in one of its periodical fits of morality'.

A few examples of what I call hypocrisy might be of interest. In the 17th Century there was a practice in Britain that men and women should separate after dinner. The ladies retired to the drawing room, the men remained in the dining room drinking port. To cater for comfort, little privies were provided for their use.

We nowadays look back on the 'roaring twenties' and the 'swinging sixties'.

In the twenties, however, the homeless and the poor were offered food at what became known as 'poor relief soup kitchens' whilst, at the same time, revellers in fancy dress were dancing the night out at the 1924 Empire Ball held in the Albert Hall.

Am I too cynical if I remark that there is almost an echo of this 'poverty scene' in what is occurring today, when we have to argue how to define the poverty level that the country is experiencing, especially in its principal cities?

During the same period, the Charleston was looked upon as the work of the devil whilst at the same time bathing costumes became relatively more revealing, although they were incredibly modest by modern standards.

The hypocrisy of the upper classes, for instance, was exemplified in the works of Noel Coward. Nor should it be forgotten that in 1921 we had 2.5million unemployed.

A strong supporter of traditional morality, James Douglas, wrote in the Sunday Express in 1920: *'The war has profoundly disturbed the feminine mind ... it has cast modesty to the winds, it has abandoned all its reserves and reticences.'*

He thundered against the 'absolutely brazen display of feminine charms' and the 'decadent and degenerate poisons of Paris' that infected English fashions. One wonders what language he might use if he were alive today!

The pornography sphere is where the hypocrisy of the English best comes to the fore. In 1922 James Joyce had published in Paris his 'Ulysses' (he could not get it published in England).

The books were seized when they come over to the UK in 1923 and condemned as obscene. In his work[66] Alan Travis points out that the Director of Public Prosecutions at the time, Sir Archibald Bodkin, who, as he writes, 'was responsible for driving James Joyce's Irish masterpiece underground in Britain for more than a decade', reached his conclusion as to the obscenity of the book after reading only 42 of its 732 pages. The vivid description that Joyce gives of Molly Bloom's orgasms was surely too much for establishment figures at the time. Sir Archibald Bodkin was, in fact, the moral watchdog of the nation, quite conscientious in upholding the rather stringent traditions in the office of the Director of Public Prosecutions. To him we owe the description of 'disgusting filth' applied to the works of Sigmund Freud...

Much greater hypocrisy resulted in the banning of Radclyffe Hall's book 'The Well of Loneliness' since, by comparison with Joyce's work, it is almost chaste.

But there is no doubt that the English liked it that way and there was general rejoicing when William Joynson-Hicks

---

[66] *Bound and Gagged – a Secret History of Obscenity in Britain', Profile Books Ltd, London, 2000*

was appointed Home Secretary in 1924. A pillar of the establishment and a strict upholder of morality, he adopted a rather inflexible stance when it came to obscenity. His was the decision to pursue Radclyffe Hall and D H Lawrence.

The Swinging Sixties did not produce a Joynson-Hicks: this may have been a blessing in disguise, since from that period onwards the English have decided that there is little 'morality' (in the sexual sense) to uphold. Even so, however, there have been some notable instances of hypocrisy, the classic being the prosecution of the Penguin Books' paperback edition of 'Lady Chatterley's Lover', which was published in May 1960. The trial that commenced on the 27 October of that year at the Old Bailey caused uproar, as well as the expression of extreme views both for and against. The result was an acquittal.

The English have gone over the top when it comes to their stance on pornography since they have moved from extreme censorship even in the theatre and for films, to the utter freedom and bad taste of Michael Bogdanov's 'The Romans in Britain' and 'Oh Calcutta'. It would appear that nowadays anything can be printed and shown on screen. What is notable, however, is the inability to distinguish the different corrupting effects of displaying sex and violence; but this seems to be a trait of Anglo-American society.

It is also worthwhile recalling that, until the 1950s, homosexual behaviour between consenting adults was still a criminal offence (as it became in the late 19th Century) although the number of prosecutions kept reducing over the years[67].

In 1954 (27th August) Sir John Wolfenden CBE and a committee of 'competent' persons were appointed 'to consider the law and practice relating to homosexual offences and to offences against the criminal law in connection with prostitution and solicitation for immoral purposes'.

The committee reported three years later (Report of the Departmental Committee on Homosexual Offences and Prostitution – September 4th 1957) and concluded that, contrary to previous long-standing practice, homosexual behaviour between consenting adults should no longer be a criminal offence. Not a minute too soon, one might observe.

More debatable, however, were its conclusions regarding prostitution, where the hypocritical stance continues to have impact on social behaviour. The committee endorsed the existing view that prostitution as such was not a crime; but nevertheless reached the conclusion that one should try to sweep it under the carpet. The appearance of prostitutes on the street was considered highly objectionable and therefore it should be made much more difficult for them to ply their trade openly in the streets.

---

[67] *I need hardly mention the treatment meted out to Oscar Wilde*

Whereas under previous law one had to establish annoyance by the prostitute to her client (potential or actual) or to the general public, Wolfenden recommended that the law should be formulated so as to eliminate the requirement of annoyance, that maximum penalties for street offences should be increased and that a system of progressively higher penalties for repeated offences should be introduced. On this issue they rejected outright the contrary recommendation of the police, who quite understandably would have preferred to know who the prostitutes were and where they could be found and feared that, as a result of the particular recommendation, they would then disappear to places where, not being visible, they could not be identified so easily.

That was the Committee's first example of hypocrisy in sexual matters, and it has not really worked.

One ought perhaps to ask oneself, rhetorically of course, whether a simpler solution might not have been to legalise the existence and provision of brothels: that might have kept prostitutes off the streets quite effectively. But this is quite a controversial issue.

The second example I should like to mention is of a slightly different nature. The reader should know that the committee took evidence from 35 professional and public bodies (the Churches, the British Medical Association, the Law Society, etc.), six government departments and 31 individual witnesses consisting of judges, magistrates, JPs, medical officers, etc. However, not a single prostitute or client was interviewed: rather like reaching a conclusion as to an illness without examining the patient...

One wonders whether, in fact, the highly respectable members of the committee were perhaps afraid of what they might learn about the male of the species by listening to what prostitutes had to say. In any event, all the evidence was heard in private.

One should keep bearing in mind what was, and still is, going on in the country, namely that although brothels were, and still are, not recognised, the unlawful practice of providing sexual services against payment was, and still is, quite extensive and it affects most types and members of society.

In 1979, for example, when the police raided the premises of Cynthia Payne in Ambleside Avenue, Streatham (London SW), who was running a brothel, they found a Member of Parliament, a Lord, three accountants, a barrister, a retired wing commander and several Anglican priests, amongst others, most of them in ladies' clothing, and one even dressed up as a waitress. Some of them were waiting to have sex by paying with £25 luncheon vouchers...

It is not suggested here that things were any better in the 19th Century. Paul Ferris records[68] that at that time a

---

[68] *'Sex and the British', Michael Joseph, London 1993, p7*

Member of Parliament's wife ran off with the Marquis of Waterford; Lord Colin Campbell married a Gertrude Blood and gave her syphilis; Sir Charles Dilke and Charles Stewart Parnell were both cited as co-respondents in divorce actions (and were politically ruined as a result).

Coming to times closer to us, I'd like to mention that the five greatest English traitors of the 1950s all came from Cambridge. Donald Maclean, Guy Burgess, Kim Philby, Anthony Blunt and Victor Rothschild, who are all said to have given information to the Russians, including radar and atom bomb particulars, were, it has been suggested, homosexuals.

In March 1995 Bishop Derek Rawcliffe publicly stated his homosexual leanings, perhaps prompted by the charitable statement made by the Cardinal Primate of Westminster on behalf of the Catholic Church, Basil Hume, that love between persons of the same sex should at least be respected.

The Bishop of London, David Hope, felt that he had to keep up with the times, and shortly after made a statement to the effect that his sexuality was ambiguous. I wonder what that really means.

One certainly does not wish to get embroiled in religious argument, but is it not David Jenkins, a former Anglican Bishop of Durham, who has been arguing against the theological history of the Christian faith? And hasn't the reverend Anthony Freeman maintained that our references to God do nothing else but transmute all our hopes and ideals of what is best in ourselves? Did I not read somewhere that there is in Bristol an Anglican priest who celebrates Mass dressed up as a clown; and am I not right to consider it worrying that in the Anglican diocese of Ely in Cambridgeshire, budding vicars and pastors have to provide signed sworn statements to the effect that they will refrain from abusing children sexually?

Nor do modern members of Parliament fare much better. In 1992 David Mellor made the news after his affair with a Spanish actress called Antonia de Sancha, as a result of which he lost his ministerial post and had to resign.
We all know, from his Diaries, of the sexual prowess of Alan Clarke, he who was an admirer of Hitler and liked to refer to Africa as 'Bongo Bongo Land'. Tim Yeo had to acknowledge an adulterous daughter, Steve Norris is on the record as saying that he has had five mistresses, when Lord Caithness acknowledged adultery his wife committed suicide, Gary Walker acknowledged an adulterous son, the fruit of a relationship that he had had with a researcher of the House of Commons; Stephen Milligan, who was also a journalist for 'The Economist' and the 'Sunday Times', was found dead, stark naked except for a pair of ladies stockings and a plastic bag on his head, having indulged in a highly dangerous erotic practice; Hartly Booth, Parliamentary Secretary, had to resign after a newspaper reported that he had had a relationship with a very young model. Nothing odd or unusual about that, save for the fact that he was

married at the time and also a lay preacher in the Methodist Church.

Just one more example. Cecil Parkinson refused for a long time to acknowledge the illegitimate child he had produced with his secretary[69].

The sexual behaviour of some of our members of Parliament is hardly better as a few examples, chosen at random, will show.

We have had in England a Labour MP who picked up a rent boy with whom he had a rather long-standing affair. If that did not suffice, he employed him as a parliamentary researcher thus utilising taxpayers' funds to support his improper and illicit behaviour.

A married father of two and Liberal Democrat MP was found with two male prostitutes in a London flat, committing a 'bizarre sex act too revolting to describe' for which act of humiliation he was paying more than £100. Bad enough, you might say; it is somewhat difficult to decide whether to laugh or to be disgusted at the hypocrisy of the man who was publicly committed to family values.

A Conservative MP, when caught with his trousers down in a Midlands brothel that was being raided by police and other officials, claimed that he was only there because,

---

[69] *There have occurred recently many more such examples. The list would be too long and too tiresome.*

whilst driving back home from a meeting, he got a stiff back and wanted a massage.

Another male MP was caught having sex with a man on Clapham Common.

A member of the Welsh Assembly, when photographed in a sex act with another male at a location off the M4 motorway, claimed that he was there because of his interest in badger and bird watching.

Nor is this all. There was, quite recently, an MP who posted pictures of himself in a state of semi-undress on the internet, together with inviting sexually explicit messages.

Again, dealing with MPs, who ought to be the cream of our society, one was accused of being on Clapham Common looking for homosexual encounters: his reply was that he had 'lost his way'.

Leo Abse, himself a member of Parliament, points out that not too long ago there was a MP who was found 'orange in mouth, oddly bedecked, hanging dead in his home'[70].

As an aside, I observe that the word 'honour' appears to have lost any meaning; in my view, it barely exists in current English usage. The expression 'doing the honourable thing' does not often occur; this is especially true in the case of

---

70 'Fellatio, Masochism, Politics and Love', Robson Books, London, 2000, p65

some of our members of Parliament, whose main concerns nowadays appear to be money and power.

I find it amusing that we continue to refer to our MPs as the honourable gentlemen or members or the right honourable gentleman or member, which appears to be almost a contradiction in terms at the moment, particularly in light of the recent 'expenses' scandal. The image that they project shows that they cling desperately to their posts, are ready to exploit the system but above all to treat any criticism of illegal, wrongful or immoral behaviour on their part with indifference, if not arrogance (of course, I make the same points concerning the expression 'honourable lady', since recently we have had a few of them showing that financial dishonesty is not a prerogative of the male...).

In my opinion, this is quite a depressing feature. As a matter of fact, I am sorry to say that honour is becoming a commodity increasingly scarce in our country.

I shall not comment on the more recent (2012/2013) discoveries of improper conduct by a number of public figures save to observe that they are symptomatic of a marked sexual 'corruption' in our society.

I will not spend too much time on the advantages and disadvantages, politically, socially and in sexual terms, of the system of public schools in England but I should wish to conclude this section by quoting from Christopher Hibbert,

'The English: A Social History 1106-1946', Grafton Books, London, 1987, p457:

> *In 1837, taking note of gambling, cockfighting and drinking in the town that went on at Eton – and echoing the belief of Henry fielding, himself an Old Etonian, that public schools were 'the nurseries of all vice and immorality' – the Quarterly Journal of Education declared, 'before an Eton Boy is ready for University he may have acquired a confirmed taste for gluttony and drunkenness, an appetite for brutal sports and a passion for female society of the most degrading kind.'*

The number of 'unlawful' if not aberrant forms of behaviour in British society do not require a reminder.

Lastly, I must admit that I find it impossible to leave this sad topic without referring to the recent discoveries of the undignified behaviour by some MPs, best summarised in the words of a daily newspaper of March 10th 2014, referring to 'lurid allegations of sexual harassment, drinking sessions and abuse of power'. No comment.

Despite the sexual excesses of one kind or another that I have mentioned and which have been occurring in England for quite some time now, it is difficult to understand why any attempt to legalise and supervise the activities of prostitutes – when acting in concert; the activities of a single prostitute are not per se illegal – is promptly stifled. If this is not hypocrisy, I do not know what is.

We are not alone, of course. Most countries in the world acknowledge that prostitution as such is not illegal although some punish the client, some the woman, some both. However, we in England seem exceptionally reluctant to acknowledge that sexual pollution needs control and that brothels are to the sexually ill what hospitals are to the sick. Most of the time it is argued that brothels are an offence to the dignity of woman, ignoring that such dignity is offended much more brutally under the present system on a daily basis.

Prostitution is legal in at least 50 countries in the world including Canada, France, Denmark, the Netherlands, Germany, Turkey, Latvia and most of South America; the regulation of brothels varies. But I should record a recent development concerning this aspect of life, an occurrence in the country (Switzerland) with which one would least associate such ample toleration of brothels.
It was reported in August 2013 that, copying what was already available in the German cities of Utrecht, Essen and Cologne, the local authority in the district of Zurich known as Alstetten has inaugurated nine specially constructed box garages that are rented out to prostitutes. They are known as 'sex boxes'.

The customer drives into the garage, out of sight, out of mind as far as the local residents are concerned. They had initially complained about the aggravation caused by the prostitutes who frequented the area. The garages are available for the use of clients during the hours from 1900 to 0500.

I wonder...

The English and Racism

'Racism? But is it not only a form of misanthropy?' Joseph Brodsky, Less Than One, 1986

To the question 'Are the English racist?' the answer, regrettably, is in the affirmative.

However, before tackling what is obviously a very difficult topic, I wish to make two points perfectly clear. The first one is that I am concerned solely with the English. Not for me to consider whether the French or the Italians or the Spaniards – to choose three nationalities about which I have some knowledge – are better or worse than the English. They are racist as well. All people are instinctively racist. All of us resent those who are different from us.

The second point I wish to record is that one has to be rather cautious when making statements 'about colour' which are a generalisation: that is obvious, but it is even more dangerous when dealing with race. The reaction to a black person by a Londoner will be totally different from that of someone who lives in the Lake District. London is such a cosmopolitan centre, there are so many people of different colours, creeds, nationalities, religions, etc., all mixing quite normally especially in schools, kindergartens, football stadia and elsewhere, that one cannot accept that the attitude to blacks, for example, by a born-and-bred Londoner is typical of England as a whole. I have no doubt that the 'little Britain' mentality is less likely to be found in Stockwell than in a provincial city.

Quite clearly therefore, as I have stated, one has to be wary of being influenced in one's judgement by either a sense of extreme liberality and tolerance or a feeling of antipathy and rejection. So much for clarity; I hope...

Whilst it is true that, technically, racism differs from xenophobia, they are but two aspects of the same approach to those who are not 'our own': such an approach is inevitable in England. We are dealing with an island race and all island races, because of their natural isolation, resent strangers almost as much as novelty. The Channel Tunnel may have joined England to the Continent but it is not of itself sufficient to compensate for centuries of 'glorious' isolationism. In psychological terms, in the case of different races, it is much more comforting to be able to assert the superiority of one's own by looking upon the immigrant population as invaders, which, if I may add in passing, is exactly the attitude that we have been developing ever since the greater liberalisation of movement for citizens of the EU has been more felt in our country.

One of the Venetian Ambassadors to London reported to his masters in the 16th Century that it was quite customary for the locals, 'with the malevolent look of pigs', to attack foreigners and wreck and loot their London property. Indeed, there were recorded rather violent riots in London in the year 1517, provoked in the main by artists and artisans who attacked foreign shopkeepers who were believed to be depriving them of business. On the other hand, envy, perhaps, was a component of this behaviour, but the natural dislike of foreigners was undoubtedly the principal cause.

This particular kind of violent reaction clashes somewhat with the fact that there was a long tradition of foreign merchants settling, especially in London, as well as of attendance by foreigners at English fairs, a tradition that goes back to the 14th Century when such fairs were well known and fairly extensive. There was a very popular one in Winchester, for example, which was visited by people from the regions that are now France, Holland, Germany and even Italy.

Many foreigners came to England to visit the tomb of Thomas à Becket in Canterbury, in the same way as the English themselves would go abroad, either to Santiago de Compostela or to other religious centres. England was a well-known place to visit and yet our antipathy towards foreigners was always there.

Moving from the 15th to the 19th Century, nothing much seems to have changed. Even in the 19th Century the English were not so keen on other races. By modern standards, both Carlyle and Cecil Rhodes were racists and would undoubtedly have been prosecuted if they had lived in our time. The English, exception made for Rudyard

Kipling, always looked upon the Australian natives as savages. Nor was it merely a question of pure racism: as far as the English are concerned, racism and xenophobia go hand in hand. The Irish Catholics and the Jews were no more liked than the Australian Aborigines and the Latin races were considered, almost by definition, soft.

I observe at this point that this is an instinctive feeling about non-English people on the part of the English, which contains, I believe, a major psychological component that tends to be forgotten: the English have no respect for those who do not stand up to them. One of the fundamental reasons why, in my view, the English ultimately have on the whole respected the Germans is because the Germans have always stood up to them, and even having lost two World Wars, proved that they were able to fight, that they were organised for fighting, and could display that kind of natural superiority that was so consistently manifested by Kaiser Wilhelm II and upon which Hitler was to play so dramatically and cruelly during the Second World War. Because the Englishman is born free, and has been accustomed to stand for himself, and to speak his mind, he looks askance upon those who, for whatever reason, do not manifest similar traits. It is almost as though he is a wolf and if he sees a sheep, he will go for it; but if he meets another wolf, he'll just pass by.

I believe, too, that this is one of the reasons why he becomes so touchy when he is caught out; and why he is so reluctant nowadays to acknowledge that the world situation has changed the standing of our country. In a sense, England is suffering from the fact that because it became an industrial power before any other country in the world, it would inevitably be the first to become somewhat out of touch with modern developments. It is not by chance that one often hears the expression 'you've never had it so good', which is usually a prelude to the conclusion that one is now suffering because one was not sufficiently competitive. Rather like a number of shopkeepers in London or elsewhere, who were owners of twenty-one year leases at low rents and could no longer compete when, at their expiry, rents caught up with inflation.

This particular feature of the English, namely that they appreciate those who endeavour to gain their respect and make themselves respected, explains why so many in this country were not prepared to condemn Hitler out of hand, at least until he invaded Poland, or felt that Mussolini was good for Italy (in fact, they praised his construction of the first motorway 'autostrada' from Milan to Varese in 1924 and his elimination of malaria from the Pontine Marshes), as well as not complaining too much when he tried to get himself and his country some glory as he unsuccessfully invaded Ethiopia. Even Winston Churchill, who met him in February 1927, didn't think that Mussolini was a bad chap.

It also explains why there is such appreciation for people who have made a financial success of their lives. Money was respected in England long before the glorification of the profit motive, which American society has inculcated into the whole of the western world, became a most prominent feature of English tendencies. It is not simply a matter of corruption: rather more of an appreciation of what money can provide, namely power. The equivalence of money with power, which goes back quite a long way in time, as witness Trollope's 'The Way We Live Now', explains certain phenomena, such as the South Sea Bubble, the grudging respect accorded to Jewish bankers and the ability of Robert Maxwell to fool all and sundry.

It is not strictly related to any question of class distinction, although the upgrading of class for those with money is inevitable. As a matter of fact, social pretension, whether arising out of having made money or otherwise, has been a notable feature of British society and, indeed, at the heart of British comedy over many years.

When, in 1968, Enoch Powell made the famous 'rivers of blood' speech[71], for which he was attacked and vilified, he did not put a date by which the blood would begin to flow; and it is true to say that no real blood has flowed, at least not river-like. This fact, however, should not blind us to the realisation that, despite their innate and almost distinctive tolerance for other people, (one of the greatest assets of this island race that has served it well through the centuries, since it has allowed it to integrate foreigners whose contributions to the well-being of the nation can never be overestimated), the English are naturally racist.

---

[71] *'As I look ahead I am filled with foreboding. Like the Romans I seem to see the River Tiber foaming with much blood.'*

We certainly would have no need for the anti-discrimination and protection of minorities' legislation which the United Kingdom has witnessed over the past three decades, if there were not a projected 'evil' which had to be curbed. The truth is that the immigrant non-white population served a purpose, namely to perform those jobs which the locals did not like: the first generation of non-white immigrants remedied that particular deficiency.

The second generation began to settle in and whereas it may be true (personally, I don't accept it, because the tone of a voice can always be identified regardless of accent; but one has to be trained to do that) that speaking over the 'phone to a black person who was born and educated in Birmingham, one would not be able to say whether that person was black or white or of some other colour, it is also regrettably true that the assimilation of the non-white individuals into British society has not only been incredibly slow, but continues to be rather painful, as witness the recent riots in a number of northern towns[72].

The other forecast Enoch Powell made did provide some indication of time and it was that 'in fifteen or twenty years the black man will have the whip hand'. Of course, he was wrong in both anticipations, but he did identify what would be one of the major challenges that the United Kingdom was going to face; a challenge which it is still facing, though not always successfully, namely the colour problem. The

---

[72] *A survey carried out by ICM between the 27th and 29th July 2001 on issues of race proved quite inconclusive.*

difficulty is that colour is a very difficult concept with which to come to terms, even though non-whites and liberal minded people generally argue that it is, in fact, an irrelevancy. When we say that what one must look at is the individual member of the human race, so that the distinctions are not between races or colour, but between individual human beings, one is making a statement which, from the Christian or moral standpoint, is obviously correct; but from the practical, entirely naïve. It is an argument that ignores that there are people who instinctively resent and reject others who have a different colour from their own. They don't even have to be black: there are many people in the southern Mediterranean or, for example, even in southern Spain, Greece or Sicily, who are, in fact, whites to all intents and purposes at least in racial terms, but who have a very dark skin. There are many of their fellow nationals who take exception to these people in the same way as they would to a black from the West Indies.

The moral argument of the equality of all human beings before God, which is irreproachable, ignores completely the differences of background, custom, living style, moral outlook, skin type, body odour, eating habits, sexual mores that are not necessarily related to colour as such (the eating habits of an Eskimo are certainly not those of a Sicilian even though their skin colour may be the same), but which skin pigmentation accentuates.

The first arrivals of non-white, Commonwealth citizens, British subjects, commenced in 1948. They were mainly men, and when they got here they needed women. Inter-relationships and inter-marriages were the very first pressures to be put on British societies where race is concerned.

I am old enough to remember that, in the early '50s, there was a great outcry, both locally and nationally, when the Bedfordshire brick industry that needed cheap labour brought over from Southern Italy thousands of workers. Newspapers and commentaries were full of remarks to the effect that the morals of the local community would be corrupted, the women molested, criminality would increase, and that the immigrants could not be trusted and so on. Strangely, the same remarks were made then – and I recall them well – which have been made more recently about immigrants of other nationalities.

Very prominent were the fears voiced about the well-being of local women; fears for their virtue, for their physical safety.

I mention the fact because I recall the names of the brick companies involved (the London Brick Company, the Marston Valley Brick Company – the latter no longer in existence). A lot of fuss about nothing. The workers blended in well and, as far as I know, they now represent a substantial law-abiding section of the Bedford community. They even have their own radio station.

The sixties might have been swinging, but did not result in a wholehearted endorsement of mixed marriages. Not only did the whites disapprove of mixed marriages, the blacks did as well; and understandably so, because the cultural and other differences already referred to are very marked.

In many cases, marriage with a black man took place only after the white woman became pregnant. These marriages resulted in children whose colour was neither white nor black, but often brown and, given the initial rejection by society generally of such children, many were given up for adoption.

Whilst it is true that to describe any person as black is to use an imprecise term, since it does not identify origin, culture or background, but merely a shade of colour that is not white, in the case of these 'brown' children the situation was, in a sense, even more serious. The loss of identity was inevitable, especially because there wasn't a correct way of describing them. Then, and now, were they or are they light black-skinned, olive-skinned, 'whiteys', half-caste, or of mixed race? Of these descriptions, mixed race seemed the least offensive and it has now, since 1991, been confirmed in usage by the Office of National Statistics not only on census forms but also generally (indeed, the mixed race group is the fastest growing ethnic group in the UK numbering at the moment 1.2 million persons). But is it a fabricated notion, even more so than the description 'black'.

As Tony Benn had observed more than once – and given the varied nature of his family, he was in an excellent position to judge – we are all members of the human race, and that's it.

The mixed race part of the England population has reacted to the situation usually with considerable strength and pride. 'Of mixed race' cannot be converted into a political statement in the same way as boasting 'I am black' can be. The children of mixed marriages have a foot in both camps and partake of both white and black culture and, in all likelihood, they represent much less of a social and psychological problem than the person whose colour is much more intense, despite the fact that in Britain we have the highest percentage of inter-marriages between whites and blacks in the whole of Europe.

If there has been a change of outlook in England, as concerns the persons of mixed race, it cannot be said that that change has also applied to those whom one nowadays has to describe as black.

The racist feelings first developed in the early '50s remain the same in England. If anything, they have got worse, also because there has developed a certain amount of confusion in the relationship between the local residents and the black population, brought about by the fact that tolerance has been converted into helplessness and fairness into weakness.

The judgment given by Mr Justice Cyril Salmon in the Notting Hill riots case (it will be recalled that this was the first instance, in 1958, of manifest violence against the West Indian immigrant population) – the judge was very tough and later became Baron Salmon of Sandwich in Kent – represented a landmark in race relations, but whilst it was hailed at the time as a victory for justice and tolerance, despite the lengthy jail sentences, of itself it could not compensate for an atavistic resentment. Nevertheless, one cannot deny that improvements have been made from the early sixties when, for instance, in many factories there were not only segregated toilet facilities but also segregated canteens.

Most dictionaries describe 'racism' as a belief in the superiority of one's own race when compared to others. The difficulty is that one can have a lengthy disquisition on colour, simply because there are so many variations on the same theme. A West Indian or an African would certainly insist upon being called black; would an Indian or a Pakistani? Of what colour are, in fact, the Chinese and the Japanese, if not yellow, that is inappropriate, as well as ungracious. There are not many Redskins left, but presumably, they ought to be described as red; of what colour are the Aborigines of Australia?
All these considerations escape the rioters in Bradford, Sutton Coldfield, Leeds, Leicester, Nottingham, Blackburn, Oldham, Bristol, Notting Hill Gate, Brixton and the Broadwater Farm Estate in London and in many other places, especially in large, busy cities. What troubles them

is a combination of what I would term 'culture' in the broadest sense, and envy in a strict sense. Not for them the consideration that the complaints about the way of living, or the eating habits, or the smells emanating from the kitchens, or the noise of their 'coloured' neighbours, are more noticeable simply because of almost an atavistic regression, an original gut feeling of aversion to what is not customary, not known, not understood and ultimately unacceptable because, perhaps, of a mode of dress, a hairstyle or the wrong accent.

Not for them the development of 'racist' feelings which may occur once one has found factual realisation of prejudices which may be the result of bitter experiences.

Their racism is instinctive.

It is true that, compared to what happened in 1958 at Notting Hill, substantial improvements have been made in racial relations; but the resentment is still there. Whether it be because of claims in many parts of the United Kingdom that the indigenous white population has been ethnically cleansed out of whole areas of some cities, or whether it is because there are too many differences and too much aggravation, or whether because many of these racist whites claim that they are discriminated against because we have been trying too hard to redress the balance between black and white, it is a fact that the so-called multicultural tourist who may visit Brixton market or Uxbridge sees only what he wants to see and has no feeling, no awareness, for the animosity that is simmering below the surface. It is equally a fact that not many Englishmen wish to live in what is now called a mixed area because they are beginning to feel what the non-whites felt when they were in a minority.

Furthermore, many whites are beginning to challenge the concept that they should be a minority in a school where most of the pupils are of Asian origin and are really concerned about sending their children to such schools. Hence the clamour for total segregation of colour in schools, in itself a bad idea and contrary to the principles of a mixed society.

Equally, there are claims that there should be state schools for separate faiths, again, not a good idea, since there is no doubt that the absence of integration would inevitably lead to an apartheid type of society and, probably, to forms of indoctrination.

All these problems were less noticeable in the sixties. But 25 or so years on they became much more marked and today, at least in this writer's opinion, they represent one of the greatest social problems that England has to face despite the noticeable progress that has been made, particularly in the last 10/15 years and especially in the major cities, towards a more general acceptability, if not toleration, by the locals of the black population.

Much more dangerous in my view is the fact that the public are not being told the true position.

Anyone with experience of the major British cities knows very well that the influx of black and 'coloured' immigrants has resulted not merely in racial tension but also, more importantly, in the establishment of 'no-go areas'. Political correctness prevents this fact being openly acknowledged, despite occasional efforts by some policemen and reporters to highlight the problems that are inherent in a kind of situation which it may be extremely difficult to rectify, and that one only hopes time will cure.

Ask any taxi driver in London how keen he is to take you, especially at night, to certain parts of Streatham or Brixton council estates or more secluded residential areas and you will learn a lot about race relations in this country; certainly much more than by reading newspapers or listening to political statements by well-meaning though either ignorant or hypocritical politicians and libertarians. The intellectual dishonesty that prevails in this matter, as in many others, in the higher echelons of British society is truly frightening[73].

In her book 'Just Law — the Changing Face of Justice and Why it Matters to us all'[74], Helena Kennedy QC mentions the case of Delroy Lindo, a civil rights activist who took legal action against the police after being stopped and searched

---

[73] *On May 5th 2014 it was reported in the national press that a major London store refused to deliver goods ordered there to Brixton on the grounds that it was 'too risky'.*
[74] *Chatto & Windus Just Law, 2005, London, p.187*

more than 37 times in eight years...... She also reminds us that black people today are 'eight times more likely to be stopped than whites' (p.189).

In common with others, I watched on 21 October 2003 a BBC documentary which showed an undercover journalist recording the racial hatred of some police officers. Most people who live in large cities know that if you are a young black or Asian and you drive a particular type of car, you will almost inevitably be stopped by the police, even where in all likelihood you have not committed any offence; and may I immediately make the point that all this has been happening in the United Kingdom long before the 11 September 2001, so one cannot justify the figures and the behaviour of the authorities by saying that they are concerned about terrorist activities. Clearly the concentration of blacks, Asians and other immigrant communities in certain areas of the larger towns does not help and I must admit that many of the observations that I make on the topic of racism are much more closely related to what happens in the larger cities than in the countryside.

Furthermore, as the territorial claims by non-whites in English cities increase, so does the envy for what the immigrants have succeeded in doing, especially in business and sport. The unemployed English factory worker, pressed by his creditors, his children, his divorced wife or unmarried partner, looks with envy at the Pakistani shopkeeper who, through the energy of a united family, thrift and hard work, continues to perform dramatically better than his white counterpart who, obviously, blames his 'coloured' neighbour for being there, in a country which is not his, and whose language he can barely speak.

This wonderful white specimen of manhood forgets that it was his own country that invited the non-whites to come and work here, whether on the buses, or as cleaners, or in any other shape or form, carrying out duties which we didn't want to perform. He forgets that we have more than 1.8m single mothers and 2.7m children who don't know what a family really is, whereas the immigrants rely on the family unit for their success. He sees only a difference in colour, even where the language and the accent might be the same.

In the case of colour, the English have a tendency to split along what one could term social lines. The upper middle class trendies believe that the mixture of cultures and colours is a good thing for the country; not for them Enoch Powell's view. Accordingly, they feel that the arrival of what are, for the English, exotic foods, whether fruit, vegetable or fish, and perhaps even some type of music, and living in the open air, trying to echo their experiences in France, Greece, Italy, Spain or the Caribbean, adds a touch (forgive the pun) of colour to their lives.

However, as the numerous riots in the city centres have proved, this is not the view of those who live in close proximity to non-whites, who would be only too pleased if there were greater segregation, claiming that would result in less violence. The pious announcements by politicians and successive government ministers are hardly reassuring.

One often hears remarks to the effect that a number of blacks have proved quite successful in their friendships with whites. Of course, if you have been to Eton or Oxbridge and you have mixed with the Maharajah of this, the Sultan of that, or the Prince of something else, it is quite understandable that, both in terms of comradeship and culture, you would find yourself at ease with such a non-white fellow student. But it is not at these levels that the more troublesome aspects of racism are manifested. It is not at Eton or at Oxbridge that there will be what has so vulgarly become known as Paki-bashing. There are no racial riots in the city centres of Oxford and Cambridge or in the township of Eton.

Indeed, it is in my view almost fraudulent to cite examples of successful relationships between whites and non-whites, fostered in a cultural climate that is as far removed from that of Bradford as French or Italian cuisine is from that of the Eskimos.

We have had a spate of legislation to try to reduce, if not eliminate, racial tension, the latest being the Race Relations (Amendment) Act 2002 that is probably the most significant piece of legislation in the field for 25 years. The law now imposes an active duty on public bodies to promote equality and not to act in a discriminatory way. A cynic would observe in passing that Lord Scarman led the enquiry into the Brixton riots in 1982: 20 years have passed before his findings could be taken on board.

However, I should not fail to mention a major drawback of our anti-racist attitudes and legislation generally: that is to say, the fear they frequently engender of being considered racist even when one clearly is not. As a result, blacks must be treated with kid gloves; any criticism or judgement of their conduct and attitudes must be tempered by softness and understanding of the kind that would seldom be extended, in similar circumstances, to a non-black person.

The result of such an approach is that very often criminal conduct goes unpunished when there is even the slightest doubt about the evidence of impropriety or illegality that would be needed for a conviction.

Regrettably, persons in command and prosecuting authorities both fall into this trap, adopting a stance which clearly aggravates relations between blacks and whites, causing resentment in the white section of our population.

Furthermore, it is interesting that most commentators on racial matters do not appear to have given sufficient prominence to an aspect which I have always thought fundamental: that is to say, to observe how some black men and women behave towards their English (white) counterparts.

Look at their eyes: when they are not full of resentment, they show reflections of irritation, where they are not condescending. The black man in particular, conscious of his alleged sexual prowess, does not look too kindly upon his English companions; deep down in his soul is the knowledge that, in many respects, he is a better man and that sooner or later he will prove it.

Time is on his side because he is patient: it is this extreme patience which distinguishes many non-whites as well as those from the southern Mediterranean and, above all, the Arab people, which is not readily visible to, nor, above all, understood by the white man, especially by the average Englishman. But it is there all the time, lurking in the background, and it is becoming more and more evidenced as black athletes continue to assert their abilities and, as in the USA, to prove themselves as good as, if not better than, their white counterparts in many fields. The number of black soccer stars is increasing all the time; indeed, I noticed that in one or two cases more than half the team is black[75].

Equally increasing is the number of blacks on rugby pitches.

Of course, we applaud loudly their victories and, when they earn gold medals, we show them draped in the Union Jack and play the National Anthem. We admire their artistry and

---

[75] *An aside: on the occasion of the European Cup Final that was played in Lisbon on May 24th 2014 between Real Madrid and Atletico Madrid, it was rather strange not to see a single black player on the pitch...*

their abilities whether on the track, or on the pitch; but how many of us would relish the thought of having them as next-door neighbours?

Casting my eye back to the 1950s I do not recall a single black player in any of the football teams I followed, but there were some around; even so, it took over two decades for a black footballer to play for England, as Viv Anderton did at Wembley on 29 November 1978 in the game against Czechoslovakia. The position is obviously quite different in 2014 where, despite the protests that flare up occasionally on the terraces, black players are taken for granted in most football teams. Indeed, one is tempted to wonder how many teams would function without them...

Nor should it be forgotten that racism does not only cut one way. It is not only the white man who might consider himself superior to the non-white or, more specific, to the black. The blacks themselves, particularly in England, very often consider themselves superior to the locals and display a contemptuous attitude towards them.

We are not thinking clearly, I believe, when it comes to racial problems.

This lack of clarity, our inability to reduce if not eliminate what I have described, I hope correctly, as our instinctive racism, was nowhere more evident than in the nation's attitude to apartheid.

The first peaceful protests against the separation of whites from blacks in South Africa started in London in the '50s and the protest movement gained strength, as it did elsewhere in the world, from year to year; but there was no way that our successive governments could, especially in the '70s and '80s when the anti-apartheid voices became louder, be prevailed upon to impose sanctions upon South Africa. In the conflict between white and black in South Africa, British governments sided almost inevitably with the whites.

The terminological distinction which arose at the time is significant; members of the ANC and especially Nelson Mandela were defined as terrorists, not freedom fighters as they themselves claimed. Our short-sightedness was extreme.

I should not be taken as decrying the bona fide efforts made by all concerned with racial problems: there is goodwill nowadays, surely, on the part of the authorities and efforts are made to integrate. Often contradictory, though, as witness the assumption, occasionally repeated even by governments, that immigrant communities are entitled to retain their religion and cultures but are obliged to integrate much more profoundly into the British way of life. Eminently sensible as a matter of principle, this view is in effect somewhat naïve, since the retention of one's religion and culture inevitably militates against fusion. It is all the more difficult to maintain as a concept at a time when different ethnic or religious groups seek independence from the stronger elements of any country. After all, we have delegated powers to the Scottish Parliament and the Welsh are following along the same road; the Basque Separatists wish to emancipate themselves from Madrid and the number of situations throughout the world, where ethnic/religious considerations are giving rise to internal social and political problems, is anything but negligible.

There is no point in trying to explain to the white rioters who, in the summer of 2001, caused havoc and civil disobedience, as well as unrest, in the northern towns of Bradford, Burnley and Oldham, that the local communities, assuming that to be a fact, were trying very hard to integrate with their British counterparts. Those white rioters were not animated by a desire to achieve integration; repatriation, yes: integration, no. And when all is said and done, that is what racism is all about. A circumstance that often escapes commentators is that the Englishman's racist attitude is not necessarily the fruit of any unkindness or nastiness; but it is a fact that the actor Warren Mitchell's character of Alf Garnett in the television series 'Till Death us do Part' struck an easily recognisable note when he used to call blacks 'coons'.

It is rather trite for our Governments quite often to suggest that Muslim immigrants should learn to speak English. Apart from the fact that it has always been a requirement that those who wish to acquire British nationality should be able to speak English, these modern stipulations are reasonably absurd. If one goes and speaks to the young Muslims who rioted in the northern cities, one will find that they know English very well. In all likelihood, the majority will have been born here and many of them may even be well qualified academically. Their problem is not that they do not speak English, but that their access to jobs and, where they have a job, their promotion prospects, are very limited indeed. It is that which makes them angry and not any failure to understand the English language. Otherwise, what would be the point of Sir Ben Kingsley CBE, who managed to get an Oscar for his interpretation of Gandhi, considering it advisable to change his name from Krishna Pandit Bhanji?

We found it reasonably easy to integrate and assimilate white immigrants, especially when they changed their name; but we are not having the same result with the blacks and the 'coloureds', despite all the tolerance and goodwill shown by both the whites and the non-whites.

It is odd. Throughout its history England has been incredibly successful at absorbing immigrant populations, in ensuring that they would become anglicised, that they would be ultimately 'one of us'. It is probably too easy to say that this has occurred because of the damp English weather, which has a softening and sobering effect in all areas of life; although the weather is a contributory factor, I find it difficult to believe that it is solely for this reason, for example, that we can no longer distinguish the Huguenots, the second or third generation Eastern European Jews, or Italians, from the natives.

One of the ways in which this has been achieved has been by stipulating that individuals should not only conform to English manners, thought and attire, if not to Shakespeare's language, but also — and this is a subtle and almost inexorable prescription — that they should anglicise their names or, at least, they should change their Christian name to an English one. There are innumerable examples of this requirement but a few classic Italian ones are the famous director of the British Museum Antonio Genesio Maria Panizzi, who becomes Sir Anthony Panizzi; the explorer Giovanni Caboto, who is turned into John Cabot; the conductor Giovanni Battista Barbirolli, who became Sir John Barbirolli; and the caterer Carlo Forte, who graduated from being Sir Charles Forte to Lord Forte (an exception, however, seems to have been established for some musicians since both Paolo Tosti and Antonio Pappano were knighted without having to change their Christian names. Progress...?).

It may be that it is because England has provided not only a free environment but also a politically stable one, coupled with much tolerance and respectability. It is not for nothing that the English have always been good at public ceremonies, providing impeccably executed parades, displaying sensibly and elegantly the pomp of an efficient and dutiful monarchy and orchestrating suitable displays of national history and patriotism, strengthened by the playing of the National Anthem. It is also difficult to determine whether this great ability on the part of the English might, to some extent, be connected with their own background. One wonders, in fact, how many English people carry Roman blood, nor should this be at all surprising given the inevitable inter-marriages.

Furthermore, it is hardly a coincidence that a psychological Roman heritage exists, in light of the fact that Britain was able to prove that it did by establishing a fairly close equivalent of the Roman Empire. One is, of course, reluctant to call the British Empire an atavistic regression to the time of Britain's emancipation from primitive life; but the pride of Macaulay in his ancestors may have had justifications that went beyond the purely historical, and might have been of a more physical/psychological nature. Whatever the explanation, England was, until the 1950/60s, a country where non-English people were proud to blend in with the local population and, even to some extent, ape local customs, often disowning their origins especially once they had changed their names. I repeat, England achieved such integration brilliantly and successfully, despite its inherent xenophobia.

But it has not been easy.

The current mood, quite properly, for once, imbued by political correctness, dictates that we should all discount entirely such differences. We can do so before God and before the law; most of us find it difficult in practice to do so with conviction, because we are − though we should certainly not be − racist. It is unfortunate that for much of the time we are not even aware of the fact.

Feminism[76]

'I want to say right here that those well-meaning friends on the outside who say that we have suffered these horrors of prison, of hunger Strikes and forcible feeding, because we desired to martyrise ourselves for the cause, are absolutely and entirely mistaken. We never went to prison in order to be martyrs. We went there in order that we might obtain the rights of citizenship. We were willing to break laws that we might force men to give us the right to make laws.' Emmeline Pankhurst

---

[76] *For a critique of feminism, v. R Goodall, The English and Sex – The Shadow of Hypocrisy, Amazon 2013*

Fine words; and undoubtedly true, as far as she was concerned. The struggle was a hard one. The parity that Mary Wortley Montague and Mary Wollstonecraft strove for had to be acquired after bitter fighting during which woman certainly showed her mettle.

But how to the point, though far removed, are Emmeline Pankhurst's words from the nonsense that is spewed out daily by modern feminists, which has continued practically uninterrupted for some fifty years on both sides of the Atlantic, despite the occasional 'recanting' by some of the major feminists of the '60s and '70s?

It might be appropriate at this stage to remind the reader of how pithily Bertrand Russell put it in his 'Marriage and Morals'[77]: 'The rights of women did not of course depend upon any belief that women were morally or in any other way superior to men; they depended solely on their rights as human beings or rather upon the general argument in favour of democracy. But as always happens when an oppressed class or nation is claiming its rights, advocates sought to strengthen the general argument by their contention that woman had peculiar merits and these merits were generally represented as belonging to the moral order.'

There is a logical inconsistency here. No one can dispute the claims by women to equal treatment with men in

---

[77] *Unwin Paperbacks, London 1976, page 59*

society and in the marketplace. Observers of society are already looking back with astonishment to women's battles for the vote, equal pay, better career prospects, maternity leave etc. and wonder how primitive and selfish we were in the bad old days when women's rights to equal treatment were not recognised. It is perfectly proper and useful that woman should be allowed and entitled to do the same jobs as men, since there seems to be no sphere of remunerated work where women should not be permitted to prove that they can perform as well as men, as many now do; if not better.

The difficulty, however, is that no matter how vigorously women's rights to equality are pursued, both by the individual and by the State, it is not easy to overcome the basic physical and psychological differences between men and women that have evolved over thousands of years. No matter how much feminists and the Advertising Standards Authority may complain, woman is physically, biologically and emotionally different from man and that is the natural order of things. On the one hand, we have attempts to defeminise woman by allowing her a suitable place in business or on the career ladder; and on the other hand, we have sexist descriptions of her. The Advertising Standards Authority on the 28 February 1990 published a report where it considered the views of the public on the way in which women are treated in advertising.

In 1963 Betty Friedan had published 'The Feminine Mystique', a book which sparked off a long debate on whether advertisers were doing women an injustice when they created models that women aspired to attain, whether it be in clothing or body shapes or smells or otherwise, which were in fact over-flattering to woman simply because they showed her principally as a sex object. It is not quite clear what the net result of the campaign and the findings of the ASA are. From nude women to Pirelli-type calendars, the choice is great but it is difficult to draw firm conclusions as to the effect on the relationship between the sexes of depicting women as objects of lust, since this is really a matter of taste and representation.

Unfortunately, England is not doing too well in coping with feminism, mainly because there is a very marked tendency to treat it as a relevant part of the politically correct scene: that is not helpful, especially since there continues to be great confusion about what is or ought to be the role of woman. English society has, until recently, functioned as perhaps the most efficient and compassionate in the world simply because every citizen, male or female, knew that there was a role to be fulfilled, knew his place; and yet, the English have really tried to take feminism to heart, although they have not even begun to realise some of the damaging consequences of the strict application of feminist principles, especially in social, political and practical terms.

As an example, our insistence on quotas in politics, teaching, public company management and so on, is not always conducive to the selection of the best people for the job. It creates an echelon of privileged human beings chosen not because of their abilities but because of their sex. In fact, I cannot help observing how absurd the situation is. We have eliminated the hereditary principle of selection for the House of Lords but are retaining, indeed fostering, the establishment of preferential choices based on what is alleged to be a different type of 'nobility'.

The mere fact that it is almost impossible to find a definition of feminism that is acceptable to all women is symptomatic. Even in their relationship with the legal system women find it difficult to decide whether the theory of equality should be preferred to that of difference, or whether the theory of male dominance should be replaced by one that relies on a more complex vision of gender and gender discrimination in what is known as a system of 'contextualisation'.

If I appear to be treating feminism as a relevant part of the political correctness picture, it is because I truly believe that the two are inseparable in the sense that feminism is a facet of politically correct attitude, and may be viewed in fact as one of its precipitating events.

One of the problems political correctness engenders is that a strict adherence to egalitarianism is counterproductive. At the moment in England every person wishes to be what he/she is not: we have an army without private soldiers, since we all wish to be at least sergeant majors, if not generals.

The greatest strength of the English people has always been that the individual was prepared to make sacrifices for the sake of the whole. The soldiers may have been a bunch of sheep but a great general (take Wellington, for example) could make them do what they themselves did not even believe could be achieved; Nelson obtained the same result with his sailors. It is true that, as George Macaulay Trevelyan put it (and as I have already observed above), the English are a people who have always 'preferred committees to dictators', but even in committees, they have always been prepared to be guided by those whom they believed to be better than themselves.

It is hardly a coincidence that England is one of the few countries I know of where disc jockeys are so popular: people are prepared to be told what music they should listen to. Not for them even the passing thought that they might know more about music than the disc jockey who is so popular. 'Desert Island Discs' has been around for many more years than I should care to remember. The format of the programme is a typical representation of this particular trait of the English, if not the British people which, it must be repeated, has always been a source of great political and historical strength.

Those days are gone.

The English are no longer prepared to accept their own individual limitations: they are no longer happy in the role that they have either adopted or has been forced upon them. The ambition, mostly frustrated, of the English male to be a general rather than a private finds its counterpart in the feminists' creed. Modern woman is determined that she can maintain a certain universality for her role in society: she claims that her independence of mind, her determination, her confidence and her non-conformity are such that she can be at any time wife, mother, mistress, sister, friend and, above all, breadwinner. She certainly has no wish to be cast in any particular role. She can procreate, fornicate, appreciate, listen sympathetically and cater for all the passions, the failings and, at times, the deviations of her man; and earn a living.

That is unsettling, to say the least.

Often feminism is stated to be a way of life and a view of woman's role which ignores and purports to nullify the different conformation of men and women, and its consequent functions and manifestations, arguing that woman is superior to man and should, accordingly, be emancipated from her historical, personal and social subservience to his power, such emancipation being achieved primarily in the sexual sphere by a reliance on masturbatory or lesbian activity. Of course, this definition as well is incomplete, but it does at least highlight the feminist concern about the 'political' aspects of the relationship between men and women resulting from the concept of power. In this context Kate Millet[78] quite

---

[78] *'Sexual Politics', Virago Press, 1977*

correctly draws attention to the writings of at least three 'macho' types of men – D H Lawrence, Henry Miller and Norman Mailer – whose whole approach proceeds from the submission and subservience of woman, and an utter lack of respect for her.

These feminist views ignore completely the two basic instincts of survival and procreation, exemplified by food and sexual activity.

Nevertheless, the feminist movement has grown in strength with the passage of each year and we in England have been very happy to import it from the USA and wholeheartedly to endorse it. As I have observed, the English have really taken feminism to heart and, in the same way as we have become subservient to the USA in our foreign policy, so we in England have become slaves to feminist beliefs and behaviour. In fact, as matters stand at present, one could argue that, if there were a competition between us and the Americans on this particular point, we would probably be ahead.

How has this come about? How have the English passed (I was about to say progressed, but stopped in time...) from the Victorian approach to woman, to the present day?

As observed above, a judge with great experience of life, Lord Scarman, expressed the view in the early seventies that the contraceptive pill was proving more powerful than the atom bomb and would have an enormous impact on society. He was, of course, quite right, since by facilitating the passage of the control of reproduction from man to woman, the Pill altered the balance (or imbalance) of power by transferring it from man to woman. The early feminists were very conscious of the importance of man's political (if not physical) power.

The rather violent arguments proffered by Mary Wollstonecraft in 'A Vindication of the Rights of a Woman' (1792, published in 1794), repeated what had been put forward previously by Mary Astell and shared by Lady Mary Wortley Montagu, namely that woman should not be treated solely as a domestic animal or creature, subject to man's whims. According to feminist writers at the time, and Katharine Macaulay is included, the conventional 'domestic' view of woman was based on a sentimental premise that was not justified on the facts. The trouble with Wollstonecraft's particular attack on men was that her own personal life was not above reproach by the standards of the times[79], so that it was far too easy to criticise her on the basis that all she was doing was claiming for women greater sexual licence simply because she was not in agreement with the view that woman's primary destination as mother could, of itself, provide fulfilment for her within the framework of a legal marriage. This was, in a sense, an

---

[79] *She had her first daughter whilst unmarried, attempted suicide and, despite her friendly relations with Dr Johnson, she was not much liked by her fellow writers, mainly because of her extreme (for the time) feminist views. In fact, Horace Walpole called her 'a hyena in petticoats'. Overall she led an unhappy life and, ironically, she died aged 38 married and a week after the birth of her second daughter, because of septicaemia.*

unfair attack, but an easy one to mount because the sermon, no matter how good it may have been, came from the wrong pulpit.

We have seen the same set-up nowadays when those members of the public, whoever they may be, who clamour for the legalisation of drugs of one kind or the other, are themselves open to attack if they admit to being drug takers; similarly, those who argue for the decriminalisation of prostitution must, if they acknowledge that they themselves use the services of prostitutes, bear the brunt of a criticism which, hypocritical though it is, relies on a well-known self-serving principle. Put differently, like Caesar's wife, all campaigners should be above suspicion, suspicion in this context meaning either that one has to lie about one's personal sexual life, or one must not have any.

In the case of Wollstonecraft, she was a little unfortunate because another 'feminist', Hannah More, proved herself quite capable of providing a balanced and sensible response to feminist claims. And yet, Hannah More was no submissive creature, since she was most insistent that, regardless of her role within the family, it was fundamental that woman should be educated, mainly because the kind of practical education that Hannah More was advocating for woman would teach her that the struggle for parity with men was self-defeating.

But the arguments that, despite or perhaps because of her 'liberation' from slavery to man, woman has not benefited as much as was expected is quite correct.

That D H Lawrence, Henry Miller and Norman Mailer are not representative of the way in which many men look at women should, however, always be borne in mind; but modern feminists' dissatisfaction with the negative traits of woman, which parity of the sexes has endorsed, should perhaps be turned against the female sex. On the whole, men treat women according to the image that woman herself projects.

Obviously no feminist approves of D H Lawrence. His gamekeeper, Mellors, is, by modern feminist standards, a male chauvinist pig. He is interested only in sexual satisfaction (rather more than power, despite what feminist philosophy decrees nowadays), the very satisfaction that, to the disapproval of feminists, Lawrence argues, brings Constance (Connie) close to him.

One cannot help wondering whether the common language of the USA and Great Britain has been the cause of the British attitude to feminism being run on almost exactly the same lines as its American counterpart.

Here in England we seem constantly to be aping our 'fellow Americans', not always – some might even say, practically never – to good advantage.

I conclude with a personal observation on the state of British society at present, namely that the application of strict feminist principles has highly damaging social, political and practical consequences.

To describe feminism as a view of nature and of life which argues that men and women are exactly the same not only by reference to their equality before the law, which is obvious, but also in the physical sense is utterly absurd. But not many inhabitants of the British Isles wish to insist on such an observation.

The premise of feminist thought seems to be that women have had enough of being slaves to men: so far so good. The trouble is that one cannot separate the factual situation of the different physical and psychological conformations from the reality of social life, nor can one overcome them merely by claiming that not all of them are acceptable to woman.

Woman's ambition to be equal to man creates certain inelegances of behaviour such as drunkenness, smoking, drug taking, promiscuity and sexual carelessness, the consequences of which we can see in our daily lives. More important, indeed much more relevant in the writer's view, is the loss of modesty and gentility, the flaunting of one's physical attributes and general vulgarity, especially in speech. It has become quite common for women, some quite well known, to use inappropriate terms. If it were merely a matter of an outburst, or of manifesting one's irritation at something, they might perhaps be forgiven, although rude words never sound good in the mouths of women. The truth is, however, that quite often such vulgarity is calculated to draw attention to oneself or to one's work or perhaps to a film or a show. It would be too much to hope that such women, specimens of femininity, have read Machiavelli…: I doubt that very much. I am much more inclined to believe that such examples of ill-manner are constitutional.

A classic representation of such 'feminist' vulgarity occurs in an American writer's book published in 1987 [80] . Dworkin's work consists of nine chapters and 191 pages of text and was claimed to be a major contribution to feminist thought. Nevertheless, it is worth noting that the word 'fuck', either as a verb or as a noun, is used throughout the text 171 times… (humorously, I remark that she clearly emerges victorious in her contest with 'Lady Chatterley's Lover', for in that book the words 'fuck' or 'fucking' appear a mere 30 times). Dworkin does not mention the word 'love' once.

Feminist women have increased their aggressiveness and lost their femininity: they have become inelegant. This observation alone should suffice to justify a particularly critical description of current feminist thought, which has overcome all boundaries of common sense. I can't help feeling that women generally should dedicate more time to

---

[80] *Andrea Dworkin: Intercourse, Martin Secker & Warburg*

asking themselves, whether under the shower or elsewhere, why God, Mother Earth, Mother Nature etc. created woman in a particular physical fashion…

One tends to forget that, in some form or other, feminism as a type of behaviour and conviction by woman of her superiority to man has always existed. In his play 'Lysistrata' the Greek Aristophanes[81] gives a good example of what women are capable of doing when they refuse to copulate in order to get their men to stop fighting and making war.

But I suppose it could be said that it was only in the 18th Century that feminism acquired a more literary and philosophical form, whilst at the same time it had to find a mast to which the feminist flag could be nailed. That mast was the unsatisfactory nature of the English laws of property. Before that, we had a less aggressive feminist, Josephine Butler, who campaigned for well over a decade to repeal the 1846 Contagious Diseases Act with a view to protecting women from venereal diseases. But it was those men and women who argued for the liberalisation of the laws dealing with property which resulted in the Married Women Property Acts 1870, 1875 and 1882 who were truly the first feminists. But not of the modern kind. They certainly were not concerned about any kind of physical, psychological or moral superiority of woman over man, but merely with ensuring that men should not have the

---

[81] *c. 446 BC – c.386 BC, the author of* The Clouds, The Wasps, The Frogs, The Knights.

advantage over women when it came to property matters, so that the two sexes should be treated equally. The feminists of this period were highly respected women.

When Octavia Hill embarked on her social crusade to reform and improve the living conditions of London's poor, she certainly wasn't thinking of any superiority by woman over man, or of intercourse.

Equally, when Dr Mary Scharlieb carried out her profession with dignity and morality, it was probable that nothing was further from her mind than any kind of glorification of female masturbation, such as has occurred in recent times.

The suffragettes had to find another mast to which to nail the feminist flag. Whilst changing the form of prayer (pray to the Lord, for She will help you...), they claimed that they were entitled to the vote. And they were quite right; they got the vote in 1918 (at least for those women over the age of 30) in return for the assistance provided by them in Lloyd George's munitions factories.

Closer to our times, the women of the 20th Century found that their claims to power were justified when the contraceptive pill became available, which event altered the balance of authority between men and women. The feminist flag was nailed to the mast of sexual independence.

In 1967 the feminist flag was nailed to the mast of abortion and the Abortion Act was enacted, which gave woman the unfettered right to decide on the outcome of her sexual proclivities.

But the combination of the legislation passed in England since the '60s, including the Divorce Reform Act 1969, resulted in a different form of feminism being established as a philosophy. A more virulent form, more aggressive, where the principle was stated belligerently that woman was superior to man and man was so obviously inferior to woman that he didn't really count for much. In fact, it can be said that during this particular period of our history, women declared for the first time their hatred of men. Whereas before they were clamouring for their rights, now that they have the rights they clamour about the insignificance of their male counterparts. Their hubris appears to become more prominent with the passage of time.

It is a sad commentary on British society that it has allowed such a situation to occur. In my view, it will be very difficult indeed to remedy it and its consequences will get worse as we move on.

In fact, I am quite certain that exasperated feminism, with its unreasonable, intolerant and dogmatic approach is proving as big a social problem for Britain as colour.

I go further. I maintain, with conviction, that all the more aggressive feminists are influenced in their beliefs by their personal, never satisfactory, sexual and marital (if any) experiences.

Beliefs such as the superiority of women, their absolute right to abortion, the inborn brutality of men, the uselessness of the interdependence between the sexes, the irrelevance, if not positive danger, of the traditional heterosexual family unit, were first voiced in the USA and became established there in the 1960s and '70s.

Nowadays, however, variations on the same theme, often bordering on the satanic, have become home-grown here. Sown on fertile soil in the garden of England and fattened by massive doses of feminist, homosexual and politically correct dogma, they have spread rampantly like bindweed. The only remedies – apart from sprays of spiritual weedkiller – would be abundant doses of common sense and traditional English values, which, alas, are conspicuously lacking.

One cannot help concluding that the feminist beliefs and arguments of the '60s and '70s have developed into a philosophy of life which is as troubling as it is detrimental to the relationship between men and women, since modern feminists appear increasingly angry, unreasonable, dogmatic, intolerant and, worst of all – and I apologise for being repetitive – inelegant.

It never seems to occur to the great British public to enquire of feminists what values they are imparting to young English girls, who regularly end their Saturday nights either picked up drunk in the street by the police or found unwell in emergency departments or selling their bodies at a very early age in exchange for drugs or other 'perks'. Are these misguided creatures inspired by up-to-date feminist values? Or are they victims of a society that does not understand them? If feminism is to be, as claimed, a new way of life for young British girls, some of its present-day manifestations are, to say the least, unpleasant where they are not obscene.

The real trouble appears to be that gutless males are taking it all lying down, causing one to wonder whether these very marked, aggressive, exasperated feminist traits may not be justified given the spinelessness of the male of the species...

But perhaps I am going too far; perhaps this is only one of the many phases that nations go through and eventually the traditional good sense of the British people will find a balance that will ensure a return to more normal relations between the sexes, to the great benefit of the individuals involved and, above all, of society[82].

---

[82] *On this topic generally, v Richard Goodall, The English and Sex – The Shadow of Hypocrisy, Amazon, 2013*

PC

'The pearl of tolerance is most readily achieved by those who are not burdened with convictions.' – Alexander Chase

No, I shall not be writing about the personal computer, indispensable though it has become. I should like to say a few words about a concept that at least in England appears to have become almost as important as the personal computer, namely what is defined as political correctness (for the purposes of the following discussion, I am assuming, without conceding, that there can be a definition of political correctness…).

My first observation is that the term is imprecise, if not fraudulent, because the correctness that it advocates is said to be political, which would lead one to believe that it is merely inspired by the need to attract votes. Unfortunately, PC discounts completely other aspects or requirements of correct behaviour such as its effect on morality, religious beliefs, social trends, the economy, the emotions and the psyche of individuals generally[83].

So what is political correctness? A description often given is that it is the recognition of better treatment and greater importance to be given to minority causes. Obviously there would be nothing wrong in that because there is no doubt that the disabled, the elderly, the ethnic minorities,

---

[83] In 'The Paris Review' of 1995 the writer P D James described political correctness as 'a form of linguistic fascism'.

homosexuals, lesbians and women generally are all deserving of greater consideration than is provided for them in present times. The trouble is that the corollary appears to be that we should all be less judgemental, more tolerant of behaviour – whether sexual or otherwise – of which we may not ourselves approve and, above all, not too dogmatic in our views. A direct consequence of this approach is the tendency to do away with powerful beliefs, so that judgements become less clear cut and much more relative, especially because what is advocated is 'political'.

Such particular tendency is all the more noticeable, and serious, when it is applied to sexual orientation, because one of its direct consequences is that the individual, male or female, tends to lose sight of what are the cardinal rules of human nature and behaviour and thus becomes disoriented.

Indeed, once the indoctrination by political correctness has proceeded successfully, the individual applies the resultant rules like a zombie: the outcome is that those essential, bitterly fought for and long-standing typical features of traditional, liberal English society, namely tolerance, reasonableness and common sense, cease to have any meaning. If they were to be taken on board, then the dictates of PC could no longer be applied.

'Once the Oxford University Press claimed to be the custodian of the English language. Its 1995 American edition of the New Testament omitted 'darkness' (as a synonym for evil or ignorance) to avoid offending blacks; 'the right hand of God' to appease left-handers; and was reluctant to mention 'the Lord', an editor explaining that 'Lord God' does not cut it these days because we don't have lords.'[84]

Furthermore, political correctness leads to absurdity and interferes with freedom of expression, as well as with information.

The 2000 edition of the Oxford Dictionary of Thematic Quotations has a number of headings dealing with sexual matters (bisexuality, celibacy, homosexuality, lesbianism, love, marriage, masturbation, pornography, relationships, seduction) but not one for prostitution. The reader ought to know that both its managing editor and its editor at the time of publication were women. I have no doubt that the omission results from the application of politically correct principles; I appreciate that prostitution is a concept that feminists do not like but it is not going away and as a social 'theme' I should have thought it is certainly interesting, if nothing else.

And if anyone doubts the prejudice that emerges from editorship, one should consider the space dedicated by the said publication to 'woman's role' and 'women' and compare it to others.

---

84 From Peter Vansittart 'In Memory of England – a Novelist's View of History', John Murray, London 1998, p13

To describe, as some have done, political correctness as the representation of dogmatism and an excessive sensitivity to minority causes is not, in my view, sufficiently pejorative. Not because the disabled, the elderly, the ethnic minorities, homosexuals, lesbians and women in general are not deserving of consideration, but simply because the concept proceeds from the premise that we should not be too judgemental and we should all be much more tolerant of behaviour, whether sexual or otherwise, of which we may not ourselves approve. It is a fairly sad fact of modern British society that relativism and 'non-judgmentalism' are spreading at the same pace as the increasingly frequent episodes of mindless violence.

The trouble is that, in my view at least, it is much too easy to be very tolerant when one has no strong beliefs. Strongly held beliefs tend to engender a mild form of intolerance and I for one would prefer to believe that our civilisation was born in Greece and not in the Congo and that Socrates and Aspasia, to mention but two characters, were, as we had always assumed, white and not black. To be told, in the absence of evidence, that what we had believed for, say, 2000 years is wrong I define neither as politically correct nor as tolerant but merely as stupid. This stupidity, I am afraid, is permeating the whole of British life, with consequences that are quite serious, though both governments and the general public prefer not to acknowledge them.

When it comes to political correctness, we are becoming like ostriches, burying our heads under the sand.

It cannot be denied that PC, as it is now termed, has often been lacking in international relations. For example, the practice of using the nationality of peoples one dislikes as adjectival qualification for things, events or illnesses is well known. As early as 1530, when the Italian physicist Girolamo Fracastoro first described syphilis in the West, he didn't realise that it had come over from America and he called it the 'French disease' (understandably, because the plague that had started in Naples in 1495 was spreading throughout Europe on an epidemic basis and he may have believed that it came from there and, of course, that the French troops – invaders – garrisoned there were responsible). The name is derived from a poem he wrote about a shepherd called Syphilus, who was struck down by this particular illness: until then, syphilis was merely known as a serious disease and did not have an official name. The Italians, the Germans, the Poles and the English, who disliked the French intensely, likewise all called it the French disease, whereas the French, who weren't getting on at all well with the Neapolitans, called it the Neapolitan disease!

In turn the Neapolitans, who hated their conquerors at the time, the Spaniards, called it the Spanish disease, and the Portuguese, for analogous reasons of hatred, called it the Castilian disease. The Turks themselves could not resist the temptation of a tit for tat and called syphilis the Christian disease. The Spanish doctor who first came across it called it the 'serpent of Hispaniola', clearly relating it to the

Spaniards' adventures in America, thus shifting the blame on the inhabitants of the New World (he was right, of course).

Everybody calls flagellation the English disease, associating it with 'Perfidious Albion' and with a fairly common practice in our country. However, I believe that we owe the first use of the expression to the French who termed it 'Le Vice Anglais'.

The French use the expression 'filer à l'anglaise' that means to retreat in silence. That marks their contempt. The English (and the Germans, for that matter) use the same expression – retreating in silence – for the French...

Furthermore, the English in turn show their contempt for both the Spanish and the Italians by saying 'thank God for the Spanish otherwise the Italians would be the last people in Europe'.

The Italians were accused of treachery by the English, probably picking up on the principles enunciated by Machiavelli. The French did not escape because we had expressions like 'French flu' and, rather more oddly, 'French dog' to describe someone fancifully dressed.

The French, with the contempt that came about in the 19th Century for contraceptive measures in their country, called the condom the 'capote Anglaise' and on their part the English called it the 'French letter'.

The English hated the Dutch and so they gave us 'Dutch courage'; the relationship of the English to the Dutch is particularly interesting in linguistic terms. In England we first started using the word 'Dutch' to refer to the people of Germany, it being clearly derived from the German word 'Deutsch'. But when a strong antipathy developed between England and Holland in the 17th Century, since they were both fighting each other at sea, the adjective Dutch began to be used in a pejorative or derogatory sense. So we have a 'Dutch auction', namely a corrupt type of auction sale where people conspire to defraud the auctioneer and/or the vendor, 'Dutch foil', namely a very malleable alloy of copper and zinc used as a cheap imitation of gold leaf, 'Dutch gilding' and 'Dutch metal' with the same pejorative meaning as Dutch foil, 'Dutch oven' in slang as describing a person's mouth and 'Dutch wife', a cane or rattan support used in the Dutch Indies to rest their limbs upon whilst in bed[85].

Even the rather common expression 'going Dutch' or 'Dutch treat', which is meant to indicate that the expense of something is shared, has a derisive element about it, at least in its origin. It is uncertain how it came about, though

---

[85] *The above commentary is obviously not exhaustive. There are many other instances where the adjective Dutch accompanies nouns or expressions, which are, on the whole, derogatory. For example, 'Dutch widow' or 'Dutch wife' to identify a prostitute, 'Dutch cap' to describe a contraceptive device, 'Dutch-bottomed' to indicate something that is empty and perhaps, more objectionable, 'double-Dutch' to indicate something incomprehensible. Linguists will, no doubt, appreciate the uncertainty of the description 'Dutch uncle', which may mean either a person giving firm but benevolent advice or a non-family member who takes too severe and strict an interest in other people's behaviour...*

it is suggested that it is related to the type of door often found in farmhouses, which is in two halves so that the bottom can stay closed whilst the top half is opened. We certainly appear not to have liked the Dutch, although one hopes that such rivalry is long forgotten...

For the sake of truth, however, I should record that the term 'Dutch Elm Disease' we have used quite unfairly since the disease did not come from Holland. It had been around for some time when in 1967 a more virulent form of the Elm Bark Beetle came to us in a consignment of logs emanating from North America. We call it Dutch elm disease because it was first identified in the 1920s by a Dutch biologist called Christine Buisman[86].

In my opinion, it is clear that nowadays the development of political correctness is inspired less by a wish, if not a need, to avoid discrimination of any kind, but much more by a strong concern about attracting votes, hence its qualification as such. But it does not follow that what is politically acceptable is necessarily right, nor that it will have positive effects on society, any more than it would inevitably be profitable for the nation, or useful to the individual.

----

[86] *Admittedly somewhat out of context, I cannot help remarking on what has come to us from the most powerful, generous and significant nation in modern history. Apart from the cited Dutch elm disease and syphilis, America has given Europe squirrel pox imported from it in the 19th Century (resulting in the practical elimination of the red squirrel to the benefit of the grey), the potato blight that almost destroyed Ireland, divorce at will, exasperated feminism, the glorification of weapons of self-defence and of war, the cult of violence, the sanctification of the profit motive and last, but not least, tobacco... It is indeed very odd.*

Political correctness is aimed at conduct, language, situations and people. Women, homosexuals (males and females) and those whose skin is not white are particularly affected. I am discounting entirely the special considerations for the handicapped, assistance to whom cannot in any sense be termed political, but is merely the result of greater thoughtfulness towards fellow human beings less fortunate than oneself. The application of preferential treatment to particular classes of society only is, in itself, discriminatory. Where does one see in any statement of political correctness a claim to preferential treatment for, say, a married woman who stays at home to look after the children, or a heterosexual husband or father?

The counter to that may well be that civilised society needs a certain amount of active discrimination (though it is fraudulent to try to project positive images for what are essentially negative features). Whilst that itself is a bland political statement which remains to be proved, let us assume for present purposes that it is accurate. Nevertheless, the consequences of political correctness are nonsensical: for that reason alone, it needs to be criticised, also because of the effect it has had, and continues to have, on England and the English.

Before providing examples, however, I should like to reiterate that, as a matter of principle, if not linguistics, what is acceptable politically need not be convenient practically. Politically, we accept that Parliament is supreme and, as one constitutional lawyer, Sir William Ivor Jennings, if I recall correctly – or was it Dicey? – said many decades ago, if it decreed that all men should be women and vice versa, that would be the law of the land no matter how absurd. This might be correct in political terms, but it is clearly a nonsense; and in any event, the fact that it is a majority in Parliament that can make and undo anything it wishes is not too valuable a feature when there is not a strong opposition or the majority is too substantial. Events in Britain in the past twenty years have shown what a large majority in Parliament is capable of producing: Thatcherism and Blairism, for instance.

But the matter goes well beyond the constitutional sphere, as a few examples may show.

It is politically and practically correct that there should be no discrimination against women, who should be treated as equal in the workplace and as regards pay. We are certainly all equal before God and, in theory at least (but only in theory) before the law. Nobody would argue otherwise. Apart from this, however, equality does not exist, save probably in the case of identical twins. By all means, women should receive remuneration as men, given parity of job and performance; but what the principle ignores is that in a country like ours where there is still substantial unemployment, it might be preferable if women were tempted to stay at home to look after their children rather than go out to work, possibly making more men unemployed. It seems to me that one of the primary disadvantages of providing equality of opportunity and pay for woman is exactly that, namely distracting her from other functions and possibly duties to which she is better suited than her male counterpart. I accept, of course, that not everybody views matters in the same light: the point I am making is simply that what is politically correct for one person might be considered either improper or nonsensical by another.

Political correctness dictates that we should not discriminate against any form of sexual leaning, or orientation; I shall not say deviation. Perfectly proper too, given that we are all equal before God and before the law, but one of the consequences of this tolerance is that younger people find it more difficult to direct their sexual development into channels which are more suited to their personality. Hence the increasing numbers of homosexuals, both male and female, and the resultant sexual instability in our society, which, depending on points of view, may or may not be beneficial for either individual or State.

By parity of reasoning, one must not discriminate against an individual on the ground of colour. That too is obvious. On the other hand, by forcing the adoption of a particular stance or the use of particular words (for example, black instead of coloured), whether in society or in the workplace, one is dealing only with appearance and not with substance.

It seems to me that what political correctness achieves is a raising in the tone of voice of those people for whose benefit it was established, whose vocal manifestations have a tendency to become hyperbolic. They themselves, in clamouring for support for their beliefs and attitudes, become less tolerant of other people's differing views, less inclined to listen to any criticism of their own approach, more determined to assert with offensive conviction their point of view and their philosophy of life, ignoring completely anything which contradicts it.

They have a tendency to avert their eyes and turn a deaf ear to the expression of ideas and beliefs that clash with their own assumptions, especially if contained in journalistic or book form. One gets the feeling that, if they could, they would gladly – Hitler-like – burn any written material that might be even mildly critical of what they are fighting for so aggressively.

Fortified by the State's decree that we should all behave in a particular fashion towards them, they become much more vociferous and belligerent, turning the situation on its head by maintaining that the political correctness that ought to prevail is not in their own favour but in favour of others. Put differently, their behaviour is the correct one and all others are wrong, but may be tolerated simply because of political correctness: the resultant intolerance is most un-English.

Thus one gets feminists telling us how much stronger, fitter, better, more intelligent and able women are than men (to some extent, of course, they are also nowadays telling the truth seeing how spineless modern man has become), lesbians advising us that 'King Phallus' is dead and 'Queen Clitoris' has succeeded him, male homosexuals decrying any kind of heterosexual activity and relationship and blacks and, to a lesser degree, other non-whites, openly showing their contempt, in many cases justified, for their white especially male counterparts. One would not want to go so far as the American humourist, Tom Lehrer, who is reported as having said in 1996 "in my youth there were words you could not say in front of a girl; now you can't say 'girl'[87]"; but we are reaching the stage where one has to be so cautious about what one says, or one does, and even how one looks at others, that the requirement of political correctness could be said to interfere with our freedoms to an increasingly damaging degree. The intolerance of other people's views and beliefs engendered by the application even mildly of concepts of political correctness is becoming, in my view, an unacceptable feature in British society.

Full credit to Tom Lehrer is due: there has recently been a case in England where a barman was dismissed from his employment because he addressed one of the female customers as 'pet'...

What political correctness, as reinterpreted in the 1990s, fails completely to acknowledge is not the inequalities in people but their different roles in society.

---

[87] *A prophetical statement... It was reported on May 27th 2014 that the BBC removed the word 'girl' used by one of its presenters in a documentary. What can I say?*

The tragedy is that what has become established as a rule for social behaviour and intercourse in Anglo-American countries is extending also to the Mediterranean where, given the more bellicose nature of the people, it manifests itself in an even more virulent form. But that is a separate issue.

A much more serious criticism of English political correctness is that it is truly 'insular'. By that I mean that it represents the crystallisation of certain intolerant views which are born within a particular kind of society. We thus have in England a political correctness which is clearly typical of a country which prided itself in its isolationism; indeed, it could not be otherwise. The fact, however, is that in applying the principles that this particular policy dictates, we inevitably discount the customs, the beliefs and the religion of other cultures.   Put differently, political correctness makes for conflict rather than peace, since we are not prepared to consider that there may be others who do not accept the way in which our society functions and whose traditions, if not religions, are different from ours and equally entitled to consideration and, where appropriate, protection.

This is a much more serious indictment of the overall concept of political correctness than any detailed aspect.

Such attitude carries with it an almost inevitable contempt for other cultures and ways of life. Gone are the days when the wives of English officials in India would go bathing fully dressed in order not to offend local sensibilities.

Shortly before the invasion of Iraq, Geri Halliwell, one of the Spice Girls, entertained the British troops in Kuwait. She was scantily-clad in a Union Jack bathing costume and was accompanied by other females equally attired, singing and dancing before an enthusiastic Army audience. Whilst one can never be certain, some would suggest that such a performance broadcast on television was highly detrimental to Anglo-Arab relations.

Not necessarily the result of political correctness, it must be admitted; but a related event, since it proceeded from the premise that any problem that might exist in Anglo-Arab relations was certainly the fault of the Arabs and not ours. One has no wish to embark upon a political debate: recording such an event is factual only.

In any case, the performance itself was wrong from whichever point of view one is approaching it, especially since it ended with the performer turning her back to the audience and displaying her backside in a stunted English imitation of a can-can pose. This particular gesture showed a total lack of consideration for the host country and an incredible failure to acknowledge the Arab mentality. Apart from any other thought, it was an offence to Arab dignity because they, the Arabs, do not view women in the same way as we do and they do not allow their women to be seen half-naked. We should have known better because, when we ruled India, we were very alert to differing local beliefs and ensured that English women were not allowed to swim in a bathing costume in order not to offend local sensibilities, as already observed above.

Furthermore, such behaviour displayed a complete failure to acknowledge that we strengthened the Arab's belief that Westerners are not fit to lord it over them. Any Arab who saw that particular transmission would have felt infinitely superior to the English, their troops, their women and their Prime Minister and that certainly does not make for peaceful relations.

Logically, one should not forget that if the display was planned before the occurrences in New York of September 11th 2001, it was in bad taste and it should have been cancelled. If it was planned after such occurrences it was a gross misjudgement, for it appeared as a callous disregard of the Arab people's feelings. In no way was it saved by the decision on the part of the Americans not to bomb anywhere on Friday October 11th 2011, the reason alleged being that on Friday the Muslims are at prayer. A bad performance whichever way one looks at it.

Political correctness has affected, some might say infected, the English language. One often reads statements like this: 'every child was responsible for their own room', or consider the following extract from one of the 'bulletins' that a well-known firm of London solicitors makes available to its private clients:

> 'Broadly speaking an individual is UK resident if <u>they</u> reside in the UK for 183 days in any one tax year.....'.
> 'Everyone is born with a domicile of origin which is generally that of the country where <u>they</u> are born and <u>their</u> father resides.'

Or even a programme on Radio 4 (17 February 2002) 'when you get a judge who becomes too fond of their own importance'.

I often wonder what replies one would get from students sitting for an English exam if one set them the following task:

> 'From an interview with a headmaster on 12 February 2002: 'The learner achieves what they are trying to achieve'. Consider and discuss (limit 250 words).'

Thanks to feminism, or political correctness (does it matter which?), the practice of using the plural after a singular in order to avoid identifying the sex of the person involved is now so common that one may be inclined to believe that the rules of English grammar have changed. Of course, in the old days one would, in similar contexts, have used the personal pronoun 'he' or the relative possessive, but this is not good enough for modern feminists. The difficulty posed by using the masculine was identified last century by the legislator because in one of the Interpretation Acts (I forget which year, but the date is immaterial) it was clearly stated that whenever the masculine personal pronoun 'he' appeared, it was deemed to include 'she'. It was a standard joke amongst pupils in chambers, or even more mature barristers, to play around with the concept that "he' is to be taken as embracing 'she"'. (Is such a statement politically correct? Probably not...)

Nowadays, the combination of the personal pronoun and the plural verb appears to have solved the problem. It may have done so from the political correctness standpoint but there is no doubt that it is grammatically offensive to find a verb that is in the singular followed by a pronoun that is in the plural or vice versa. But even well-educated persons now indulge in this solecism, which is insidious and an offence to Shakespeare's language.

Furthermore, we can no longer say 'he is one of the chaps', the noun having been replaced by 'guy(s)', an Americanism that is meant to have no gender, and which is gaining currency even here in England (a short trawl through the internet will provide very many examples, some most amusing, of the nonsensical application of PC ideas).

To replace 'mankind' with 'human kind' or 'chairman' with 'chairperson' or, even worse, 'chair' I find abhorrent; also because it runs contrary to a long-established practice according to which everyone knew that whenever the masculine was used in any context it would, if the context so permitted, include the feminine as a matter of course. To insist upon an identification of gender neutral descriptions is to ignore what happens in nature and is totally inappropriate (indeed, unnecessary) in the case of Latin languages, for example. Well apart from the gender of the nouns often identified by the endings, the definite articles in French and Italian, to choose these two, are of themselves sufficient to provide a correct identification of the object or subject. To pray in aid the fact that in Greek we have also a neuter gender seems to me somewhat short-sighted because the Greek neuter gender refers to inanimate objects...

In any event, one must be rather weary of playing about with language because, as Sir Francis Bacon wrote, it is not we who control the language but it is the language that controls us, and this was no bland statement. George Orwell's Newspeak should not be converted into Feministspeak.

It is not what the language expresses but what it is understood to convey. Does it really matter whether a noun is masculine or feminine? Certainly not as far as Latin is concerned where the male sexual organ ('mentula') is feminine and the female ('cunnus') is masculine...

Another consequence of the 'non-judgmentalism' which has become so popular in modern Britain, has been the psychological manipulation or, if that sounds somewhat extreme, the change that has come about in our English language, which is often claimed to be a coincidence; but I'm not too sure about that.

We have made a few changes to the vocabulary and have adopted a tendency to prefer words which relate to conduct or activities which may be deemed unpleasant, to make them gentler, more suave. For instance, good old-fashioned descriptions are no longer popular: we seem to have been brainwashed into applying wrong definitions or using words that are superficially more pleasant.

A few examples might illustrate my point. Those who have come to the end of their lives because they have drunk too much are now said to have died because of alcohol poisoning: no longer because of alcohol abuse. It is as though by changing words we have relieved the person from responsibility for past conduct. The prostitute is more often termed a call girl, the dustbin man a refuse collector, a flat has graduated to an apartment (although I appreciate, of course, that the linguistic choice may have been influenced quite substantially by American usage...).

STDs – sexually transmitted diseases – are now called STIs – sexually transmitted infections – as though we wished to relieve the person affected of blame. Maybe it is less blameworthy to contract an infection than a disease.

Not too many years ago, the Marriage Guidance Council, which had been established for quite some time (in fact, it was founded in 1938 as the National Marriage Guidance Council; the name was changed 50 years later), altered its name to 'Relate', clearly showing, in my view, that relationships are more important than marriage...

Even the common and unfortunately too frequent use of the term 'paedophile' (linguistically correct and sounding more elegant) instead of child molester or child abuser appears to hide the true significance of the conduct of which complaint is being made. The prefix or suffix -phil(e) derives from the Greek to like or to be fond of. It usually denotes (except possibly for philander/er) a favourable, dignified activity (philately, philosophy, philanthropy, philharmonic). I suggest it is not only confusing but wrong to use it as a noun that describes the abuse of children.

Similarly, a number of nouns and adjectives used until 20 years ago to describe homosexual activity are now almost universally converted into 'gay', which gives a tone of cheerfulness to a particular type of conduct.

I believe the psychological manipulation is there and causes one to wonder whether it is right to describe idiomatic changes as an evolution of the language rather than artificially produced terminological pollution.

Of course, it will be countered that political correctness cuts both ways; but the requirement of political correctness that men should be treated in exactly the same manner as women does cause unusual results. On 12 January 2000 a Sheffield publican was ordered to pay £566 compensation to a prospective barman (£500 for injury to feelings and £66 for loss of earnings). The Employment Tribunal heard that the publican cut short a job interview when the barman refused point blank to chop his ponytail (reaching much further down than his shoulders) on the ground that he felt personally violated and, why should he, when there were females behind the bar with long hair.

The publican's argument that he ran a traditional establishment where a man with long hair would not fit, was brushed aside.

Not too long ago the fact was advertised that the abbreviations 'BC' (before Christ) and 'AD' (Annus Domini) are gradually being replaced in school text books, and elsewhere, by 'before the common era' (BCE) and 'after the common era' (ACE). The justification given for this is that one should not offend the sensitivity of religious minorities or atheists.

What does 'common era' mean? Common how, to whom? A wit might say that it offends the sensitivity of all Christians in the British Isles that 2000 years of history should be wiped out simply because Christ is no longer such an important figure, assuming he ever existed. What is the real meaning of a 'common era'? Pandering to minorities turns democracies into unofficial dictatorships. To protect, as one should, minority interests is laudable only if those interests do not override the legitimate, established expectations of the majority.

Not too long ago (1994) there was published a book by Philip K Howard by the title 'The Death of Common Sense:

how law is suffocating America'[88]. The author complains amongst other things about the excesses of government agents who have to measure the number of inches surrounding a railing. I don't know America well enough to say whether he is right or wrong; but I believe I know England sufficiently well to state that whilst here common sense is not yet dead, it is certainly moribund. That is indeed a pity, for the greatest virtue that the British people, if not the English, have always displayed and used to advantage especially in creating an Empire, was, in fact, common sense without which, it was said centuries ago, 'a man is foolish or insane'. The Shorter Oxford Dictionary defines common sense as 'good sound practical sense; general sagacity' as well as 'ordinary, normal, or average understanding'.

Leaving dictionary definitions aside, it is quite clear that common sense can only be what is common to a particular race. What may make sense to a citizen of the Gold Coast is not the same as what would have meaning for a Frenchman and what is common sense to the man on the Clapham Omnibus need not necessarily be acceptable to an Aboriginal from Australia. Indeed, one can go further and say that sense common is not the same as good. Many things are common which are not good: for example, smoking, divorce, promiscuity, drunkenness, etc. In many languages there is no equivalent to our English expression 'common sense' where it is normally replaced by either good sense or a healthy approach to life.

---

88 Random House, 1994

There are, in fact, some languages where the expression is simply not to be found and no conclusion whatsoever can be drawn from such linguistic variations. For example, in Italy we say 'buon senso' underlining the fact that this is good for society, although it need not necessarily be common to society. France is similar to Italy but Spain and Portugal use 'common' rather than good sense. It is interesting to note that both the French and the Italians prefer the expression 'good sense' to 'common sense'. I assume that this is because they rely on their citizens' individuality so that they maintain that their 'sense' is good, but it is their own 'sense' and they don't care about anybody else's: to that extent, it does not even have to be common! Still, there are disadvantages in such an approach that are somewhat outside the scope of this review.

Whichever way one looks at it, there is no doubt that throughout the world good sense and common sense are terms that are defined by acting in accordance with nature. Regrettably, this is something that is clearly not happening in our country.

We no longer have common sense in England: the reason is that we are obsessed by political correctness. Political correctness in turn is the creature of exasperated feminism and racial hypersensitivity, both hyperbolic manifestations that have come to England from the USA. Indeed, it is my view that the ever-increasing Americanisation of European culture generally is the principal reason why we have a tendency in this country to do some pretty silly, if not awful, things.

Consider, for example, how political correctness has brought about a 'compensation culture'.

Until 1976 there were in the UK no particular rules protecting employees in their contracts of employment and reliance for any form of indemnity or damages had to be placed upon contract law or the general common law. Given that until then it was not even necessary that a contract of employment should be recorded in writing, one can see how employers had the upper hand.

It was, of course, perfectly proper that, as happens in other countries in the world (though not in the USA, as I understand the position) greater protection should be given to employees generally. But practically at the same time as this occurred, a new development became noticeable which was to turn itself in to what can only be considered an illness of our society, namely the greedy need to seek compensation at all costs in any set of circumstances, even where, if one adopted a common (good?) sense approach, no fault could be attributed.

Way back in January 2000 a council warden received over £200,000 in compensation from its local authority for stress; a similar sum was awarded by a different local authority to a council official again for stress.

The sum paid out by NHS Trusts in compensation for clinical negligence runs to millions of pounds. Whatever happens, somebody must pay, someone must be made a defendant, very often the police authorities.

If it were merely a matter of establishing a principle of general responsibility of public bodies, then the sums involved could not possibly be so great. It is outrageous that public resources that could more profitably be employed in cardiac surgery, kidney transplants, hip operations and so on, should be diverted for the private gain of the individual.

If it were merely a matter of money, however, one might be forgiven for arguing that there is no reason why the private individual should not gain at the expense of the State, which is a very common present-day philosophy applicable to situations which are far too numerous to mention. But the social and psychological imbalances that this desperate need to litigate in order to make money gives rise to are very often ignored.

In the first place, most public sector organisations now spend more time adopting practices to defend themselves against the citizen than in increasing their efficiency. Doctors and lawyers are just as concerned about the risk of being sued by their patients and clients as they are by health and propriety considerations. Suspicion breeds both suspicion and conflict. Even if we discount – and as a lawyer, I am only too well aware of it – the worry that any kind of litigation imposes upon human relations, the fact that as soon as an incident occurs, in order to get some kind of compensation, the individual rushes to see his solicitors (or, which is even worse, solicitors rush to see him), we have established a set-up that, whilst of benefit to the legal profession, is highly detrimental to the individual's ability firstly, to take responsibility for his own actions, and, secondly, to try to sort out his own problems. Just as we are becoming more and more dependent on the State, so we appear to be reaching the stage where anything negative that occurs in the individual's life is somebody else's fault: misfortune has ceased to exist and is replaced by someone else's liability to cough up.

That may well be unfair, apart from increasing insurance premiums.

But then, fairness no longer guides the Englishman's approach to today's life: political correctness has taken over, matched only by extreme sentimentalism, the narcissism of 'confessionalism', the seeking of attention and publicity and the lack of any kind of shame in respect of wickedness.

And now that we are all Europeans, political correctness also governs our patriotic outlook. Why should anyone be proud of being British?

Not too long ago a TV programme was broadcast which purported to ascertain what it meant to be English; no conclusion could be reached. In any event, we came out of it rather badly, especially since what seems to be prevalent in England today is a mood of self-vilification. As a result, it is hardly surprising that fairly nonsensical applications of so-called political correctness give rise to situations or suggestions that are not merely patently absurd, but that almost nullify the centuries of fairly glorious history.

What about the suggestion (fortunately, not yet adopted) that there should be no more 'Rule Britannia' at the last night of the Proms? Can one be surprised then if Britannia stairlifts advertises with the slogan 'Rule Britannia! Britannia rules the stairs!'?

Coupled with the invitation by the same firm 'buy a quality Britannia stairlift and support British jobs', this is a small example of a denial of the dignity of patriotism, and an appeal to a sense of solidarity which is almost meaningless if it is divorced from belief in one's country, no more God etc.

Another result of our adoption of politically correct stances is that we seem to have lost any sense of reasonableness. Like sound bites on television, our society clamours for what is extreme whether in terms of violence, indecency or misbehaviour. The more extravagant and aberrant a conduct, whether sexual or otherwise, the more it is publicised.

One final aspect of the nonsense established by the strict application of politically correct canons is what is happening to the Christian religion in this country.

It may well be true, as atheists, secularists and others of different opinion or belief have been maintaining for some years with increasingly raucous voices, that England is no longer a Christian country. From this follows the prescription that it is politically correct not to attach any special significance to Christianity, of which there should be no public evidence, no too obvious crosses as necklaces (unless, of course, the European Court of Justice wishes to extend the scope of its judgement in the BA employee case), none on crematorium buildings and no more traditional prayers at council meetings. Put differently, we should not 'upset' those who do not believe in the Resurrection.

Consequently, what is the point of having a YWCA (Young Women's Christian Association) when its members may not necessarily be Christians? Let us by all means change the name of that organisation to 'Platform 51', as was done in 2011. Furthermore, at practically the same time, the oath taken for years by Girl Guides had its wording changed by deleting any reference to God. This was an initial decision that had to be altered because of protests and complaints that were voiced and, as a result, the Association decided upon a compromise solution to the effect that those who did not wish to take the ordinary form of oath containing references to God did not have to take the oath at all. One wonders whether the fact that God is no longer mentioned detracts from any belief that in fact He (or perhaps 'he') does exist...

By the way, I was forgetting. The name change to Platform 51 has, apparently, been adopted only in England since other countries have refused to go along with it.

And who says that our God, if He exists, is male and should be identified as such? Certainly this was not the view of the Scottish Episcopal Church when in 2010 it deleted from its liturgy all references to Father, Son and Holy Ghost since they were obviously male characters; who can say whether in fact the Holy Trinity should not consist of a mother, a daughter and... what? A blithe spirit? Who knows?

Before I forget, allow me to wonder whether in fact it is politically correct to describe the Supreme Being by using the capital G. Referring to him with a possessive, should 'His' also not be written with a capital H...?[89]

I can't help wondering how long it will be before it is suggested that we should have a 'Mother Christmas'. Why are we concentrating so much on a male deliverer of gifts...? (Can't a woman be trusted to 'drive' a sleigh?) Maybe, to be politically correct, we could have both a Father and a Mother Christmas riding the sleigh together...?

---

[89] *The same considerations apply to the non-use of capital letters in written prayers or invocation to the Lord: Your, and You...*

Jocularly, I remark again that perhaps it will not be too long before we change the words of our national anthem since, as I see the position, there appears to be no point whatever in praying for the health of the monarch to God if He does not exist...

A final, jocular aside. In the centre of the City of London there are two addresses bearing the names of the two principal prayers in the Christian religion: namely, Paternoster (Our Father) Square (Row) and Ave Maria (Hail Mary) Lane. If we wish to be consistent in our suggested disregard of the manifestations of Christianity, should the City authorities not be asked to change the names of these two addresses...?

I have never been able to understand the origin of the present-day attacks on Christianity in this country, a tradition, if I may term it such, which goes back nearly 1,500 years.

Incidentally, I should like to observe that, in a curious sense, it could be said that the bringing of Christianity to England occurred quite by chance. Alban Butler was an English Roman Catholic priest who between 1756 and 1759 published his 'The Lives of the Fathers, Martyrs and Other Principal Saints'[90].

---

[90] *Edited by Michael Walsh, Burns and Oates, 1987*

He records that in the year 573 Pope Gregory the Great, a doctor of the Church who died in 604, happened to see in a market three golden-haired, fair complexioned boys for sale.

Having enquired about their nationality he got the reply that 'they are angles or angli' which he then countered by saying: 'they are well named, for they have angelic faces and it becomes such to be companions with the angels in heaven' (a quotation usually shortened to 'non angli sed angeli').

Whereupon he was so touched by the vision that he decided to send Saint Augustine to convert England to Christianity.

He organised for Augustine, who was later to become Archbishop of Canterbury, to lead a mission to Britain with the aim of converting the pagan king Aethelberht of Kent.

Off Augustine went in 595, having left the Rome church of San Gregorio al Celio for England with a group of Benedictine monks. His mission was a great success. It is recorded at Christmas 597 that 10,000 angli were baptised as Christians.

We owe to Augustine, who was later made a saint, the founding of a monastery and of Canterbury Cathedral in 602. But enough of that; let's go back to present days.

Angered by the obvious lowering of standards and the frequently occurring absurdities, the citizen reacts with annoyance, equating his beloved country to an inferior type of society which he describes as being of the third order (more about that later).

Quite a long time ago English judges established the concept of reasonableness in many spheres, both criminal and civil; and to ascertain what the standard meant it was suggested that one should look at the behaviour, reaction and comments of the 'man on the Clapham omnibus' who was intended to represent the kind of Englishman who could be trusted to be fair and reasonable in all circumstances, and to display the kind of common sense that made our country great[91].

The notion seems to have gone out of fashion, perhaps because, I would suggest, there are not many Englishmen who can be found nowadays on buses going to Clapham.

---

[91] *See the Court of Appeal libel cases of Mcquire v. Western Morning News (1903) and Hall v. Brooklands Auto-Racing Club 1932/3*

A Third World Country?

'If you want to tell people the truth, make them laugh, otherwise they'll kill you.' – Oscar Wilde, The Nightingale and The Rose

Maybe not, at least not yet: but we are getting close!

Surely not, you will say – that is an exaggeration. It is, in a sense, but one cannot challenge the fact that for many years now the expression has been heard being spoken when least expected. It would be too simple to justify these occurrences by the often repeated observation that typical of English people is their tendency to complain (not about food, though... nor, especially in 2014, of the far too numerous, and often quite dangerous, potholes in our roads that are not repaired so promptly or as well as they should be).

Used by sensible people it does not mean, obviously, that life in England is the same as in the Congo; but it is meant to convey the idea that our people have learnt to put up with the extreme number of inefficiencies and absurdities of our present-day English social and governmental organisation. Acquiescence in them is not approval; silence does not imply acceptance, especially when, as is so common nowadays, the citizen knows that there is no point in complaining, that there is practically nothing he can do since protest is either misunderstood or ignored.

We have reached a situation in England where it is not merely a matter of thinking that 'fings ain't what they used to be' but, above all, that the standards of efficiency reliability propriety lawfulness simplicity equality morality loyalty honesty integrity patriotism honour solidarity discipline respect for authority pride charity tolerance unity of purpose sense of history dignity reasonableness modesty and, above all, common sense, which not only made England great but also allowed it to be a civilised country in which to live, appear on the way out, where they are not already dead and buried.

I am afraid it is far too easy to blame foreigners for what I can only call comparative degradation although they, of course (all of them), must carry a certain amount of responsibility.

Over the top? I am not sure.

The title of this chapter is factually inaccurate. Ours is still a modern, civilised country; but if we compare it with the England of the Victorians or of the days of the Empire or even with those of the '30s and '40s, there is no doubt, at least in my mind, that we are justified in considering that, in relative terms, we are beginning to sink rather low, despite all the technical advances that have been made, especially in public health matters, now that there are increasing signs of losses of integrity in many of the institutions of our country; an aspect of our society that is particularly troubling.

This realisation escapes the masses, who do not see that many of the features that made our country great are disappearing.

Of course, it can be argued that it was inevitable that sooner or later England would exhaust its historical function, its mantle as a world power having been taken over by the USA, Russia and probably also China (until recently, the second biggest world economy after the USA but now – October 2014 – the principal world economy).

To say that the political system of a rich country, as Great Britain was, no longer operates successfully in the third millennium, when both its power and its riches have reduced and the country seems incapable of coming to terms with its changed economic and moral circumstances, is as valid an observation as any other.

Equally, there is much truth in the theory that the British economy has grown weak also because of the destruction of its manufacturing base and the ever-increasing reliance upon a service industry mentality and a financial system which, for reasons that are far too numerous to be mentioned here, are proving unreliable, if not corrupt.

In his book 'Our Age – Portrait of a Generation'[92], the historian Noel Annan records the decline of Great Britain as follows: *'In 1955 we had been the strongest economic*

---

[92] *Noel Annan, Our Age – Portrait of a Generation;, Weidenfeld & Nicolson, London, 1990, page 335*

military power in Europe and the leader in atomic energy. In 1979 we were not even in the front rank of European, let alone world, powers.' Matters have certainly not improved since then...

The counter to that is to blame what are seen as evils of present-day Britain on the fact that the English race has been polluted by the influx of foreigners. Whilst it cannot be denied that, since the 1950s, the face of England, if not of the whole of Britain, has changed dramatically, this is an oversimplification. It is not merely a matter of colour but also of attitudes and it is conceivable that the change was probably inevitable. But this type of argument belies an inability to understand that the causes of what is most objectionable in our present-day behaviour are much more profound and cannot always be laid at the door of the immigrants, of whatever race or nationality they might be.

England has always received with open arms all political refugees, all persecuted foreigners of all nationalities. It has always been a beacon for democracy and freedom and acknowledged as such throughout the world.

Admittedly, nowadays the numbers are greater and the impact is much more noticeable, visually, aurally, and temperamentally; however, the causes of our inability to assimilate successfully the foreigners who have come to England over the past 30 years, or at least so successfully as we had done previously, are to be traced elsewhere.

(Although once more I cannot resist the temptation of observing that, to some extent, the English themselves are also to blame, especially nowadays with the great influx of immigrants, because quite often we allow tolerance to be misunderstood for helplessness and our fairness for weakness.)

In my view, the most obvious one is our loss of a national character, of our Englishness, which has gone not only out of football. This is due to the fragmentation of society, nowadays composed of a diversity of groups, each of which is keen to assert its own existence and has become intolerant of the views of others to such an extent that polarisations are common place. They hardly make for any kind of order.

With this fragmentation there has developed over the years a loss of direction, of the value of our history and, as a result, as an old Italian proverb puts it, 'if you don't know where you are coming from, you cannot possibly know where you are going'; and in my view, England certainly doesn't know in which direction it either is moving or ought to move.

Furthermore, our social and personal relations seem to have gone awry and give way to many problems and much confusion of thought, especially as a result of our changing sexual customs which have been developing over a range that goes inconsistently from hypocrisy to a brutal, obscene free-for-all.

As an example of such inconsistency I cannot resist the temptation of mentioning a rather humorous event, namely the fact that not too many years ago the local magistrates in the town of Swindon ordered the seizure, as obscene, of Boccaccio's Decameron, one of the classics of world literature!

But I should also observe that in England there appears to be in such matters both confusion and constraint, aggravated by grey skies and the rapidly developing multi-racial society, as well as compounded by an uneven historical, cultural, religious and educational background.

Again (I am sorry...), I cannot resist temptation. I list in the Appendix some information and certain statistical data that highlight the parlous state in which the country finds itself. I suggest that it deserves a glance.

If you do not share my concern at what is happening nowadays in Great Britain or have decided not to be bothered by it, then I apologise for having wasted your time.

You do share my concern? You have read it?

Yes? I am delighted. The following pages will, I hope, provide further ideas, bearing in mind that the data recorded in it appear to have been totally ignored by the inhabitants of the British Isles.

Decline, but not yet Fall
(with acknowledgements to Gibbon)

*'Facts do not cease to exist because they are ignored.' –
Aldous Huxley, Complete Essays II, 1926-1929*

The question that I really believe it would be useful for us as a nation to pose is not when Britain will fall; nowadays nations do not fall as empires used to. Britain has lost its Empire; more correctly, perhaps, it gave it away. But even if its prestige were reduced to a minimum, the country would survive because it is still part of a much larger supra-national organism, Europe, of which it would become a mere region.

No, it is not a matter of Britain's fall, rather of the manner in which its decline in power and its position in the world order take effect and, more particularly, what the consequences will be for the citizens of this country. It certainly will not happen overnight, since it is not conceivable that over two and a half centuries of greatness can be nullified in a few years.

The problem, in my view, is at what speed we are moving downhill. On that, opinions differ. Though our descent is not in doubt, its rate must remain a matter for debate.

There will continue to be a future for humanity despite all the problems our modern world has to face; but predicting what part our country will play in human development seems to become more difficult as time passes.

The reason for this is that we are torn from one direction to the other by barbarians. Unlike what happened to the Roman Empire, when the barbarians were at the frontier, in our case they are already among us. Thanks to the power of television and the printed word, they are inside our homes. For example, they are all those who wish to ignore nearly 2,000 years of Christian veneration and belief; agnostics and atheists, who do not dare even try to explain away the fruits of a belief in God which we see in centuries of beautiful and meaningful examples of the human spirit available to all of us in architecture, sculpture and paintings.

It is often claimed that we are becoming an atheist country. Serious though the problem of the reducing significance of religious faith in our country may be, it is not really, in my opinion at least, the most significant factor in our decline. I have always subscribed to the view that atheists lack the crusading spirit. What I mean is that they will not go out of their way to try to convert believers to their non-believing point of view. Whether this is because they are inherently more thoughtful and less aggressive or whether, on the other hand, they feel deep down that they are unlikely to succeed since the believer, because of his faith, is stronger in mind and less likely to be swayed, is a little difficult to say. What is certain, however, is that those with beliefs of any kind – religious not merely, but also social and political – are more inclined to try to convert others to their point of view.

The stronger their belief, the greater the incentive to pass it on to the rest of the world. It might well be that, deep down, atheists realise this and that's why they don't waste their time trying to convert believers to spiritual nihilism.

Much more dangerous, however, and leaving aside the all-important colour problem, are the other barbarians among us, namely proponents and supporters of the two major evils that affect present-day British society: that is, exasperated feminism and political correctness, the philosophies of two groups who certainly do not lack the crusading spirit.

I have referred partly to both in previous pages, but I should like to revert briefly to them given that, in my opinion, the difficulties posed for our country as a whole by these 'theories of life' are in reality quite serious.

One of the major ones that it seems to me the English have to contend with, if they wish to deal with the existing instability caused by what I call, again, the barbarians amongst us, is the fact that we are islanders. As such, we have developed over the centuries, to a very marked degree, the ability to close ranks against foreigners and invaders, of course, but above all, we have a tendency to resent criticism. As islanders, we have developed a feeling of superiority and almost a belief that we can do no wrong; our insularity has forged our way of thinking and of behaving through the ages: the creation of the British Empire is proof of this particular fact.

There has thus been realised what has become known as the 'great British character', namely, the resilience in the face of adversity and the ability to overcome problems at a national level, even if often enough we have to 'muddle through'.

This basic, instinctive, objection to criticism of the way in which we do things, the closing of ranks, the ability to sacrifice individuality for the common good, have proved a boon historically and a good feature politically. It has however a serious drawback, namely the tendency to be oversensitive about criticism and, more particularly, to reject outright without due consideration any objection that may be made to our way of life, especially when emanating from foreign observers.

This is a disadvantage which is not helping us in dealing with the difficulties we have to face and has become much more noticeable as the country has grown less significant in world affairs and, very often reluctantly, more involved in Europe.

As a result, we seem to be looking at ourselves though rose-tinted glasses and to have developed a totally absurd type of sentimentality that is replacing truth.

The judgements we make of situations and of problems are no longer inspired by our centuries-old common sense — rather by this wonderful, reasonably novel addition to our intellect and to our emotions. It is odd: we who have always, condescendingly and critically, ascribed sentimentality to the Latin races now find ourselves enslaved by it. Sentimentality is not conducive to good judgement.

At the same time, we seem to incline much more than previously to trust in hope; the hope that, even when we see the evil around us we believe that, by not confronting it, it will go away. We are guided by a passive – I was tempted to say voyeuristic –, despondent attitude which contradicts all that the English have stood for throughout their history.

It is not even a matter of sweeping the evil we see under the carpet since, in my view, doing so would require some action, movement, or a decision to eliminate something whereas – and I admit I may be exaggerating – we are becoming incapable even of doing that.

There is definitely narrow-mindedness about this approach.

We muddle through, fearful of speaking out in opposition to what might be a general view.

One of the most detrimental results of this attitude is the fact that we tend to keep our critical views to ourselves, concerned that if we were permitted (a big if...) to publicise them, we would certainly be open to attack, whether by the press or others in a position of power. This, I suggest, is proving to be one of our principal weaknesses in the 21st Century.

The English people's reaction to criticism of them, of their way of life and of their habits is a particularly interesting national trait. The closing of ranks that occurs when objections are made to the English views, policies or attitudes is truly extraordinary. I go further: in my opinion, it is unique.

It manifests itself in what would, on first consideration, appear to be a conspiracy of silence.

The critical points raised are not even contradicted. No attempt is made to prove that they are mistaken, inaccurate, wrong and incapable of having the consequences that are stated to follow. They are simply ignored, silence surrounds them, dead silence, as if the words of complaint had never been uttered or the written criticism never published.

However, the peculiar aspect of this behaviour is that, contrary to appearances, there is really no conspiracy. It is not as though newspaper editors, television producers, politicians or whosoever is allowed to express an opinion, had really got together and had conspired to keep silent. People just behave that way: their reaction is instinctive.

They do not wish to know, they do not want to hear more about what does not please them. It is, in effect, a form of self-protection from having to do something, especially where the realisation occurs that the criticism might well be justified. This is all the more common when the objections that are raised relate to matters the rectification of which calls for drastic action, or at least for unpopular measures being taken, that may interfere with vested interests or modes of thought established over long periods of time[93].

I have already quoted the 50 years that are said to elapse between the English people thinking of something and doing it. That, of course, is an exaggeration but there have been other examples, namely the 20 years that elapsed from the date of Lord Scarman's report into the Brixton Riots or the same period of time that it took to give effect to the recommendations resulting from the King's Cross fire.

Often, this kind of situation develops along more sophisticated, if not subtle, lines.

In the early 1990s a Parliamentary committee considered whether prostitution should be legalised. The usual objections were raised, especially by the MP Diane Abbott, and no action was taken. Obviously, inactivity seldom cures major problems and prostitution continued to flourish. So what was decided should be done? Officially, nothing, given the attitude referred to above; anyone who knows

---

[93] *I should record that, recently, this attitude appears to be changing, especially as a result of the much publicised and extremely upsetting instances of child abuse and pornography.*

what really occurs in our country is aware of the fact that a blind eye is turned regularly by the authorities to the existence of 'brothels' (unofficial, of course) in our major cities. Problem solved. Well, maybe, but others have been created, especially when it comes to public health. Something similar occurred when it was decided to ban hunting. It was officially banned in 2004 despite major protests by countryside communities; but those of us who live in the country know full well that other 'sporting' solutions have been found.

In justification of such a way – a typically English way, if I may say so, of approaching problems (that is to say, to avoid having to face them frontally) – it is said that, as a result, attitudes are less confrontational and differing approaches, which might be frustrated, create less anger; possibly, there will be less public disorder.

A fairly interesting manifestation of this approach is the way in which nowadays we, as a country, are reacting to whistle-blowers (an apt description of such individuals for, rather like referees at sporting matches, they make themselves heard when they see a breach of the rules of the game). They are treated as though they had done something wrong, as if by exposing inadequacies, inefficiencies and improprieties as well as an overall waste of public money they were, in a sense, betraying their function within the organisation denounced, almost as if the whistle-blowers themselves were letting the side down. It is odd: those who criticise them fail completely to see that it is their attitude to the whistle-blowers that is letting society and the country down, rather than the reverse. The criticisms voiced about the failings thus revealed are seldom contradicted; little attempt is made to prove that they may be erroneous or incapable of having the consequences which are attributed to them. They are simply ignored[94].

It is as though there were a mafia type of mentality at work, capable of ensuring that certain matters should be kept under wraps. We have had striking and highly disgusting examples of this in the recent cases of Jimmy Savile and Cyril Smith (and, regrettably, others).

But apart from those and similar cases, this particular type of approach is widespread and much as I spend time in trying to work out why, I have to confess my utter failure. I can only attribute it to what I have generally described above as an ostrich-like way of thinking fostered by an instinctive aversion to criticism, no matter how justified. What I fear is completely overlooked is that problems continue to fester and usually much harsher measures than otherwise necessary are needed when it comes to the crunch, the situation having got out of control.

Before concluding, I should like to make a few more observations on the state of our society. I do so not in any

---

94 On April 18th 2014 the national press reported on the unsuccessful attempt by the NHS – lasting 13 years! – to silence a cardiologist who had spoken out against irregularities and inefficiencies in the hospital system...

critical sense, but merely almost to remind myself that the irritation that I constantly feel at the way in which the country is developing has some justification.

I shall start with the behaviour of our politicians, of which a few examples have been provided earlier on. To put it mildly, it must be admitted that many of them are conducting themselves with extravagant sexual and financial laxity. There have been recently a number of other instances of conduct by them that is highly questionable, disgusting and mostly of a criminal nature: the conclusion must be drawn that a good number of them are quite undeserving of the honour of representing their constituents. In fact, as of today's date six members of our Parliament have been prosecuted, and convicted, for fiddling their expenses; other police enquiries are pending.

This is regrettable because, at least in principle, our political representatives are supposed to be a better part of the population of the British Isles, just a theoretical top. It is quite clear, however, that they are not quite so good as they claim to be and I am reminded of the Italian saying that when a fish goes bad, it starts rotting at the head...

I should not omit to mention that the months of June and July 2014 have witnessed the revival of dirty stories of extensive sexual abuse of young boys both in Westminster and among titled personages, government officials and other political creatures going back to the 1980s.

There has been repeated talk of a conspiracy of silence, a disappearing informative dossier and at least one possibly related prosecution and conviction.

It is well beyond the scope of this work to deal in any manner with such sad stories, old and new. However, if they were true, they would provide some support for the increasingly held view that the English male has an inclination towards paedophilia (a most unwarranted generalisation, of course. But is it?). No more said.

One does not wish to establish a litany of 'bad' things but I think it is not unreasonable to argue that, since the end of the Second World War, the quality of our politicians, as well as of our Prime Ministers, has not been of the highest. Many of them can be accused of lack of vision, of being constantly inspired by political dogma and some of them even of having gone into politics solely to feather their nests. The combination of a lower calibre of man with the inevitable loss of our national identity (as well as of our sense of direction) is quite serious. Whilst it remains debatable whether the former has caused our inability to see in which direction our future lies (for example, by reference to Europe) or whether it is the latter that has resulted in the failure to preserve what had been, at least until the Second World War, our fairly individual, clear-cut characteristics and identities, is a chicken-and-egg situation with which one is not really too concerned for present purposes. Suffice it to acknowledge that it exists.

I have already remarked on the Americanisation of our culture, our loss of honour and on the weakening of the traditional family, as well as of the significance of our Christian morality.

Our mood of self-denigration does not help, particularly when it coincides with the development of a sense of intolerance for other people. At the same time, it is turning to a form of masochism which leads us to the belief, almost widespread now in the country, that England is becoming an underdog. That would only be true if we believed it; but it would appear that some of us do.

Simultaneously with the loss of our sense of pride in the country's history and traditions, we have also surrendered any kind of shame and of social stigma in respect of wickedness. For example, when did one hear of an MP resigning his seat when caught out committing an illegal act? Not too often... This may or may not be related to our lack of discipline and be the result of contempt for constituted authority, of which we see regular depressing examples in everyday life; but it must be acknowledged.

Another aspect of our behaviour which is puzzling (and on which, I am sorry to say, I have already remarked) is the manner in which we seem to have become more intolerant of our neighbours and other people generally. It seems to me that this has occurred because we have lost our sense of culture. One cannot have toleration where there are no moral standards, because it is only when the difference between right and wrong can be appreciated that one can afford to be tolerant of those who do not act morally. Toleration, after all, comes from the habits that establish a way of life and not from the creation of philosophical theories about one's sexual behaviour.

It is really no news to say that we do have problems[95].

And yet, in some ways England is a surprising place! Against the pessimism of many of my observations one has to put that, in several respects, our country can be at the cutting edge in certain activities. Leaving on one side the enormous success of its popular bands (The Beatles etc.), its engineering, musical and theatre activities, fashions and fashion houses, its popularity in the world is still quite substantial. It may be that most of it occurs because of the existence of centres of excellence for certain activities.

London, in particular, remains probably one of the most appealing venues in the world. Its displays of art and entertainment (the Royal Academy, the National Gallery, the Royal Albert Hall, the Royal Festival Hall, its theatres, the Tate Gallery, its numerous palaces and buildings open to the public; the list of places to visit and enjoy would be very long indeed) continue to attract visitors. Interestingly, the number of foreigners who take up residence there increases almost on a daily basis. Perhaps they look at England with different eyes; the novelty of it – we even drive on the left and not too many countries

---

[95] *No need, I suppose, to mention the recent illegal behaving by some journalists...*

follow that example – may fade after a while. Who knows?

Despite all such positive features, I have reluctantly come to the conclusion that whilst there is a grain of truth in all the theories that are put forward, by myself included, to provide an explanation why we are a country that has ceased to deserve the respect in which it was held by the remainder of the world and that, each in their own way, contribute to our decline, they all pale in comparison with what I would term generally the present-day moral weakness of England as a whole. I am not trying to make a religious point; whether England is a more or less religious country than, say, it was in the '30s, might be extremely relevant in the final analysis, but my concern is somewhat different: I use the adjective 'moral' in a much wider acceptation than as referring purely to religion, in contradistinction to the frenzy of individualism that grips us all..

The premises of my approach are not historical, political or economic. England might have made a mistake in misunderstanding its role in Europe or, depending on your view, in joining it in the first place and it can be argued that it is now spending a lot of time in trying to make up for the fact that it wasn't in Europe when it was first established; it may need a written constitution to remedy some of the more obvious deficiencies in the political system; it might require the help of modern Friedmans, Galbraithes or Keyneses to try to anticipate, and find a cure for, its financial difficulties when the present panacea for its economic ills, namely North Sea Oil and Gas, run out; it will certainly need inspiration to decide how far to allow fracking activities to interfere with individual liberties and rights of way; it will suffer much heartache and will have to deal with serious doubts in deciding what policies to adopt to resolve, or at least minimise the impact, of the very serious problems inevitably posed by an ever-increasing aged population; and so on. I am not really qualified to comment on that and on similar problems, but I do know that the country will have to search for a lot of help to compensate for the prevailing mood which discounts completely any spiritual approach to everyday life.

It does not suffice to say that we are becoming a much more equal and fair society, even assuming – and I do not believe it – such statement to be true. One of our major difficulties is that political correctness is, at least in theory, nothing but an exaggerated extension of the concept of equality. What we have done, however, is to take it to extremes which over the years have proved to be the most destructive element in the elimination of the principal virtue that has, throughout the centuries, inspired and protected this country, namely its common sense. If I may be permitted to use rather extreme language once more (but for the last time...), I should say that political correctness has resulted in the rape of common sense. One need hardly mention the absurdities that, combined with an idiotic and strict application of philosophical concepts of human rights and extreme health and safety requirements, it has brought about: absurdities and stupidities which are so evident and damaging in everyday life.

We have all become obsessed by our 'human rights' but it is not often that one hears any reference to our duties. We are reluctant to realise that in respect of each right that we claim there is someone somewhere who owes a corresponding duty; that is not mentioned. Indeed, it is difficult to imagine how popular a politician might be who advocated a convention on 'human duties'...

Karl Marx was wont to observe that 'religion is the opium of the people'; nowadays we ought to say that exasperated feminism and political correctness are the opium of British society and it is becoming increasingly more awkward to determine, no matter how objectively the situation is viewed, which of the two is more damaging.

The German philologist and philosopher, Friedrich Nietzsche, had, some years ago, propounded the view that the Christian identification of conscience, of good and evil, of morality, makes slaves of human beings. What he appears to have ignored is that the neglect of conscience results in the glorification of a system which is aimed solely at ensuring self-fulfilment and self-expression, without any limitation in the interest of other people, of the country as a whole. The lack of any sense of belonging to a community encourages licence and anonymity which prosper in the rootlessness brought about by city life.

Our morality has become our exasperated individualism, obsession with matters sexual and constant search for profit. I suggest it is surely better for us to be slaves to god-like beliefs, rather than to sex and money.

Envoi

What now? What will my English friends say? Have I been too unkind to the inhabitants of the British Isles?

I am not sure, but I am convinced that I have tried to be objective. If I have erred, it was probably as an overreaction to the almost too-perfect picture that Jeremy Paxman painted: it is difficult for me to determine how much that might have coloured my view. In truth, not that much: I am sure his was merely a provocation, which brought to the fore thoughts and beliefs developed by me over the years.

In the overall picture, I think that any criticisms I have made, apart from being well-meaning, are also well founded.

But that is not the end of the world, at least in this sense; better that a long-standing resident (nay, more than that: an 'Englishman' of choice) should, without dislike, draw attention to negative features than that an enemy should do so with viciousness and spite.

In any event, truly, it is not all that bad...!

I still think that the majority of the English are less perfidious than the French have observed, more passionate than the Italians consider them to be, more generous than the Greeks maintain, less inclined to sexual deviation than lots of people believe (despite all recent extraordinarily perverse examples and the ever more virulent obsession with matters sexual), less xenophobic than even they sometimes think they are. But their history does not help.

Furthermore, today's press and TV reports have a tendency to magnify inappropriate conduct; nor should it be forgotten that it is probably true that the picture thus projected reflects more the principal cities of the UK than the country and the countryside as a whole.

The hypocrisy and racism, to which I myself pointedly draw attention, are in the general picture less damaging to everyday life than they need be. There is a reason for this.

Despite occasional episodes of unexpected nastiness, the English are not unkind. The behaviour of their hooligans cannot be generalised. Their tolerance is considerable, their gregariousness is quite significant and useful, their discipline (though reducing...) praiseworthy, their patriotism – also reducing – is still notable, their generosity great; in fact, at times it is also out of place. More importantly, perhaps, they are still very fond of their gardens...

If they succeeded in ceasing to be shackled to US foreign policy they might even see their future more clearly.

Have I, by even the remotest chance, been of some help to the English in enabling them better to understand some of their attitudes and reactions? I doubt it; but I have enjoyed writing about them and I think I shall pay England the compliment of saying that, despite all my criticisms of the past, but more particularly present behaviour of its nationals, I should not wish to live elsewhere. That is saying a lot...! (Pity about the weather, though...)

Appendix

- ❖ The number of abortions in 2011 exceeded 250,000. The equivalent figure for 1976 was 180,000 and for 2008, it just exceeded 200,000. It was reported on May 25th 2011 that in 2010 there were over 20,000 abortions carried out on women under 25 years of age who had already undergone one or more abortion intervention.
- ❖ The number of divorces in 2013 was 129,763. 63% of these divorces occurred where couples had children.
- ❖ Statistics published on November 2nd 2012 show that only half of 15 year olds now live with both parents.
- ❖ After Denmark (58%), the United Kingdom has the highest percentage of mothers working when the child is 12 months old, namely 50% (OECD Report, April 2011).
- ❖ Statistics published in May 2012 indicate that one in 11 couples splits up before a child of the marriage is five years old.
- ❖ UK Births outside marriage are at their highest in 2013 for 200 years and it is now recorded that 50% of children can expect their parents to divorce or separate by the time they reach the age of 16.
- ❖ Just under 50% of children born in England are born to unmarried mothers.
- ❖ In the same year (2012), we spent 5.8% of our GDP on care for the elderly whereas Italy and France spent respectively 11.7% and 11.1%.
- ❖ We now have close to two million single mothers, having one or more children each, and three million children live in households where there is only one parent (ONS, January 2012).

- ❖ Every year half a million children and adults are drawn into the legal system and, at the moment (2013), 3.8million children are currently caught up in family litigation.
- ❖ Figures received under the Freedom of Information Act 2000 from 34 out of 43 Police Authorities (excluding those for West Midlands, Greater Manchester and the London Metropolitan area) and published by the NSPCC on March 4th 2013 show that over the past three years there were more than 5,000 formal investigations into the behaviour of youngsters under 18 accused of crimes including rape and sexual assault.
- ❖ The same figures show that the number of sex offences committed by under-18s has increased by 38% from 1,432 in 2009/10 to 1,978 in 2011/12. Extrapolation would show that every day our police are dealing with at least five 'children' accused of sexual offences.
- ❖ Statistics published in April 2011 show that no less than 31% of habitable units in England are in the occupation of one person only.
- ❖ Statistics published in November 2012 indicate that nearly 2.5 million adults between the ages of 45 and 64 live alone (an increase of over 50% since 1996).
- ❖ 70% of young offenders come from broken homes.
- ❖ The NSPCC reported on April 4th 2012 that between April 2010 and March 2011 there were over 23,000 sex offences against children under the age of 18.
- ❖ 38% of all rapes recorded by the police in England and Wales in the same period were committed against children under the age of 16 years.
- ❖ 18,915 sexual crimes were recorded in total against children under 16 in 2013; 32% of the total of sexual crimes recorded generally in England and Wales (54,982) were also against

children under 16. One in 20 children under 16 had been sexually abused.

❖ The OECD reported in 2007 that the United Kingdom lies 27th in the percentage of children aged up to 14 who live in the same household as both parents, namely 68.9% (compared with Finland 95.2%, Greece 93.6% and Italy 92.1%)

❖ The UK has the highest rate of venereal disease (as traditionally defined in the Venereal Diseases Act 1917) in the whole of Europe. Sorry, a politically incorrect expression: I should have said sexually transmitted infections...

❖ English girls under the age of 15 have the second highest (after Denmark at 58%) percentage of having been drunk at least twice. They share it (44%) with Finland (OECD Statistics, 'Health at a Glance', 2013). The percentage for Russian girls is 19%, for French 15% and for Italian 14%.

❖ And finally, to be up-to-date, I should not fail to record that in August 2014, Professor Alexis Jay published her Report into 16 years of abuse (1997-2013) in the South Yorkshire city of Rotherham.

It had been preceded by her August 2003 Report (commissioned by the South Yorkshire Police), that had found 'a significant number of girls and some boys who are being sexually exploited' in Rotherham. A later report was published in 2006 which claimed that the situation was continuing 'as it had done for a number of years', with an organised and established sexual exploitation scene.

In November 2010 there followed the conviction of five Pakistanis from Rotherham for sexual exploitation (including rape) and physical abuse upon underage young girls. They were sentenced to varying terms of imprisonment (from four to 11 years).

The 2014 Report highlighted the fact that girls as young as 11 were being raped 'by large numbers of male perpetrators and abducted, trafficked to other cities in England, beaten and intimidated' as well as 'collective failures' by political, police and social care authorities over the first 12 years covered by it.

The Report found that, over the period covered by it, at least 1,400 youngsters, mainly though not exclusively female, were abused sexually, assaulted and beaten.

The most damaging feature, however, is that, according to the Report, schools, police, officers/members of the Rotherham City Council <u>knew</u> what was going on and, for different reasons, <u>took no action</u>. One is tempted to exclaim: 'well done, Rotherham'.

Although there are problems in other English cities, it is not unreasonable to say that Northern England in particular has proved over the past few decades to be a dangerous area for young girls. In 2012, nine men were sent to prison for up to 12 years for their part in what became known as 'the Rochdale grooming scandal', namely their constant and consistent sexual abuse of girls underage.

For god's sake, what is happening to England?

Bibliography

Abse, Leo: *Fellatio Masochism Politics and Love*, Robson Books, London, 2000

Adonis, Andrew and Pollard, Stephen: *A Class Act – The Myth of Britain's Classless Society*, Hamish Hamilton, London

Anderson, Digby: *The Loss of Virtue*, Social Affairs Unit, London, 1992

Annan, Noel: *Our Age – Portrait of a Generation*, Weidenfeld & Nicolson, London, 1990

Bennett, H S: *Life on the English Manor – A Study of Peasant Conditions 1150-1400*, Alan Sutton, 1987

Bennett, Henry Stanley: *Life on the English Manor (A Study of Peasant Conditions 1150-1400)*, OUP, 1937

Black, Jeremy: *Modern British History Since 1900*, Macmillan Press, 2000

Boswell, James: *Life of Johnson*, 11th April 1776

Brady, F & Pottle, F: *James Boswell on the Grand Tour 1765-1766*, London, 1955

Burford, E J: *Royal St James's: Being a Story of Kings, Clubmen and Courtesans*, London 1988

Butler, Alban: *The Lives of the Fathers, Martyrs and Other Principal Saints*, Burns & Oates, 1987

Butler, Lawrence & Jones, Harriet: *Britain in the Twentieth Century – A Documentary Reader*, Heinemann, 1995

Cannadine, David: *History in Our Time*, Yale University Press, 1998

Clarke, Peter: *Hope and Glory – Britain 1990-1990*, Allen Lane, 1996

Colley, Linda: *Britons – Forging the Nation 1707-1837*, Random House, 1992

Congreve, William: *The Double Dealer*, 1694

Coward, Barry: *The Stuart Age – England 1603-1714*, Longman, London, 1980

Darwin, Charles: *The Expressions of the Emotions in Man and Animals*, 1872

Davies, Norman: *The Isles – A History*, Macmillan, 1999

Defoe, Daniel: *A True-Born Englishman: A Satyr*, 1701

Dickens, A G: *The English Reformation*, Batsford Ltd, 1964

Ferguson, Niall: *Empire – How Britain Made the Modern World*, Allen Lane, Penguin Books, London 2004

Freedman, Betty: *The Feminine Mystique*, 1963

Golby, J M: *Culture & Society in Britain 1850-1890*, Oxford University Press, 1986

Hibbert, Christopher: *The English – A Social History 1066-1945*, Grafton Books, London 1987

Howard, Philip K: *The Death of Common Sense: How Law is Suffocating America*, Random House, 1994

Hutton, Will: *The State We're In*, Jonathan Cape, London, 1995

James, Lawrence: *Warrior Race – A History of the British at War*, 2001

Joseph, Michael: *Sex and the British*, London 1993, p7

Keen, Maurice: *English Society in the Later Middle Ages 1348-1500*, Penguin Press, 1990

Kennedy, Baroness, Helena: *Just Law*, Chatto & Windus, London 2004

Kennedy, Helena: Chatto and Windus, London, 2004

Loyn, H R: *The Making of the English Nation*, Thames & Hudson, London, 1991

Marotta, Giuseppe: *L'Oro di Napoli*, Bompiani, Milan, 1956

Martin, Howard: *Britain Since 1800 – Towards the Welfare State*, Macmillan Education Ltd, 1988

Marwick, Arthur: *The Sixties*, Oxford University Press, 1998

McKinstrey, Leo: *Turning the Tide – A Personal Manifesto for Modern Britain*, Michael Joseph, London, 1997

Millett, Kate: *Sexual Politics*, Virago Press, 1977

Mitchell, Graham: *The Roaring Twenties*, 1986

Morgan, Kenneth O: *The People's Peace – British History 1945-1989*, Oxford University Press, 1990

Murray, Charles: *Underclass – Losing Ground*, IEA, H&W Unit, London 1996

O'Pie, Swayne: Why *Britain Hates Men – Exposing Feminism*, The Men's Press, Bath, 2011

Orwell, George: *The Lion and The Unicorn*, Secker and Warburg, London, 1962

Paxman, Jeremy: *The English – Portrait of a People*, Michael Joseph 1998, Penguin 1999

Pearce, Malcolm & Stewart, Geoffrey: *British Political History 1867-1990*, Routledge, London, 1992

Plowden, Alison: *Elizabethan England – Life in an Age of Adventure*, Reader's Digest, 1982

Price, Richard: *British Society 1680-1880*, Cambridge University Press, 1991, p316

Purdue, A W & Golby, J M: *The Civilisation of the Crowd – Popular Culture in England 1750-1900*, Sutton Publishing, 1999

Richardson, Nigel: *Life in Britain in the 1960s*, B T Batsford Ltd, London, 1986

Rule, John: *The Vital Century – England's Developing Economy*, Longman Group UK, 1992

Ruskin, John*: Letters to his Parents*, October 23rd 1845

Ruskin, John: *Works*, Vol.36, p48,

Russell, Bertrand: *Marriage & Morals*, Unwin Paperbacks, London 1976, page 59

Salmond and Heuston: *The Law of Torts*, Sweet & Maxwell, London, 1996

Sampson, Anthony: *Who Runs This Place?*, John Murray, Great Britain, 2004

Santayana, George: *Dominations and Powers: Reflections on Liberty, Society and Government*, 1951 (check publishers)

Saul, Nigel: *The Oxford Illustrated History of Medieval England*, Oxford University Press, 1997

Schama, Simon: *A History of Britain – The British Wars 1603-1776*, BBC Worldwide Ltd, 2001

Shapiro, Harold: *Ruskin in Italy: Letters to His Parents 1845*, Clarendon Press, 1972

Social Affairs Unit: *Faking It, The Sentimentalisation of Modern Society*, London 1998 (p.121)

Storks, Christopher: *Forgotten Fruits*, Windmill Books, Great Britain 2009

Travis, Alan: *Bound and Gagged – A Secret of Obscenity in Britain*, Profile Books, London, 2000

Vansittart, Peter: *In Memory of England*, John Murray, London, 1998

Wellings, Kaye, Field, Julie, Johnson, Anne M & Wadsworth, Jane: *Sexual Behaviour in Britain*, Penguin Books, 1994

Wilson, A N: *God's Funeral*, John Murray, London, 1999

Woodward, Sir Llewellyn: *The Age of Reform 1815-1870*, Clarendon Press, Oxford University Press, 1962